ALEXANDER
or
JESUS?

Best wishes

Bill Brod

ALEXANDER

or

JESUS?

The Origin of the Title "Son of God"

W. E. L. BROAD

Foreword by William R. Telford

PICKWICK *Publications* · Eugene, Oregon

ALEXANDER OR JESUS?
The Origin of the Title "Son of God"

Pickwick Publications
An Imprint of Wipf and Stock Publishers
199 W. 8th Ave., Suite 3
Eugene, OR 97401

www.wipfandstock.com

ISBN 13: 978–1-62564–861-7

Cataloging-in-Publication data:

Broad, William Ernest Lionel

Alexander or Jesus? : the origin of the title "Son of God" / William Ernest Lionel Broad.

xxii + 182 p. ; 23 cm. —Includes bibliographical references and index(es).

ISBN 13: 978–1-62564–861-7

1. Jesus Christ—Person and offices. 2. Alexander the Great, 356 B.C.—323 B.C. I. Title.

DF234.2 B75 2015

Manufactured in the U.S.A.   03/09/2015

For Daphne, Kate and Sarah who encouraged me to embark on my first period of research in my 69th year of life and for Dr. Bill Telford of Durham University whose unremitting tutoring and care meant that I not only obtained a degree but produced a work which may be found to have merit.

Contents

Foreword

In seeking to express his significance for them, what inspired early Christians to apply the designation "Son of God" to Jesus of Nazareth, a figure who, historically speaking, can be said to have been no more than a Jewish teacher, prophet and exorcist? When did they come to apply the description to him, and what did they mean by it? These fundamental, and indeed challenging, questions are at the heart of New Testament Christology, and they are taken up in a bold and original way by William Broad in this compelling new book.

Christianity began as an apocalyptic sect within Judaism, a monotheistic faith that was reluctant to blur the distinction between God, the Creator, and man, the created, and had little truck with the notion that humans were divine, or could become so. A common view among New Testament scholars is that the term "Son of God" was first applied to Jesus within a Jewish context to identify him as God's suffering, righteous or obedient servant or even as Israel's messianic king, but only in a metaphorical and not in a metaphysical way. When Christianity spread out into the wider Gentile world, however, an epithet describing his filial relationship to God in an ethical or adoptionist sense came to be understood in a more Hellenistic way as pointing to his divine or supernatural nature or status.

It is this common view that William Broad challenges in *Alexander or Jesus?* The first Christians may have been Jews, but they were embedded from the beginning in the Hellenistic world, and the propagandistic tools for their mission to that world were already at hand, in Graeco-Roman culture, for the application to Jesus of the descriptor "Son of God." The precedent for the ascription to an outstanding human being of the title "Son of God" had been set three centuries before by Alexander the Great. The Emperor Augustus, who presided over the birth of Christianity, was also termed *divi filius*, and succeeding Roman emperors of the Julio-Claudian family, who reigned while Christianity spread, were regarded as "sons of the deified." In an age of religious propaganda, and the need to "sell" one's heroes or gods to others, the acclamation "Son of God" for Jesus was prepared for him by others, therefore, and the development of the appellation as a major title for him by Christians depended principally, William Broad maintains, on Alexander and Augustus.

This is an audacious claim for a lifelong Anglican cleric, prison chaplain and parish priest, now retired from full-time ministry and Honorary Canon of Durham Cathedral. Ordained in 1966, Reverend Canon Broad served as assistant curate, team rector, priest in charge and vicar in a number of dioceses (Sheffield, Liverpool, Chelmsford and Durham) and is no stranger to challenges. He was, after all, prison chaplain at Wormwood Scrubs (as well as Albany and Risley). A sailor himself, in 1984, he became Executive Officer, and, in 2002, Chairman of the Cirdan Sailing Trust, a charity aimed at providing opportunities for young people from poor backgrounds to go to sea. My wife, Andrena, and I sailed with him and his family on the 75th Anniversary (2012) of the Trust's twin-masted sailing ship, Queen Galadriel, and stormy seas, I can safely say, are obstacles he easily takes in his stride. In 2006, he became Chairman of Justice First Limited, a charity aimed at assisting destitute asylum seekers in the UK, and in 2010, Chairman of the Scotland's Great Glen Shipping Company, an ecological venture to reduce carbon emissions.

William Broad has also demonstrated a distinctive eagerness to take on academic challenges, and New Testament Christology is one of the toughest. After reading for a BSc at the University of St Andrews in 1958, and doing his initial theological training at Ridley Hall, Cambridge, in 1964, he fulfilled a lifelong ambition to pursue scholary research after his retirement by applying to the Department of Theology and Religion at Durham University, firstly for a Master of Theology and Religion degree, and subsequently for a Master of Letters, both of which he completed with aplomb. Alexander the Great (as well as Jesus of Nazareth) has been a longstanding interest of his, and this interest combined with his critical theological skills, his links with the Classics Department (especially with Dr Andrej Petrovic, whose lectures on Alexander he attended), his familiarity with the primary sources on Alexander such as Arrian, Rufius Curtius, Diodorus, Trogus and Plutarch, and above all, his intellectual energy and enthusiasm, made him a natural candidate for the MLitt, and a constant delight to supervise. This book, based on his thesis, is the result of that scholarly work, and its excellence speaks for itself.

In his Introduction, Canon Broad sets out his aims and agenda, and these need not be repeated here, but he also states: "For 'Son of God' to become a major appellation used of Jesus by his followers within 40 years of his death indicates that some strong influence other than Judaism was operating on the writers of the New Testament" (p. xix). The reader is then taken on a fascinating but focused journey into the ancient world, one that skilfully charts the "strong influence" that he deems to have operated on the development of early Christian "Son of God" Christology. The voyage presents us with a host of ideas, facts and discoveries that inform, delight and challenge, and some of the landmarks are worth noting: a lucid account of the pedigree of the term "Son of God" prior to Alexander's time (and Jesus'), in Persian, Egyptian and Greek cultures, and with particular reference to the notion of kingship (Chapter 1)—here the application of the term 'Son of God' by Greeks, for example, to an individual with special powers and significant achievements is especially enlightening; an informed summary of the life and achievement of Alexander the Great (Chapter 2)—here his deification following the Siwa experience invites striking comparisons with Jesus; a comprehensive tour of "Son of God" references in canonical and extra-canonical Jewish writings (Chapter 3)—here he demonstrates how few passages, indeed, offer sustenance for Christological germination; a critical review of the "Son of God" title in the New Testament (Chapter 4)—here, *per contrarium*, the evident prominence of the title attests to the NT writers' interaction with Greek rather than Jewish culture; an acute appraisal of "Son of God" in extra-canonical writings to 165 CE (Chapter 5)—here the growth of the title to a position of pre-eminence coincides with the early church's distanciation from Judaism and adjustment to Hellenism; an illuminating exploration of the "Son of God" appellation in the Roman Empire (Chapter 6)—here the well-known and powerfully symbolic application of the title to emperors such as Claudius, Domitian and supremely Augustus could not have failed to have had an impact on nascent Christianity and its claims for Jesus (particularly with respect to the birth stories); a concise and persuasive summation of the argument (Chapter 7)—here the case for the modelling of Christian claims for Jesus as Son of God on those for Alexander the Great and the early Roman emperors, or for their direct influence on such claims, is robustly reiterated.

If the reader is willing to take this journey with Canon Broad, then there is much of value to be learned from this book. Alexander or Jesus? Both, in their own way, can be said to be the most significant figures to have come down to us from Graeco-Roman antiquity, and both have had their biographers—the evangelists in the case of Jesus, and Plutarch, among others, in the case of Alexander. As exemplified in his *Parallel Lives*, Plutarch's method, Canon Broad reminds us, "was to take two famous figures of history and contrast them. By comparing Alexander with Julius Caesar, he produced for both lives that are rich in history and legend" (p. 18). By comparing Alexander with Jesus, and the history and legend that surround each, Canon Broad himself has followed in the footsteps of his illustrious predecessor.

William R. Telford, Visiting Fellow, St John's College, Durham University, Thursday, July 31, 2014

Abbreviations

Acts Pil.	*Acts of Pilate.* Translated by M. R. James. In *The Apocryphal New Testament*, edited by J. K. Elliott, 169–84. Oxford: Clarendon, 1993.
Ael.	Aelian. *Varia Historia.* Edited and translated by N. G. Wilson. Cambridge, MA: Harvard University Press, 1997.
Aland Greek NT	B. Aland, K. Aland, and others, eds. *The Greek New Testament.* Nordlingen: C. H. Beck, 2001.
Annals	Tacitus. *Annals.* Translated by C. Damon. London: Penguin, 2012.
Ant.	Josephus. *The Antiquities of the Jews.* Translated by W. Whiston. London: William Heinemann, 1943.
1 Apol.	Justin Martyr. "The First Apology of Justin Martyr." In *Justin Martyr: The First and Second Apologies,* translated by L. W. Barnard, Ancient Christian Writers, 23–72. New York: Paulist, 1997.
Arrian	Arrian, L. F. A. *The Campaigns of Alexander.* Translated by A. de Selincourt. London: Penguin, 1971.
CBQ	*Catholic Biblical Quarterly*
CH	Church History
CP	*Classical Philology*
Curtius	Curtius, Q. R. *The History of Alexander.* London: Penguin, 1946.
CurtiusLoeb	Curtius, Q. R. *The History of Alexander the Great.* Translated by J. C. Rolfe. The Loeb Classical Library. London: Heinemann, 1946.

Deipn.	Athenaeus. *Deipnosophistae.* Vol. 5. Translated by C. D. Gulick. London: Heinemann, 1933.
Des. Inf.	*Christs Descent into Hell* from *The Pilate Cycle.* In *The Apocryphal New Testament,* edited and translated by J. K. Elliott, 185–204. Oxford: Clarendon, 1993.
Dinar.	*Dinarchus and Hyperides: Greek Orators.* Translated by I. Worthington. Warminster: Arris and Phillips, 1999.
Dio	Cassius Dio. *Dio's Roman History.* Translated by E. Carey. London: Heinemann, 1968.
Diod.	Diodorus. *Diodorus of Siculus.* Translated by C. B. Welles. London: Heinemann, 1963.
Diogn.	*The Epistle to Diognetus.* In *The Apostolic Fathers,* vol. 2, translated and edited by B. D. Ehrman, 121–60. LCL 25. London: Harvard University Press, 2003.
Div. Aug.	Suetonius. *The Deified Augustus.* In *Lives of the Caesars,* vol. 1, 151–309. Translated by R. Graves. LCL 31. London: Harvard University Press, 2001.
Div. Clau.	Suetonius. *The Deified Claudius.* In *Lives of the Caesars,* vol. 2, 3–81. Translated by R. Graves. LCL 38. London: Harvard University Press, 2001.
Div. Jul.	Suetonius. *The Deified Julius.* In *Lives of the Caesars,* vol. 1, 37–149. Translated by R. Graves. LCL 31. London: Harvard University Press, 2001.
Div. Vesp.	Suetonius. *The Deified Vespasian.* In *Lives of the Caesars,* vol. 2, 265–303. Translated by R. Graves. LCL 38. London: Harvard University Press, 2001.
Dom.	Suetonius. *Domitian.* In *Lives of the Caesars,* vol. 2, 321–65. Translated by R. Graves. LCL 38. London: Harvard University Press, 2001.
Ebr.	Philo. *On Drunkenness.* In *Philo,* vol. 3, translated by F. H. Colson and G. H. Whitaker, 318–435. London: William Heinemann, 1979.
ETR	*Etudes théologiques et religieuses*
ExpTim	*Expository Times*

Gaius Cal.	Suetonius. *Gaius Caligula.* In *Lives of the Caesars,* vol. 1, 419–507. Translated by R. Graves. LCL 31. London: Harvard University Press, 2001.
Gos. Pet.	*The Gospel of Peter.* In *The Apocryphal New Testament,* edited by J. K. Elliott, 150–58. Oxford: Clarendon, 1993.
Hist. eccl.	Eusebius. *Ecclesiastical History.* Translated by K. Lake. London: Heinemann, 1926.
Herod.	Herodotus. *Herodotus.* Translated by A. D. Godley. London: Heinemann, 1920–1925.
Historia	*Historia: Zeitschrift für alte Geschichte*
HSPC	*Harvard Studies in Classical Philology*
HT	*History Today*
HTR	*Harvard Theological Review*
Ign. *Eph.*	Ignatius. *Letter to the Ephesians.* In *The Apostolic Fathers,* vol. 1, translated and edited by B. D. Ehrman, 201–332. LCL 24. London: Harvard University Press, 2003.
Ign. *Smyrn.*	Ignatius. *Letter to the Smyrnaeans.* In *The Apostolic Fathers,* vol. 1, translated and edited by B. D. Ehrman, 294–301. LCL 24. London: Harvard University Press, 2003.
Iliad	Homer. *The Iliad.* Translated by A. T. Murray. LCL 171–72. London: Heinemann, 1924–1925.
Int	*Interpretation*
IrAnt	*Iranica Antiqua*
JHS	*Journal of Hellenic Studies*
JNES	*Journal of Near Eastern Studies*
JSS	*Journal of Semitic Studies*
LCL	Loeb Classical Library
Livy, *History*	Livy. *The Early History of Rome.* London: Penguin, 1971.
Mnemosyne	*Mnemosyne: A Journal of Classical Studies*
Moralia	Plutarch. *Moralia.* Translated by F. C. Babbit. Oxford: Clarendon, 1913–1918.

Nero	Suetonius. *Nero*. In *Lives of the Caesars,* vol. 2, 83–179. Translated by R. Graves. LCL 38. London: Harvard University Press, 2001.
NTS	*New Testament Studies*
Numen	*Numen: International Review for the History of Religions*
OCD	*Oxford Classical Dictionary.* Edited by Simon Hornblower and Antony Spawforth. 4th ed. Oxford: Oxford University Press, 2012
Odys.	Homer. *The Odyssey.* Cambridge, MA: Harvard University Press, 1995.
OGIS	*Orientis Graeci Inscriptiones Selectae.* Edited by W. Dittenberger. Hildesheim: G. Olms, 1986.
Pliny	Pliny. *Naturalis Historia.* Translated by H. Rackham. London: Heinemann, 1938–1966.
Plutarch	Plutarch. *Alexander.* In *Plutarchs Lives*, vol. 7, translated by B. Perrin, edited by E. Capps, T. E. Page, and W. H. D. Rouse, 225–439. London: William Heinemann, 1919.
Plutarch (D)	Plutarch. *The Life of Alexander the Great.* Translated J. Dryden. New York: The Modern Library, 2004.
Prot. Jas.	*The Protevangelium of James.* In *The Apocryphal New Testament,* edited by J. K. Elliott, 48–67. Oxford: Clarendon, 1993.
Ps.-Mat.	*The Gospel of Pseudo-Matthew.* In *The Apocryphal New Testament,* edited and translated by J. K. Elliott, 84–99. Oxford: Clarendon, 1993.
PTMS	Princeton Theological Monograph Series
Quaest. in Gen.	Philo. *Questions and Answers on Genesis.* In *Philo Supplement,* vol. 1, R. Marcus, 2–551. London: William Heinemann, 1979.
Res Gestae	Augustus. *Res Gestae Divi Augusti.* In *Velleius Paterculus and Res Gestae Divi Augustus,* edited by E. H. Warmington, translated by F. W. Shipley, 304–405. London: Heinemann, 1967.
RevQ	*Revue de Qumran*

Romance	*The Greek Alexander Romance.* Edited by R. Stoneman. London: Penguin, 1991.
SBT	Studies in Biblical Theology
SJT	*Scottish Journal of Theology*
SNTSMS	Society for New Testament Studies Monograph Series
Strabo	Strabo. *The Geography of Strabo.* London: Bell, 1913.
Tacitus, *Histories*	Tacitus. *The Histories, Books 1–3.* Translated by H. C. Hamilton. London: William Heinemann, 1987.
TDNT	*Theological Dictionary of the New Testament.* Edited by Gerhard Kittel and Gerhard Friedrich. Translated by Geoffrey W. Bromiley. 10 vols. Grand Rapids: Eerdmans, 1964–1976
Tiberius	Suetonius. *Tiberius.* In *Lives of the Caesars,* vol. 1, 311–417. Translated by R. Graves. LCL 31. London: Harvard University Press, 2001.
Trogus	Justin. *Epitome of the Philippic History of Pompeius Trogus.* Translated by J. C. Yardley. Oxford: Clarendon, 1997.
Trypho	Justin Martyr. *Dialogue with Trypho the Jew.* Translated by T. B. Falls. Washington, DC: Catholic University of America Press.
TS	*Theological Studies*
Valerius	Valerius Maximus. *Memorable Doings and Sayings.* Vol. 1. Edited and translated by D. R. Shackleton. London: Harvard University Press, 2000.
Vermes	*The Complete Dead Sea Scrolls in English.* Edited and Translated by G. Vermes. London: Penguin, 1998.
Vita Apoll.	Philostratus. *Life of Appolonius of Tyana.* Edited and translated by C. P. Jones. Harmondsworth: Penguin, 1970.
War	Josephus. *The Jewish War.* Translated by G. A. Williamson. London: Penguin, 1981.
WBC	Word Biblical Commentary
ZTK	*Zeitschrift für Theologie und Kirche*

Introduction

SON OF GOD-THE TITLE

In about 35 CE Jesus of Nazareth was killed by order of the Roman authorities. Forty years later, the Gospel narratives described him as a "Son of God." After a further two centuries, the meaning of this title was to divide the newly Christianized Roman Empire between those who saw this as meaning that Jesus was the only begotten Son of God "of one substance" with his heavenly Father and those who believed that he was created and hence a lesser god than his Father. The rights and wrongs of the argument do not affect this work; what is abundantly clear is that by the end of the second century CE there was universal acceptance by the Church that Jesus was indeed the Son of God and this had become his most significant title. This book is concerned with the origin of the appellation and what led Jesus to be so titled. As Chapter 3 will make plain, the title was one little used by the Jews in the first century CE. The Hebrew Scriptures refer to angels as sons of God and to Israel as God's son but hardly ever to a human being as the "Son of God," and in this practice they are followed by the writings of the Apocrypha and the Pseudepigrapha. The "Son of God" is certainly mentioned in the Dead Sea Scrolls but its use in them is unclear, while the first century writer Josephus never uses the title. For "Son of God" to become a major appellation used of Jesus by his followers within 40 years of his death indicates that some strong influence other than Judaism was operating on the writers of the New Testament. Indications of what this was to be are found by retelling a well-known story.

A man called Jesus, born in Nazareth around the beginning of the first century CE, becomes a wandering exorcist and teacher and is executed by the Roman authorities. His followers, however, remain convinced that he is still alive and that the message of his life continues to be of the greatest importance to the human race. They tell people about the significance that Jesus has for the Jewish religion and so become involved in a major confrontation with the Jewish authorities in Jerusalem. Believers in a living Jesus then spread outwards from that city, telling people everywhere that Jesus was a prophet and a messiah, an activity that leads to the formation of a new religious group within Judaism. The normal practice of followers of Jesus, notably Paul of Tarsus, is to preach in Jewish synagogues, particularly to the proselytes who, though not Jews, are impressed by Jewish beliefs. Soon non-Jews are admitted into the new faith without having to fully comply with the *Torah*[1] and this inevitably creates a schism between the followers of Jesus and those who followed the strict faith of Judaism.

A significant change occurs towards the end of the fifth decade of the century when the bearers of the message of Jesus enter the Greek peninsula. The New Testament describes it in the following way. While at Troas, Paul has a vision in which a man of Macedonia pleads with him to cross the Aegean Sea.[2] So Paul sets foot in the land of the Greeks, where he seems to be increasingly concerned to react with Gentiles rather than with the Jews. According to Acts, he does not go to the synagogue but to a place of prayer[3] and talks to the women he finds there. He talks in the market place at Athens and in front of the Areopagus and, while in Corinth, he ceases to preach to the Jews at all and concentrates on the Gentiles.[4] A separate religion, now called Christianity, is born.

The founder of this faith was, of course, Jesus of Nazareth, and there was the major problem "as "Son of Man,"[5] a title which clearly had an apocalyptic element,[6] but the meaning of which is otherwise uncertain. In the absence of any consensus on this subject, I accept that Hurtado's explanation is probably the right one. He argues that the disciples simply recorded that Jesus had called himself "Son of Man" without understanding why he had done so. According to the New Testament, followers of Jesus referred to him as a prophet and addressed him as Rabbi or teacher. Later they used the title Lord and referred to him as a messiah.[7] "Teacher" and "Lord" were words in common use throughout the Greek world, but "Messiah" was not. The further the messengers proclaiming the risen Jesus got from Jerusalem

1. Acts 15.
2. Acts 16:9; 2 Cor 2:12–13.
3. Acts 16:13.
4. Acts 18:6.
5. Mark 10:33; 13:26; 14:21
6. Dan 7:13.
7. Hurtado, *Mark*, 41–42.

and the more he was preached about among non-Jews, the less the hearers understood the identity of the messiah or what this person signified. The concept of a messiah might have been familiar to people in Antioch but very few would have heard of it in Asia Minor. In Macedonian, however, the title Messiah would have meant nothing to any except worshippers at Jewish synagogues. People began to speak about Jesus Christ without understanding the significance of the word Christ.[8] And if this title no longer conveyed the crucial importance of Jesus, a new descriptive title was needed and in Greece there was one ready to hand–Son of God. As Chapters 1 and 2 of this book will show, this was a title of great significance among the Greeks, used of both legendary heroes and more modern rulers. To speak of Jesus Christ as a Son of God suited the gospel message well, exalting Jesus to the highest plane and guaranteeing a hearing for those who spoke about him.

This had, however, two very important ramifications. The first began when the Church in Jerusalem learned that Jesus was being referred to as a "Son of God," a title startling to a Jewish constituency. For whereas Greek legend was redolent with stories of gods who came down from Olympus and begot sons of human women, such activities could not be applied to the God of the Hebrew Scriptures who was so holy that his name could not be spoken. So the begetting of Jesus began to assume mystic proportions; his mother became the "Virgin Mary" and Jesus the only begotten Son of God. Such nomenclature nullified the claim that Jesus was of the house and lineage of David for though Matthew and Luke demonstrate that Joseph was descended from David, they then show that Jesus was not Josephs son! The concept of Jesus as Son of God had far-reaching effects in the longer term. Jesus came to be recognized as part of the godhead himself, a vision which was to lead to the concept of the Trinity and which elevated his mother from Palestinian housewife to Mother of God and Queen of Heaven.

The second ramification lay in the effect that the title Son of God was to have on the Jesus story. Heracles, Perseus and Theseus had all been called sons of god because ancient myth taught that they were the result of the sexual union between a god and a mortal woman (see Chapter 1). But more recently there had been a figure whose activities may have become the subject of legend, but whose existence and many of whose deeds was entirely historic. As Chapter 2 will demonstrate, Alexander the Great believed himself to be, and was believed by many to be, a son of god. It seems to me inevitable that tales of the life of Alexander should significantly affect the way the life of Jesus was understood and presented to the followers of the latter.

---

8. The Greek translation of the Hebrew "Messiah" was "Christ."

This book explores the thesis that Alexander, as the greatest and most significant figure in the world of the fourth century BCE (including Judaea), was widely known as a son of god and as such provided the growing Church with an example for its founder. It also examines the idea that the life and deification of Alexander provided one template for the written life of Jesus as portrayed in the four Canonical Gospels. Little, it will be argued, is known of the life of the historical Jesus, so tales of his divine begetting, self-discovery, epiphany and affirmation had to be constructed (see Chapters 4 and 5). It is possible to see the story of Jesus aligned in some way to that of Alexander. Both are said to have had abnormal and divine births; both were said to be affirmed by their god as his son in remarkable circumstances; both were said to have been major victors; Alexander over powers both human and super human and Jesus over sin and death. Finally, both are recorded as dying at the age of 32, and it will be argued that Jesus is said to have died at this age because this was the age of Alexander when he died (see Chapter 7).

Chapter 6 shows the interplay between the titles of the Emperors and those given to Jesus. It will, for example, be argued that the Apostle Thomas adulation of the risen Jesus. My Lord and My God,[9] was based on the titles given to Domitian. It will also be shown that when an emperor was referred to as son of god the name of the god was not specified. So Augustus could be styled son of god without saying that the god in question was the recently deified Julius Caesar. This may have led to confusion.

A great climax in the Gospel of Mark is the statement by a Roman soldier at the foot of the cross as he observed the death of Jesus of Nazareth. Now when the centurion, who stood facing him, saw that in this way he breathed his last, he said, "Truly this man was God's Son!" (KJV: "Truly this man was the Son of God").[10] Such a statement is remarkable and has had a far-reaching effect. One tradition identifies this centurion with another of the same rank who appealed to Jesus to heal his servant.[11] From ten thousand pulpits the utterance of a Roman officer about a crucified Jew is proclaimed as a reason for believing in the divine son-ship of Jesus of Nazareth. When George Stevens produced his film *The Greatest Story Ever Told* in 1965, no lesser person than John Wayne was brought in to speak the single line, "Truly this man was the Son of God."

But almost certainly the words of the Roman soldier are fictitious and are certainly misrepresented. The supporters of Jesus who were present are

9. John 20:28.

10. Mark 15:39.

11. Matt 8:5–13.

said by Mark to be women looking on from a distance[12] and these cannot have realistically have heard what the centurion said. What the soldier actually said is different from the normal English translations given, for the Greek from which it is translated reads truly this man was *a* son of *a* god (*uios theou*). There is no reason to believe that the centurion was a believer in the God (who would surely have been written *the* god–*ho theos*) of the Jews; his deity was almost certainly Jupiter or Mars. Doubts about the historicity of the statement are strengthened by the report in Luke's Gospel where the centurion is said to have praised God (*ho theos*) and said, "Certainly this man was innocent." The use of son of god can lead to misunderstanding. This subject is explored further in Appendix 3.

12. Mark 15:49.

1

The Pedigree of the Term Son of God
(pre 350 BCE)

The area with which this book is concerned stretches from the river Danube to the upper reaches of the river Nile and from the Adriatic Sea to Hindu Kush. From the sixth until the second century BCE, this was an area dominated by three cultures: Persian, Egyptian and Greek. The struggles between these cultures form the background to the thesis. Ideas about their gods were worked out against a background of war and conquest.

What immediately emerges from an examination of the cultures of Persia and Egypt is that the king was an essential part of them. As Frankfort points out: "The ancient Near East considered kingship the very basis of civilization."[1] This is not just because the king was the person who held temporal power, though that was an important factor, but because the whole ethos of the cultures was based on the concept of monarchy. As will be seen, the king was a significant part of the religious practices of such cultures. The same had been true of Greece and Macedon, but by 350 BCE Athens had experimented with democracy and the role of the king was being reassessed throughout Greece.

The purpose of this chapter is to establish the religious beliefs and practices of Persian, Egyptian and Greek cultures and to investigate the part played by the king in each. When that is done, the nature and authority of kingship will be explored and as will the kings relationship with the gods of his realm. Finally the question must be asked as to whether the term "Son of God" had meaning in each culture, and if so, in what way?

1. Frankfort, *Kingship*, 3.

1

The religions of all three cultures were polytheistic. Each religion, it is widely accepted, had developed from the interaction of humans with the force of nature and the efforts of men and women to exercise some influence over this force by prayer, sacrifice and ritual. "At first the supreme force would seem awesome and mysterious," writes Silverman, "but once it could be comprehended as an entity, it could be recognized, understood, and then reinterpreted in a familiar and recurrent form. In a way, it could be harnessed. *It became humanized* [my italics]." That is, it was put in terms that the individual could understand. He goes on: "Once the form of the deity had been developed, a legend, myth, or story was formulated to explain its origin and associations, and in this process the god received a name. Stories were told about these deities. They went into battle and travelled by boat. Some even drank to excess . . ."[2] In other words, the gods were like men in almost every respect, capable of loving and hating, rewarding and punishing those in their power. Indeed, it was their immortality that seemed alone to differentiate them from humankind.

The religions of these three societies had also this in common; they had no definitive scripture and no identifiable founder. They had no Bible and no Koran and they had no Jesus and no Buddha. Knowledge of the religions of ancient Persia and ancient Egypt depends upon ostraca, carvings and murals, amplified by some writings of Greeks who had visited them. Though the Greeks wrote about their own religion, this tended (as will be seen) to be in the form of stories, myths and legends rather than descriptive accounts It follows that there can be no certainty of what was and what was not to be held as true. Further, since the religions were constantly evolving, it can be little more than speculation as to what is held to be the religious view of the peoples for much of the time.

ANCIENT PERSIA

The area known to the world as Mesopotamia produced societies of great antiquity—the Hittite, Assyrian and Babylonian empires to name but three. They were ruled by kings who were first and foremost war leaders and as such had absolute power.[3] Success in war to both king and people meant expansion, wealth and security; failure meant annexation, annihilation and slavery. So a strong king was a good king, able to protect the people that he ruled, and, by conquering surrounding territory, increase his nation's wealth and security, and perhaps even create an empire. For example, when in 550

2. Silverman, *Divinities and Deities*, 15–22.

3. Frankfort, *Kingship*, 52.

BCE Cyrus (the Great) acceded to the throne of Persia (then a province of the Babylonian empire), he established the new Persian empire by conquest. He overran Lydia and Babylon; his son, Cambyses I, conquered Egypt, and Darius I (next in line) annexed Afghanistan, making him king of the largest empire yet seen in the Middle East. In only one enterprise Darius failed; his move westward was checked at the battle of Marathon in 492 BCE and this began a long series of wars which was only to end with the total success of a Greco-Macedonian army under the command of Alexander the Great, which led to him becoming the Great King of Persia.

The pantheon of gods worshipped by the Persians was forever expanding and changing, though it is clear that by the time of Cyrus the chief of their gods was Ahura–Mazda, a name which means either "God of Iran" or "Wise Lord."[4] This very changeability led to religious tolerance, the Persians being able to adapt to or to assimilate the religions of the people they conquered. So when Cyrus entered Babylon in triumph, he took the hand of Bel Marduk (the Babylonian divinity) to signify that he had been adopted as his son.[5] When he discovered a Jewish enclave in Babylon, Cyrus permitted those who wished to return to Jerusalem and provided them with financial assistance to rebuild their temple,[6] actions which earned him the title Messiah.[7] And for similar generosity, when Darius became ruler of Egypt, he was accorded the title Setetu-Ra (Ra hath begotten him) and took his place in the hierarchy of the religion of Egypt.[8] The religion of the Persians grew and expanded. Westerners found it an easy religion to accept; ancient writers equated Ahura–Mazda with Zeus and Jupiter.[9]

The Persians were in due course to receive the wisdom of the prophet Zarathustra or Zoroaster though exactly when he lived is unclear. Although his ideas were to transform the faith of the Persians by the introduction of the reverence for fire, his teaching are irrelevant to this book in that they did not involve the role of the king and nowhere did Zarathustra teach that the king was a god.[10]

In fact, the kings of Persia had never been divine. "Contrary to the opinion of some Greek authors," writes Briant, "the king himself was never

---

4. Razmjou, "Religion and Burial Customs," 15; Olmstead, *History*, 24.

5. Rogers, *A History*, 65.

6. Ezra 1:2–8.

7. Isa 45:1.

8. Rogers, *A History*, 162.

9. Herod. 1.131; Curtius, 3.3.11.

10. Olmstead, *History*, 24; Razmjou, "Religion and Burial Customs," 15. Wieshofer, *Ancient Persia*, 30; Briant, *From Cyrus to Alexander*, 241.

considered a god."[11] Frankfort provides a rationale for this fact. The royal rulers received their authority from the gods and had to respond to this by reacting to the way those gods showed their power in the lands they ruled. Mesopotamia, literally the land between the rivers Tigris and Euphrates, was dominated by those rivers and they were unpredictable in the extreme. The king of Persia ruled over a land of constant change and had to cope with whatever happened. He stood between the gods and his people, an earnest of the sympathetic but unpredictable will of the Persian gods and he was mortal.[12] Alexander, by becoming Great King of the Persian Empire, *did not become a god or son of a god.*

ANCIENT EGYPT

Ancient Egypt was originally a country whose borders were determined by the watershed of the lower reaches of the river Nile. This river floods and dries on a yearly pattern and the people that live on its banks enjoy excellent irrigation for their crops, flocks and herds as a result. The Nile was nothing less than their source of life and their stability, something further guaranteed by their insularity. Egypt was surrounded by desert lands, the tribes of which were generally small and disunited. The Mediterranean Sea was a source of trade and only occasionally did forces of aggression emerge from it. It is small wonder that for 6000 years, Egypt retained its cohesive stability. The one danger spot lay to its north east, from where, beyond the Sinai Peninsula, forces from successive and increasingly powerful Mesopotamian empires would seek to conquer the fertile plains of Egypt. In 1299 BCE, the Egyptian Pharaoh, Ramesses II, made a pre-emptive strike against one of them and the drawn Battle of Kadesh bought Egypt a further 600 years of freedom from incursion.[13] But by seventh century BCE, Egypt could no longer resist and became a province by turn of Babylon, Persia and Macedon, before recovering independence under the rule of the Greek Ptolemies.

Egyptians were great traders and their harbors were open to Greek ships and merchants. There is evidence that the Greeks were trading with Egypt before 700 BCE and this trade led the Greeks to explore something of the Nile and experience Egyptian culture. Indeed, Egypt had a unique influence on Greek culture; the impression given by the huge temples and statues produced a permanent effect. But if the Greeks were admirers of Egypt, the Egyptians did not entirely welcome the Greeks. From 570 BCE the latter

12. Frankfort, *Kingship,* 4–6, 230.
13. Goodenough, *Tactical Genius,* 29–32.

were confined to the "treaty port" of Naucratis in the western delta of the Nile.[14] Denied access to the center of Egypt, the Greeks of this community explored the land to the west of Naucratis and established links with the oasis of Siwa and with the Greek community at Cyrene.

By about 3000 BCE the Egyptians were starting to codify their gods, giving coherence to their beliefs and names, and also ascribing personalities to their gods. This done, they produced images of those gods, which frequently took the form of animals engaged in human activities. A myth was then created to explain the name and origin of each divinity, for the Egyptians believed that to know the name of the god was to gain some control over both him and the powers he represented. The natural elements were deified more than in Persia or Greece and soon took human form; Geb (earth), Nut (sky) were worshipped alongside Khonsu and Thoth (moon gods) and Ra[15] (sun god).[16]

Though the Nile provided a superb channel of communication and as such united Egypt, its great length ensured that there was no one supreme religious center for the Egyptians. Thebes, Memphis, Heliopolis and Hermopolis along the banks of the Nile were independent religious communities and each had their own creation myths and their own gods who were preeminent figures in their regions. But, after a thousand years of bickering over names, two of these divinities, Ammon and Ptah, became gods who had national significance. Further, "in Dynasty 18, Amun (Ammon) and Re (Ra) were combined to form the deity Men (Ammon)—Re (Ra)," writes David, "who was worshipped as "King of the Gods" and supreme deity of the Egyptian Empire." As in the case of Ahura–Mazda of Persia, the composite god Ammon–Ra of Egypt was soon recognized by the Greeks as Zeus, the father of the gods.[17]

In his introduction to *The Gods of the Egyptians*, Budge writes: "The Egyptians . . . believed that they were a divine nation and that they were ruled by kings who were themselves gods incarnate. . . When the gods ceased to reign in their proper persons on earth, they were succeeded by a series of demi-gods and these were followed by the kings."[18]

The Egyptians understood that they needed a ruler who was both god and man to intercede between the human and divine world. Their king not

---

14. Burn, *History,* 95–96.

15. The spelling and names of the Egyptian gods vary considerably. I have used Ra and Ammon for the ones most important to this book.

16. For details of Egyptian deities refer to Silverman, *Divinities and Deities,* 13–33.

17. David, *Religion,* 402.

18. Budge, *The Gods,* 3.

only functioned as the high priest of every god but he stood between the god and humankind as god and man. Pharaoh was not only of divine essence but a god incarnate.[19]

There is equal agreement that Pharaoh was styled Son of Ra and that this appellation tended to emphasize his divinity.[20] There is doubt as to whether the actual coronation of Pharaoh made him a god or whether his acclamation as king simply recognized him as such but as Son of Ra Pharaoh was a divinity. This has crucial significance for, as Green writes: "When Alexander reached Memphis, he was acclaimed Pharaoh and on 14th November 332, he was instituted as Pharaoh. He became simultaneously god and king, the incarnation and son of Ra and Osiris."[21] To the Egyptians Alexander had become a son of god.

If a Greek explorer travelled south across the sea in the fourth century BCE, he would have discovered Egypt, a place of mystery and legend. He would have brought back exotic tales of pyramids and vast temples, of sacred processions and gods who were depicted as part animal and part human. He would have seen the advantages of trade with this Eldorado and, on his return to Greece, would have encouraged it. In this wonderland he would have heard tell of the semi-divine Pharaoh, who ruled as a god and whose royal trappings were those of the god–priest. He would have spoken of him with admiration and reverence.

But had the explorer travelled east by land, he would have found himself in Persia. This country had for nearly 200 years been the enemy of Greece, the bogey man that troubled their assemblies and councils. Greek stories told of the pomp and luxury that surrounded the king of Persia, which they regarded with a mixture of awe and derision. The explorer would have seen the reverence with which the subjects of the Great King greeted him and would have easily misunderstood it. Historical research may reveal to the modern student that the Great King was not a god, but would the explorer accept this? Would he not have believed that all this adulation was the offering of divine honors to the king and reported on his return to Greece that he had seen a god? The explorer, surely, would have mocked the effeteness of the Persian court but not doubted that it was the setting for a divine person.

After his decisive victory over the Persians at Issus in 333, Alexander took a bath in the captured tent of the Great King. "Here, when he beheld the bathing vessels, the water pots, the pans, and the ointment boxes, all of gold curiously wrought, and smelt the fragrant odors with which the whole

19. Frankfort, *Kingship*, 5–6; Goedicke, *Religion*, 57–58.

20. Silverman, *Divinities and Deities*, 59–65; David, *Religion*, 90.

21. Green, *Alexander*, 269.

palace was exquisitely perfumed, and from thence passed into a pavilion of great size and height, where couches and tables and preparations for entertainment were perfectly magnificent, he turned to those about him and said, 'This, it seems, is royalty.'[22] Alexander may have understood that these trappings were for a mortal man but it is likely that many soldiers (like the mythical explorer) would see them as symbols of divinity.

ANCIENT GREECE

Whereas Mesopotamia and Egypt were societies dominated by rivers, Greece was dominated by the sea. It is mistaken to see Greece as a peninsula, for the hundreds of islands, many of which are very close to Asia Minor, are an integral part of Greece. The biggest of the islands, Crete, provided an impetus for development, for its Minoan civilization was to be a rival to the Mycenaean civilization of the Greek Peloponnese and so created a stimulating conflict of trade and ideas that was to prove a founding factor in the development of Greece.

The Minoan and Mycenaean civilizations essentially sought pre-eminence over surrounding areas through trade alone and perhaps for that reason imperialism was not a part of Greek civilization. There were a myriad of small kingdoms around Mycenae and each had their own king, the High King of Mycenae itself being *primus inter pares* (the first among equals). This was to be an earnest of things to come for there was never to be a king or an emperor of Greece. The peninsula and its islands were to have many small kingdoms or city states, and though some, like Athens and Sparta, were to become more significant than others, and at times came to dominate much of Greece, independent the city states and small kingdoms remained. During the first 700 years of the first millennium BCE, the small states perpetually squabbled and fought with one another, like bad tempered children in a garden.

But to extend the metaphor, there was a dangerous man in the next-door garden. Twice the massive Persian Empire tried to conquer Greece and twice it failed; many of the city states uniting to prevent it. The campaign of Marathon in 490 BCE and in that of Salamis in 480 ensured that Greece retained its independence. After these failures, Persia contented itself with the policy of supporting one Greek faction against another and thereby preventing any Greek city from becoming strong enough to seriously trouble Persia. This policy was remarkably successful until the middle of the fourth century when Philip II of Macedon assumed control of Greece.

22. Plutarch 11.232.

Religion

This subject of religion of Greece must be approached in a different way to the religion of Persia or Egypt; indeed Calame doubts whether it is an appropriate subject for study. He writes: "Neither myth nor religion constitutes a category native to Greek thought. Neither myth nor religion were conceived of as such by the Greeks—neither myth as a corpus of (fabulous) tales of gods and heroes dependent on a frame of comprehensive thought, nor religion as a set of beliefs and practices relative to a divine configuration. The aetiological relationship between the divine story and the cult practices . . . is thus established by essentially poetic and discursive means."[23]

Burkert similarly emphasizes the paramount importance of the poetic writing: practically the whole of ancient poetry is our principle evidence for Greek religion.[24] Thus the student of Greek spirituality must turn to the poets and notably to the writings of Homer, whose classic stories, *The Iliad* and *The Odyssey,* have been described as the Greek Bible.[25]

In his introduction to *The Iliad,* Jones states:

> Herodotus argued that Homer (and Hesiod . . . who composed The Theogony [The Birth of the Gods]) gave the Greeks their divinities. His point was that, from time immemorial, gods had been worshipped, through ritual, as faceless powers representing almost every aspect of human existence, who needed appeasing in order to stop them acting against humans with all the blind, irresistible force of, say, gravity. But Homer and Hesiod for the first time gave gods an individual, human face and made a community out of them, informing us of their birth, family relationships, characteristics and everyday activities.[26]

The most powerful gods and goddesses (called the Olympians) had their home on Mount Olympus where Homer portrays them as a big quarrelsome family with an interest in the affairs of mortal men with whom they interact. Two examples of their behaviors are particularly instructive. The war-god Ares is stabbed in the belly by a mortal (Diomedes) and complains to Zeus, the king of the gods. He receives a chilling reply: "You shifty hypocrite, don't come whining to me. I hate you more than any other god on Olympus."[27] On another occasion Aphrodite, goddess of love instructs

---

23. Calame, *Greek Myth,* 259.
24. Burkbert, *Greek Religion,* 4.
25. Burn, *Greece,* 79.
26. From the introduction to *Iliad,* edited by Jones.
27. *Iliad* 5.889.

Helen of Sparta to make love to Paris, prince of Troy. Helen feels able to reply "No, go sit with him yourself. Forget you are a goddess. Never set foot on Olympus again but go and agonize over Paris, go and pamper him, and one day he may make you his wife—or his concubine." Helen's use of such an abrasive tone to a goddess prompts this terrifying reply from Aphrodite: "Obstinate wretch! Don't get the wrong side of me, or I may desert you in my anger and detest you as vehemently as I have loved you up till now, and provoke Greeks and Trojans alike to such hatred of you that you would come to a dreadful end."[28]

Three important points are established by these quotations. First, the gods think, react and generally behave as human beings and have the same capacity for anger, capriciousness and self-interest. Mortals can identify with them and talk about them in play, in ritual and around the campfire with humor and bawdiness, in much the same way that people of today mock those in political power. Secondly, the morality of the gods does not exceed that of mortals; indeed sometimes it seems inferior to it. For example, at the time of the instruction by Aphrodite to Helen, the latter was married to the king of Sparta. Helen was being *commanded* to commit adultery. But thirdly, there is an altogether darker side to the gods; they are to be feared and obeyed, however doubtful their motives and morality. When Homer describes gods in the third-person, they can be majestic beings. Even the gods acknowledge Zeus as their master, however reluctantly.[29]

Sons of God

A feature of Greek religion was that the gods delighted in sex, something clearly illustrated in Book 14 of The *Iliad*. When Hera wishes to distract Zeus, she borrows Aphrodites girdle and flaunts herself before him. The king of the gods says to her:

> Come; let us to bed and the delights of love. Never has such desire, for goddess or mortal overwhelmed my heart; no, not when I loved Ixion's wife who bore Perithous, wise as the gods; or Danae of the slim ankles, daughter of Acrisius, who gave birth to Perseus, the greatest hero of his time; or the far-famed daughter of Phoenix, who bore me Minos and godlike Rhadamanthus; or Semele, or Alcmene in Thebes, whose son was lion-hearted Heracles, while Semele bore Dionysus, mankinds delight; or lady Demeter with her lovely hair, or incomparable Leto; or you

28. *Iliad* 3.406–20.
29. *Iliad* 1.528.

yourself—never have I felt such desire for you, or has such sweet longing overwhelmed me.[30]

So Heracles and Perseus (among others) are portrayed as sons of god by virtue of a sexual union between a god and a woman. This grants them the legendary powers that enable Heracles to accomplish his twelve labors and Perseus to destroy the Medusa. Perseus, Heracles and Theseus typify what it means to be a son of god; heroic, possessed of special powers and gifts, a doer of good deeds and beloved of gods and men.

However, the sexual union of a god and a mortal woman does not preclude their issue having a mortal father as well. This is delightfully illustrated by the legend of Theseus. Aigeus, king of Athens, visits the King of Troizen, who leads him, while drunk, to the bed of his virgin daughter, Aithra. The consummation does not satisfy Aithra who leaves her bed and crosses to a small island where she has intercourse with Poseidon, the sea god. The resulting child, Theseus, is son of Aigeus and able to claim the crown of Athens on Aigeus' death, but he is also son of Poseidon and as such receives superhuman powers, which enable him to overcome such monsters as the Cretan Minotaur.[31]

Similarly Heracles, who is generally recognized as the greatest Greek hero, was not only hailed as a son of god but also believed to have attained full divinity after his death. In legend, he is part mortal (son of Alcmene) and part divine (son of Zeus).[32] His life is spent in performing good deeds, notably accomplishing his Twelve Labors. After his death, he is introduced to Olympus by the goddess Athene, granted the divine Hebe as wife and becomes a god. *Son of god by virtue of his birth, Heracles becomes god by virtue of his labors.* As a god, his cult became widespread; he was worshiped as a god in Egypt and identified with the Phoenician god Melqart.[33] His story and subsequent deification were to have a powerful effect on Alexander the Great.

The small Greek states were originally ruled by kings who, in the period of pre-history, were sometimes accounted sons of god. The legendary Theseus, for example, was king of Athens. But it must be noted that in the *Iliad* and the *Odyssey* kings were often depicted as mortal beings; neither King Priam of Troy nor King Agamemnon of the Greeks were hailed as divine by Homer. As the history of Greece unfolded, the importance of kingship diminished. The growth of political debate in Athens led to widespread

---

30. *Iliad* 14.312–40.

31. Plutarch 3.4; Renault, *The King Must Die,* 369–70.

32. Herod. 4, 9.

33. Herod. 2.44; Rawlings and Bowden, *Heracles and Hercules,* vii.

changes throughout Greece and the significant figures emerged who were not kings. So Lysander of Sparta and Epaminondas of Thebes became great military commanders and Pericles of Athens a noted statesman. Though all these were crucial to the development of Greece, they were not kings. Nowhere is this better illustrated than in the Thermopylae/Salamis campaign of 480 BCE; the Greek commander at Thermopylae was Leonidas, king of Sparta, while the non-royal Themistocles was the victor of Salamis. There seems to have been no problem among the Greek allies in soldiers serving under a royal or non-royal general.[34] Though in the fourth century BCE some states, including Macedon, were ruled by kings, kingship was no longer seen as essential for good order and political stability.

This is a significant point. Philip of Macedon and his son Alexander were in some sense anachronistic figures in the Greek world, belonging rather to a bygone age than typical of contemporary Greek practice. It was their immense ability on the field of battle that occasioned their acceptance as leader of the Greek coalition and not their royal status. The idea that they were in any sense perceived sons of god in the mythological pattern of Heracles or Perseus is to be dismissed. When Alexander invaded Persia in 334 he was certainly not thought by anyone to be a son of god.

Oracles

Throughout Greece there were many temples to the variety of gods and these religious buildings were generally under the control of the civic authorities, who laid down the dates and times of sacrifices and employed the priests. There was no central control, structure or authority in Greek religion and no prophets were attached to these temples. Those who wanted divine advice had to look elsewhere and therefore visited what they called an oracle. Oracles were to be found in specific shrines and there a question could be put to a god and an answer received. Parke writes: "To the Greeks the method of ascertaining the will of the gods was of particular importance because they possessed, generally speaking, no sacred books. Within the wide field of prophecy the oracular center with its fixed location and its traditional methods of enquiry provides a particular manifestation of Greek religion and life."[35]

There were originally two important centers of oracular utterance in Greece; that of Zeus at Dodona and that of Apollo at Delphi. From the start there was rivalry between them and the myths that surrounded their

34. Goodenough, *Tactical Genius*, 89–92.
35. Parke, *Oracles*, 9–10.

foundation laid stress to their pre-eminence. According to the myths surrounding Dodona, Jason, when building the good ship Argo to go in search
of the Golden Fleece, went to Dodona to get a bough from the sacred oak
to be part of his vessel and Dodona provided him with a prophet to go with
it. But in the Delphic story the Argonauts were accompanied by Idmon, a
son of Apollo. Clearly the seeker for truth had two centers competing for
his custom.

The oracles were of considerable antiquity and brief reference to both
is to be found in Homer. In the *Iliad*, Achilles refers to the stone threshold
of Phoebus Apollo in rocky Delphi. In the *Odyssey*, when the hero wants
to know whether to return home openly or in disguise, the reader learns
that Odysseus had gone to Dodona to learn the will of Zeus from the great
oak tree that is sacred to the god. How the suppliants learned the will of
the god in early times is not known, but in due course the mutterings and
murmuring of the Dodona oak were interpreted by devotees of the god,
who were famed for the fact that they did not wash their feet and slept on
the ground.[36] At Delphi a priestess, known as the Pythia, muttered in a kind
of trance and her utterances were in due course presented to the supplicant
by the adherent priests in hexamic verse. Some oracular utterances have
been handed down to modern day scholars, perhaps the most famous being
when Athens was threatened by the hordes of Xerxes in 480 and was told to
rely on her wooden walls, which Athenians rightly interpreted as being their
fleet. But there were other reasons than a national emergency for consulting
an oracle. Members of a city state, for example, went if they were thinking
of founding another city.

Parke tells us: "It is in the period of Greek colonisation from the last
third of the eighth century that the Delphic oracle first emerges prominently
in Greek history. This was particular appropriate because of the importance
and significance to the Greeks of founding a colony . . . it was a religious
innovation. The colony would need to found on its site temples and sanc-
tuaries to the gods and heroes and for this purpose must carry the blessing
of heaven."[37]

As the founding of a new city or town established no political links
with its mother city, a religious link was of considerable importance. Before
the development of the Greek part of the city of Cyrene could be undertaken, the approval of the Delphic oracle had first to be sought. The resulting center of Greek culture in Libya had divine sanction, so the ties between
Cyrene and Greece were religious.

36. Ibid., 20–31.
37. Ibid., 44.

But it was not only cities that sought advice from an oracle; individuals might do so as well. An individual might go to an oracle to seek cleansing of blood guilt after he had killed someone. Whereas in Homer the slaying of a man was not regarded as an act of impurity, but one for which the victim's family would demand a blood price, by the seventh century BCE the killing of someone was increasingly regarded as contaminating the whole community from which he came and so visits to oracles for ritual purification became a normal activity.[38]

Siwa is one of the most significant oases in the desert west of North Africa. It came to recent prominence as the base for the Long Range Desert Group of the 8th Army in World War 2. Following the defeat of the Axis armies in North Africa, Fakhry undertook a study of the history of the oasis at Siwa on behalf of the Egyptian government and his report remains the most significant work on Siwa to this day.[39] Since ancient times, he argues, the inhabitants of this [Siwa] oasis have been distinct from the Egyptians and connected more closely with North Africa than with the Nile Valley. When, in 671 BCE, King Esarhaddon of Assyria invaded Egypt and the country descended into chaos, goods from the East, which had come through Egypt, came through the Sudan to Cyrene and this trade led to an increase of wealth for the whole area. This development was obviously the reason for Greek interest in Libya, an interest that further developed with the treaty port of Naucratis.

The existence of an oracle at Siwa, which was originally a branch of the temple of Ammon at Thebes, can be traced back to 1500 BCE when the then Pharaoh made two obelisks to fulfill a promise to Ammon. But not until the sixth century BCE did that oracle become known to the wider world; concern at Greek interest led the Egyptians to take an interest in Siwa and to dominate the area from 500 BCE. Siwa was one of the seven oracles consulted by Croesus and was certainly consulted by both the Athenians and Spartans during the Peloponnesian War.

CONCLUSION

In 350 BCE both Persia and Egypt enjoyed a polytheistic culture and neither of them had anything which could be described as Sacred Scriptures. Persians initially displayed a remarkable religious tolerance to the religions of other cultures and though Egyptians were defensive of their own religion for themselves, they showed no sign of wishing to impose their faith on

38. Ibid., 60–62.
39. Fakhry, *Siwa Oasis* forms the basis of these paragraphs on Siwa.

other societies. In 350 both societies had come to recognize a supreme god; Ahura–Mazda in Persia and Ammon–Ra in Egypt. The Greeks regarded these gods as their own supreme god, Zeus.

To Persians and Egyptians the king was an essential part of the religion, but whereas the Persians regarded their Great King as human and in no sense a god, Egyptians saw their Pharaoh as becoming semi–divine through adoption by their gods at the time of his coronation and referred to him as son of Ra (the sun god). Persia and Egypt differed in that while the title Son of God had no meaning in Persian religion, it had deep significance to Egypt.

Greek religion was also polytheistic and though it had no Sacred Scripture, Greeks had in the works of Homer and Hesiod stories of their gods and these tales permeated their faith. Greeks accepted that these gods lived on Mount Olympus from whence they came among humans and begot sons and daughters, beings of mythological significance who were called sons of god, such as Heracles and Perseus. It follows that Son of God was an appellation with much meaning in Greece.

Greeks believed that the will of the gods could be understood through sacred oracles. Of these the most famous were Delphi and Dodona in Greece but there were others, notably Siwa in the Libyan Desert, which was sacred to the Egyptian god Ammon, whom the Greeks knew as Zeus. This oracle's most famous visitor was Alexander the Great, who, in a life-changing visit, went to Siwa in 331 BCE. The crucial significance of this occasion will be discussed in Chapter 2.

2

What We Know of Alexander the Great

INTRODUCTION

In Chapter 1 it was shown that the Greeks believed that their gods came to earth and mated with humans, producing a semi-divine being called a hero or a son of god. Such beings had special powers (e.g., Hercules had great strength; Achilles could not be wounded other than in his heel) and were credited with historic achievements (e.g., Theseus founded Athens and Perseus slew the Gorgon). But they all had this in common, that although they were given histories by Greek writers, *they belonged to the world of myth.* Even if they owed their origin to an historical figure, the sons of god were legendary characters. However, this was to change in the fourth century with the life and career of King Alexander III of Macedon, known to history as Alexander the Great. Indisputably a historical character, he was believed by many to be a son of god. The story of how he (as well as many who encountered him) came to believe this was to transform the title Son of God from an appellation of a mythical character to the description of a historical figure and thereby opened the way for its use to describe other people from history, one of whom was Jesus of Nazareth. This chapter explores the reasons why Alexander was accorded the title of Son of God.

In 331 BCE, Alexander visited the shrine of the oracle at Siwa in the Libyan Desert. This was sacred to the god Ammon and had attracted the attention of the Greeks by the seventh century BCE, who identified the Egyptian Ammon with the Greek Zeus. According to some of the sources, to be discussed later in this chapter, the senior priest or prophet greeted Alexander with the words "welcome, son of god." Any examination of the claim that Alexander was regarded as a son of god must surely have a major regard for what is supposed to have been said by the priest at the temple of Ammon—Zeus at Siwa.

In Chapter 1, the significance of the title Son of God in Persia, Egypt and Greece has been examined and it is quite possible to assess what the hearers of the prophet's words might have believed he meant. However, the question must be asked, is there any real evidence that these words were ever uttered? Could they simply be myth or human invention? What is actually known about Alexander? There are, indeed, a number of sources that describe his life and their accuracy must be assessed. But it is also pertinent to ask if this was the only occasion that such a suggestion was made about Alexander and why Siwa was to prove so important an event in his life. Only when these points are clear can there be a detailed reconstruction of what may actually have happened at Siwa and an examination of what recent historians have written about it be undertaken.

But the reconstruction must also consider *The Romance of Alexander*. This ever-growing collection of myths and folk tales contains stories of Alexander, compiled mainly by those he conquered, and also includes various accounts of Alexander's birth. Though never intending to be regarded as history, these myths and legends reveal how Alexander was viewed in many parts of the world and, where they refer to his divinity, they are pertinent to this thesis. The written collection of these stories used in this book is *The Greek Alexander Romance*, edited by Stoneman and published in 1991 by Penguin Books. Its value is discussed in the Appendix 1.

It has been established in Chapter 1 that Pharaoh was styled Son of Ra and, therefore, if Alexander became Pharaoh, he could be appropriately addressed in this way. But it has also been shown that in the Egyptian pantheon, the god Ra was associated with the god Ammon to form a supreme god, Ammon-Ra, who the Greeks recognized as Zeus. It does not require a serious stretch of the imagination to believe that a Pharaoh might be referred to as "Son of Zeus," particularly at the shrine of Ammon–Zeus. An Egyptian who heard his Pharaoh referred to as a son of Zeus would see this as a sign of respect by the Greek speaker who uttered it. It may have been that the greeting of the priest meant little more than, "Welcome, Your Majesty."

However, Siwa was not an Egyptian shrine, but an international one and Greeks had been involved with it for centuries. In Chapter 1, it was established that the Greeks worshipped gods who came down from their home on Mount Olympus, took human (or even animal) form and fathered children, who were known as sons of god. Such progeny included Heracles, Perseus and Theseus, all of whom were legendary characters and possessed supernatural powers. A Greek who heard someone of the exceptional prowess of Alexander referred to as Son of God by a respected oracle would not find this an impossible concept but he would be impressed beyond measure. It would be something he would talk about for the rest of his life; he would feel a sense of reverence for that person and would expect mighty happenings at his hands. And if a Greek bystander would react in this way, how much more would Alexander himself be affected? The words of the priest could mean nothing less than "you are divine!" So how would Alexander accept the welcome the greeting: "Hail, Son of God?" Would he hear it with Egyptian ears or with Greek ears? Would he accept it as respectful flattery or a real statement from Ammon-Zeus, the god of the shrine? To answer such a question there is a need to understand Alexander and recognize what his known about him.

Alexander was the natural inspirer of legends and many surround his name. His modern biographer is presented with a great deal of material, some of which is more legend than history. More than twenty contemporaries of Alexander wrote books about him but not one of these survives. There are, however, five biographies of Alexander from antiquity and they were written by Diodorus, Trogus, Curtius, Plutarch, and Arrian.

Diodorus Siculus

Probably the earliest of the five to write was Diodorus, whose only surviving work is the forty books of his *Universal History*. These were probably written in the latter part of the first century BCE and in some ways paralleled Pliny's *Natural History*. Diodorus's account of Alexander (in Book 17) is sandwiched between his report on Greece in fourth century BCE (Book 15), his life of Philip II (Book 16) and his history of Alexander's successors (Book 18). Therefore Diodorus puts Alexander in a historical context and compares him with other rulers, generals and philosophers of his epoch, greatly to his advantage.

Justin—Pompeius Trogus

Trogus was a Gaul, a contemporary of Diodorus and the son of a secretary of Julius Caesar, who also wrote a universal history, of forty-four books, entitled *The Philippic Histories*. These have survived only in fragments quoted by other authors, one of whom was a teacher of rhetoric called Justin who, visiting Rome in about 200 CE, wrote an *Epitome of the Philippic History of Pompeius Trogus.*[1] Books 11 and 12 of this work are concerned with Alexander the Great.

Quintus Rufus Curtius

Curtius is generally assumed to have been a soldier and a politician who lost office under Tiberius but regained it under Claudius, employing his period of disgrace writing his *History of Alexander the Great.*[2] There were originally twelve books, but only the last ten survive and the narrative of Book 3 takes up the story with Alexander already in Asia Minor. "At a time when contemporary Roman themes, or else universal histories were popular," writes Yardley, "Curtius' semi-biographical account of a Macedonian conqueror from the remote past seems somewhat an oddity."[3] Curtius is the only one of the five biographers to write in Latin.

Plutarch

Plutarch grew up in central Greece in the late first century CE and became a senior administrative figure of the Roman administration and also a priest at the shrine of the Delphic oracle. Late in life he wrote his *The Parallel Lives,* the great work of his life. His method was to take two famous figures of history and contrast them. By comparing Alexander with Julius Caesar, he produced for both lives that are rich in history and legend.

Arrian (Flavius Arrianus Xenophon)

Arrian was a wealthy Greek, whose father had obtained Roman citizenship and enabled Arrian to pursue a career in the imperial service. Around 135 CE, he served as a general in Cappadocia before retiring to Athens to write about Alexander. Having been fascinated by the Athenian soldier Xenophon, after whom he was named, he modeled his history on Xenophon's *Anabasis* and called it *Anabasis Alexandrii (Campaigns of Alexander).*

All five of these authors tell the same story. They tell the story of Alexander's remarkable journey of conquest, his four great victories of Granicus, Issus, Gaugamela and Hydaspes, his siege of Tyre, his visits to Afghanistan

1. From the introduction by Yardley *Epitome of the Philippic History,* 2.

2. Worthington, *Alexander,* 234.

3. Quoted from the introduction by Yardley, *The History of Alexander,* 9.

and India and his early death. They reveal a very remarkable young man and a superb general and it will become clear that Alexander would never have been considered as a son of god but for this general picture. However the actual claim to divine sonship depends upon certain specific stories and these vary from biography to biography. Some of these variations may be due to the bias of the author, while others are perhaps due to the sources available to some but not to others. Some examples of each are given below.

An example of bias may be seen when Persepolis was deliberately set on fire and damaged during its occupation by the Macedonian army in 330. Trogus alone does not make Alexander responsible for this arson. Arrian sees it as an act of revenge for the burning of Athens during the Thermopylae campaign. Diodorus, Curtius and Plutarch attribute the destruction to an Athenian courtesan named Thais, who urged the drunken Macedonian troops to vandalism. Diodorus claims that the arson was during a celebration in honor of the god Dionysius, Plutarch that it was purely an act of revenge with Alexander's support while Curtius attributes it to drink alone.

This bias may well be due to the period of history in which each wrote. Diodorus wrote at a time when there was, in Augustus, a popular emerging world ruler, and so had a reason for showing the idea of a world ruler to advantage. Plutarch wrote about famous men and having chosen Alexander as a subject was likely to view him in a favorable light. On the other hand, Curtius, writing in Latin in the era of Tiberius and Caligula, was perhaps prejudiced against emperors in general and did not hesitate to show that emperors can be guilty of cruelty and excessive drinking. Arrian, writing in the age of Hadrian and Antoninus, was perhaps keen to show emperors at their most majestic. The bias of Trogus is difficult to assess in this way since we do not know how Justin altered what he originally wrote.

Cutting the Gordian knot is a well-known English proverb and derives from an incident in the life of Alexander. Although, Trogus, Plutarch, Curtius and Arrian tell this story, Diodorus does not mention it.

Plutarch tells the famous story of a meeting between Alexander and the philosopher Diogenes of Sinope, who was lying in the sun at Corinth. When the Macedonian kindly asked Diogenes if he could help him in any way, the philosopher replied," I would have you stand from between me and the sun."[4] This incident is also mentioned by Arrian[5] and according to Hamilton by twenty other authors[6] but not by Diodorus, Trogus, or Curtius.

---

4. Plutarch 14.2.

5. Arrian 7.2.1–3.

6. Hamilton , *The Campaigns of Alexander,* 350n4.

Arrian tells of an incident involving Alexander journeying through the desert of Gedrosia, which he describes as the finest thing that Alexander ever did. When his army was dying of thirst, some soldiers found a tiny pool of water; enough to half fill a helmet, which they offered to Alexander. He refused to drink it but poured it out as an offering to the gods.[7] This same story is told in the Jewish Scriptures where David in similar circumstances does exactly the same thing.[8] Curtius and Plutarch, however, tell a similar story but set it in Sogdiana with the thirsty army approaching a river. Two men who did reach it are said to have filled a water skin and were carrying it to their sons when they encountered Alexander. He refused to drink what they offered until all had reached the river, standing there thirsty until all others had slaked their thirst.[9] Trogus and Diodorus do not mention this story.

A primary reason for these variations is almost certainly that the five were reliant on material they received from the works of the twenty writers who were contemporary to Alexander. To take one example, none of the three tales above are recorded by Diodorus. Either they were not found in his sources, or they were there and he rejected them. Since Diodorus work is highly flattering to Alexander, the former seems the likely explanation.

The main known writers contemporary with Alexander are listed below.

Alexander the Great

The kings of Macedon kept records of their doings in the Royal Diaries (called the *Ephemerides*), which, on their deaths, were stored in the royal Macedonian city of Pella.[10] In Alexander's case, it is believed that Ptolemy (see below) captured them and stored them in the library at Alexandria.[11]

Callisthenes of Olynthus

A nephew of Aristotle and friend of Alexander, Callisthenes[12] accompanied the expedition as a war correspondent until his death in Bactria in 327. *The*

---

7. Arrian 6.26.3–6.

8. 1 Chr 11:17–19.

9. Curtius, 7.5.9–13; Plutarch 42.4.

10. Arrian 7.24.5.

11. Hammond, *Alexander*, 1–2.

12. Arrian 4.10.1–4.

Deeds of Alexander by Callisthenes were, therefore, the earliest of the lost histories, and they are believed to have been annexed by Ptolemy and kept at Alexandria.[13]

Aristobulus

Aristobulus was one of the pioneers of the expedition and is believed to have written an account of Alexander's campaign in his old age early in the third century BCE.[14] Tarn suggests that though he was not likely to be the intimate of the generals of Alexander's staff, at a professional level he must have known Alexander fairly well.

Ptolemy

Ptolemy was a boyhood friend of Alexander and one of the generals in the expedition. Seizing Egypt as his kingdom after Alexander's death, Ptolemy made Alexandria his capital and buried the great Macedonian there. Having access to the *Ephemerides* and Callithenes' *The Deeds of Alexander*, he wrote a history of Alexander in his old age.[15]

Cleitarchus

Cleitarchus was the author of a twelve volume *History of Alexander,* a work that seems to have been popular and sensational. Tarn has exhaustively proved that Cleitarchus did not accompany the expedition and, therefore, was not an eyewitness to the events he described.[16]

Other eyewitness accounts

Chares of Mytilene, who was the Royal Chamberlain, and two admirals, Nearchus and Onesicritus, also wrote accounts of the expedition.[17] The

---

13. Tarn, *Alexander,* 1:120.

14. Ibid., 2:120.

15. Hammond, *Alexander,* 3–4.

16. Tarn, *Alexander,* 2:3–19; see also Hammond, *Alexander,* 82–83.

17. Lane Fox, *Alexander,* 364.

account of the first is thought to have been highly romanticized,[18] that of Nearchus technical and that of Onesicritus a historical romance.[19]

SUMMARY OF THE SOURCES

The way the authors of the five primary sources used the contemporary writings has been subjected to source criticism by Tarn, Pearson, and more recently and exhaustively by Hammond.[20] They all agree that the writings of Cleitarchus, which they suspect of being substantially comprised of barrack room gossip, heavily influenced the writings of Diodorus, Trogus and Curtius. They see Arrian providing a biography based more on Ptolemy and Aristobulus and suggest that Plutarch was partly influenced by the writing of Chares.

Modern researchers have, therefore, five coherent accounts of the life of Alexander, based partly on material written within fifty years of his death. Three of these were part of a more general work but two (the lives of Curtius and Arrian) concerned Alexander alone. What must be stressed is that none were written from within an Alexander cult and not one was written in a society in which the heirs of Alexander carried political authority. It is true that some showed greater affection for their subject than others but it must be remarked that Arrian, who gives the most sympathetic account of the life of Alexander, also gives the least extravagant one.

A full discussion of the writings on the life of Jesus of Nazareth belongs to Chapter 4. It is worth commenting here that the gospels were compiled by people who were part of the Jesus cult and that when they describe him as Son of God, it is because they believed him so to be. There is no life of Jesus written by an independent historian and only the most disputed reference to him in general histories. It must be accounted as remarkable that Josephus, who might have been expected to refer to Jesus in his detailed account of first century Palestine in his *War of the Jews*, is silent on the subject.[21] The writers from antiquity who wrote about Alexander were altogether different, for though they had affection for their subject, they did not lend full credence to stories of his divinity, nor did they apparently pay worship to him. Indeed, Ptolemy, one of Alexander's generals who were cer-

---

18. Cartledge, *Alexander*, 276.

19. Arrian 7.21.1–3; Hammond, *Alexander,* 3–4.

20. Tarn, *Alexander,* vol. 2; Pearson, *Lost Histories;* Hammond, *Three Historians;* Hammond, *Sources.*

21. Josephus did write briefly about Jesus in his *Antiquities* (18.3.3) but authenticity of the passage is highly disputed.

tainly present at Siwa, who succeeded him as Pharaoh and had every reason for inflating Alexander's claim to sonship of Ammon, does nothing of the kind. We have a much fuller and more balanced picture of Alexander than we do of Jesus.

A BRIEF HISTORY OF ALEXANDER'S EARLY LIFE

Philip II of Macedon (382–336 BCE) was a military genius and it was during his reign that Macedonia, a small and rugged country to the north of Greece, emerged as the dominant military power of the area. In 357 he married Olympias, a princess of the neighboring country of Epirus, who a year later bore him his first son in wedlock, Alexander. The young prince grew up at Philip's capital city of Pella and at the age of twelve had his first famous achievement by taming the wild stallion, Bucephalas, which no one but he was able to master. He was tutored by the philosopher Aristotle, whom his father brought from Athens to Pella. At the age of seventeen Alexander was given regency over Macedon when his father was on campaign and the following year commanded the victorious wing of the Macedonian army at Chaeronea in 338 in a battle that guaranteed Philips mastery over Greece. But his pre-eminence lasted only two years; Philip was assassinated and was succeeded by Alexander.[22]

Already popular with Macedonian army after Chaeronea, Alexander secured his throne and the hegemony of Greece in a series of lightning military campaigns. Crossing to Asia, he defeated the Persian army in the battles of Granicus and Issus, cleared the Persians forces from Asia Minor and moved on towards Egypt. He was held up by prolonged sieges of the cities of Tyre and Gaza but in 332 at the age of twenty-four he occupied Egypt where he was crowned as Pharaoh. He then founded the great city of Alexandria and visited the oracle of Ammon-Zeus at the oasis of Siwa.

His Motivation and Personality

What drove him to do this? His military skill and the superb army that he inherited made it possible but does not answer the question why. Was it simply his youthful desire to be a Homeric hero and conquer? Was it his wish to Hellenize the world and educate it to live as a unit? Did he want to outdo all who went before him? Did he just enjoy warfare? How important was his *pothos*, the semi–religious yearning for achievement to which

22. Tarn, *Alexander*, 1:1–3; Lane Fox, *Alexander*, 28–42.

Arrian refers?[23] Was it a case of insatiable ambition? Much ink has been expended in debating these questions but what emerges from all pens is that Alexander was a complicated and complex personality. His acts of kindness mingle with occasional acts of brutality. The same Alexander, for example, who dragged the defeated defender of Gaza to a horrific death behind his chariot,[24] was the Alexander who honored the defeated Indian rajah, Porus, and restored his rule over his people.[25] He was personally extremely brave, though very quick tempered; his troops would follow him almost anywhere and remained loyal to him to the end, but some who disputed with him paid the ultimate price. Unquestionably dark forces worked within him and some of these were the result of his upbringing.

In the 1956 film, *Alexander the Great*, written and directed by Robert Rossen, there is a telling scene. Alexander is planning to move east and his mistress, Barsine, objects. "You fear I leave you for another woman," says Alexander. "I fear no other woman save your mother," says Barsine, "and your insane desire to outdo your father." Though fictional, Barsine's remark is extremely apt. In his youth Alexander was dominated by Philip and Olympias and both undoubtedly cast long shadows over his life. Fortunately, Philip wanted Alexander taught philosophy and so invited Aristotle to tutor him.

Philip

Born of the royal house of Macedon, Philip, at the age of fifteen, was sent as a hostage to the city of Thebes where he lived in the household of Epaminondas. It was to be the turning point of his life, for not only was his host one of the greatest military commanders of the age[26] but he allowed Philip to be taught by a Pythagorean. Philip, therefore, was given the opportunity to study war at the hands of a genius and develop a love of Greek culture.[27] That he was a formidable personality was quickly realized when his brother, Perdiccas III of Macedon died in 359 in a frontier war. There were five claimants to the throne but so competently did Philip handle the situation that he was able to claim the kingship outright and begin his outstanding career as a general and trainer of troops. He obviously trained his son in the craft of warfare and bequeathed to him a superb army.

---

23. Arian 3.3.3.

24. Curtius, 4.6.29.

25. Ibid., 8.10.45.

26. Goodenough, *Tactical Genius*, 9–12.

27. Dio 16.2.2–3.

Aristotle

With Aristotle as his tutor, Alexander was exposed to Greek politics and to Greek history.[28] Fuller writes that "Aristotle instilled into his youthful charge that insatiable curiosity and love of knowledge which as a man he conspicuously displayed. He instructed him in philosophy, in scientific inquiry, in medicine, botany, zoology and geography, and inspired him with a deep love of poetry and Greek culture; he annotated for him a copy of the *Iliad* which, it is said, was Alexander's constant companion."[29] To be the most distinguished pupil of one of the greatest philosophers in history is not the least of Alexander's accomplishments. It is simplistic but true to point out that if Socrates' star pupil was Plato and Plato's star pupil was Aristotle, then Aristotle's was Alexander.

Olympias

But if Aristotle taught Alexander that moderation alone could hold a kingdom together, his mother (Olympias) was a woman for whom the word moderation was unknown. She is supposed to have been a devotee of the orgiastic worship of Thrace, a Maenad, who kept large snakes as pets.[30] Her relationship with Philip was stormy for he was clearly polygamous and was married several times, as well as having a variety of mistresses. The real passion of her life was Alexander himself and when Philip married the Macedonian Cleopatra in 338 BCE, a union that might produce a fully Macedonian child who would be a rival to Alexander's claim to monarchy, the tension for Olympias was unbearable and she went into exile.

The royal house of Macedon, called the Argeads, claimed that they were descended from the legendary hero Heracles and, since he was the son of Zeus, described themselves as Zeus born. Olympias came from a family who claimed to be directly descended from the nymph Thetis, whose son Achilles was half divine. They were also said to have the blood of Helen of Troy in their veins. Taught to reverence the works of Homer by the greatest living philosopher, Alexander was surrounded by visions of human blood mingling with the divine, with tales of heroes, of honor in war and combat. The heroes he sought to emulate lived in a twelfth century world; the glory

---

28. Cartledge, *Alexander*, 51.
29. Fuller, *Generalship*, 36.
30. Plutarch 2.1–6; *Trogus* 12.16.2

he sought was that of a time long passed.[31] There is a certain parallel, in this respect, between Alexander and the fictional Don Quixote.

If his attitude to war was outdated, his treatment of women was extremely modern. As Fuller says: "it was in his attitude to women—in nearly all ages considered the legitimate spoil of the soldier—that Alexander stood in a totally different moral world compared with the one inhabited by his contemporaries."[32] After the Battle of Issus, Darius wife, mother and daughters were captured and in terror awaited their fate. Instead of the anticipated rape and slavery, they were visited by Alexander who promised that they would continue to enjoy their royal status.[33] At the same time, he had two soldiers put to death for rape "as wild beasts born for the destruction of mankind,"[34] the first documented case of soldiers so prosecuted. And when the viceroy of Media presented him with a hundred girls armed and dressed as Amazons, he ordered them from the camp for they might have met with unseemly treatment from the troops. Such an attitude is more reminiscent of Sir Lancelot du Lac or St. Louis of France than of a fourth century BCE army commander.

Macedonian religion was essentially the religion of the Greeks. Its culture had no priestly cast; the king was their chief priest and so Alexander gained that office with the crown. It is clear that he took his duties seriously. Even when suffering from the illness that was to kill him, he never failed to attend to the daily sacrifices.[35] But there are clear indications that his enquiring mind led him to have sympathy with other religions and even study them. His attitude to religion in Egypt (as will be seen) was so encouraging that the Egyptian priests immediately made him Pharaoh. Josephus tells of Alexander's sympathetic visit to the temple in Jerusalem and Arrian of his humble approach to Indian mystics.[36] Alexander's conversation with the philosopher Psammon reveals his conviction that the gods are gods of all people on earth.[37] But Alexander remained a devotee of the religion taught him through Homer and the sacred oracles were a significant part of this.

It has already be shown in Chapter 1 that divine oracles were a very important part of Greek religion and that the shrine at Siwa was one of the most important of these. It was as important as the shrine of Apollo at

---

31. Lane Fox, *Alexander,* 61.
32. Fuller, *Generalship,* 90.
33. Curtius, 3.12.17; Green, *Alexander,* 237.
34. Plutarch 22.3.
35. Arrian 7.25.6.
36. Arrian 7.2.1, 2.
37. Plutarch 27.6.

Delphi and that of Zeus at Dodona. Though it was to Siwa that Alexander went on a life-changing mission in 331 BCE, he is reported as visiting other shrines and what happened in these is relevant.

Delphi

Only one of the primary sources refers to Alexander visiting another Greek oracle and that was to the shrine of Apollo at Delphi. According to Plutarch, after Alexander had destroyed the city of Thebes and made himself master of Greece, he went on to a meeting of the heads of Greek states at Corinth. There he was proclaimed their general and the leaders (with the exception of those from Sparta) agreed to support the war against Persia. It was a staggering achievement; Alexander was twenty-one years old, Greece with its thousand years of turbulence seemed united behind him and he had just been appointed general of Greece. Few in history have met with such success, and Alexander's subsequent and even greater achievements should not overshadow it. Such a moment calls for a pause for reflection and Plutarch gives an account of what is said to have happened.

Alexander is described as "going to Delphi to consult Apollo concerning the success of the war he had undertaken." Now Delphi lay close to the route between Corinth and Macedon and Alexander must have made an unplanned visit, for he arrived on a forbidden day when oracles were not given. When the Pythian priestess refused to officiate, Alexander entered her quarters and dragged her by force to the oracle seat until "tired and overcome with his opportunity, 'My son,' she said, 'thou art invincible.' This satisfied Alexander who declared that this was just what he wished to hear and that there was no need to consult the god any further."[38]

Did this really happen? Stoneman and Lane Fox[39] think not, the latter arguing that the unfavorable days for the giving of oracles belong to a later period of history. Certain is it that the story is not told by the other four biographers. Yet Plutarch had been a priest at Delphi[40] and it must be possible that the story was remembered in Delphi if not elsewhere. And, as a precursor to what was later to happen at Siwa, the story is apt, for Alexander's question at Delphi was concerned with his destiny.

---

38. Plutarch, 14.4.
39. Stoneman, *Alexander*, 22; Lane Fox, *Alexander*, 71.
40. Plutarch, Dryden, v.

Didyma

According to Strabo, Alexander the Great visited the shrine of Didyma after his conquest of Miletus.[41] This shrine to Apollo had been sacked in the time of Xerxes and its sacred spring had ceased to flow. When Alexander arrived, the story goes, the spring began to flow again and the oracle's silence was ended. Alexander installed a new priestess, who prophesied his future victory over the Persian.[42] Apollo began to speak again during Alexander time in Egypt and proclaimed that Alexander was born of Zeus, a story which Tarn attributes to Callisthenes.[43]

This story is less well attested than that of Alexander's visit to Delphi since none of the five primary sources mention it. But even if it belongs more to the *Romance* than to the history of Alexander, it is a clear indication that the idea of Alexander as Son of Zeus had wide acceptance and credence soon after his death.

Gordium

Though not actually a visit to an oracle, it is appropriate to mention the anecdote of Alexander and the Gordian knot, a story told by all biographers from antiquity except Diodorus. There was a traditional belief in Asia Minor that concerned a wagon that had once been driven by King Midas and was afterwards housed in the temple of Zeus at Gordium. Whoever, went the prophecy, could undo the knot that fixed its yoke to the wagon shaft was destined to be Lord of Asia.[44] To undo the knot was almost impossible, for the cord was made of bark from a cornel tree and the ends were folded back into the knot and, as such, were undetectable.

Following his great victory over the Persians at Granicus in 334, Alexander visited Gordium and undid the knot, though whether by severing it with a sword or (as Aristoboulus said) by drawing out the pin that held it is not certain. Suffice it to say that Alexander left Gordium with the oracle fulfilled and, according to Arrian, his action was confirmed by thunder and lightning. The fulfillment of the oracle concerning the knot was further evidence for Alexander of divine approval that it was his destiny to conquer Asia.

41. Strabo 17.1.43

42. Worthington, *Alexander*, 59–60.

43. Tarn, *Alexander*, 2:274.

44. The story of the Gordian knot is covered by Arrian 2.3.5–7; Curtius, 3.15, 16–18; Plutarch 18.1–2; *Trogus* 11.7.5–16.

Two significant points may be drawn from the visits to Delphi, Didyma and Gordium. Firstly, all three followed momentous successes, for if the Peloponnesian conference of 335 was a major achievement for Alexander, the victory at Granicus was no less so, being the first Greek victory on the Persian mainland. Secondly, Alexander did not seem to be concerned with what he was to do next but with his destiny. In the Peloponnese, he had been granted leadership of Greece, and was that not enough? After Granicus, he had freed Asia Minor of Persian control, but was that not enough? The answer in each case was no. At Delphi, the message was clear, he would prove invincible if he invaded Asia, and at Gordium he understood that he was to rule Asia. The visit to Siwa followed the pattern of his other visits to oracles and shrines.

Alexander's Visit to Egypt

From a military point of view, Alexander's skill at the battles of Granicus and Issus was not outstanding but his skill in capturing Tyre, a city that had withstood many sieges, was sufficient to reveal him as one of the great military leaders of all time. After capturing Tyre, Alexander's unique abilities as a commander were clear to all, and it was with supreme confidence that his troops marched into Egypt where, having advanced over a thousand miles in less than two years through hostile territory, they were welcomed with open arms by a grateful populace. "The Egyptians . . . turned out in force to welcome the Macedonian king, so great was their hatred of Persian rule."[45]

The effect on Alexander's troops must have been overwhelming. When soldiers occupy a major city, it is their usual custom to have a victory parade and the nature of this parade depends upon the attitude of the populace. In the 1971 television series, The World at War, there is a significant sequence. German troops are shown occupying the Sudetenland in 1938. The inhabitants, being ethnically German, greet the troops with delight; the soldiers are feted, given flowers and kisses and showered with good will and they respond by breaking ranks, hugging girls and giving sweets. The camera picks up the expression on their faces, happiness, gratification and fulfillment. But the same faces are shown when, a few months later, they are filmed entering Prague, where they are received in silence and apathy by the populace. The troops are shown as surly, grim, disciplined and plainly unhappy, just as the Macedonians entering Tyre must have appeared. The entry to Egypt, however, must have been akin to the German entry to the Sudetenland and was, for Alexander's troops, a euphoric experience. As shown in Chapter 1,

45. Worthington, *Alexander*, 85.

the Greeks saw Egypt as a cultural center with a religious magnificence that they had long envied. To be welcomed and feted in such a setting was, for a Greek soldier, the most satisfying happening imaginable.

If this was the effect on his troops, what of the commander? As one concerned with his destiny, Alexander would have found the loving welcome of a whole people a blissful but also a challenging experience. At Delphi and at Gordium he had sought affirmation that he was to rule over Asia and here was evidence that he was succeeding. He was being hailed as a liberator, escorted up the Nile and, according to Heckel, recognized as the legitimate successor of the Pharaohs.[46] Whether he was actually crowned as Pharaoh in the temple at Ptah, as was the invariable custom for Pharaohs, is disputed. A formal enthronement is only mentioned by Pseudo-Callisthenes but Wilchen is clear that the adoption of the royal state must have found expression in some official act[47] in which assertion the support of Fredricksmeyer. Alexander immediately showed himself worthy of the trust imposed in him, for, according to Green, his wisdom and great heartedness inspired him to rebuild temples and hence guarantee Egyptian self-esteem.[48] His popularity soared to incredible heights, as did adulation for his extraordinary achievements. He had been king of Macedon for only four years.

Alexander's three most enduring effects upon the world are generally regarded as the founding of Alexandria in Egypt, the development of Koine Greek as the *lingua franca* of most of the known world and his concept of empire. It is my contention of that there was a fourth—the recognition that the appellation Son of God was a historic as well as a mythical title. All four found their genesis in Egypt and all are interwoven.

ALEXANDRIA IN EGYPT

In Chapter 1, the importance of the port of Naucratis as a Greek treaty port in Egypt was stressed, as was the part played by religion in founding a city. Alexandria was built to connect Egypt and Greece and it became the capital of Egypt and for a time the most important city in the world. Its library was to become one of the Seven Wonders of the World.[49]

---

46. Heckel, *Alexander*, 71.

47. Wilchen, *Alexander*, 114.

48. Green, *Alexander*, 270.

49. Tarn, *Alexander*, 1:41; Lane Fox, *Alexander*, 195–99.

Koine Greek

Alexander's army was made up of Macedonians and Greeks and the language used was a basic form of Greek, a distillation of the various dialects from various city states. This was clearly the language used in the new city of Alexandria, the center where the Septuagint text of the Jewish Scriptures originated and arguably the center where Greek became the language of empire and of the future Church. "It was thus ultimately thanks to him [i.e. Alexander]" writes Cartledge, "that the Hebrew Bible was translated into Greek at Egyptian Alexandria, and that St. Paul . . . wrote in koine Greek."[50]

ALEXANDER'S VISIT TO SIWA

While in Egypt, Alexander developed a *pothos*[51] to visit the shrine at Siwa to consult the oracle of Ammon.[52] His reasons for doing this have been widely discussed and emerge in the questions he is said to have put to the oracle and the responses he received. But one seems to have superseded the others for, according to Arrian:

> One reason (for visiting Siwa) was his wish to consult the oracle there, as it had a reputation for infallibility, and also because Perseus and Heracles were supposed to have consulted it . . . But there was another reason: Alexander longed to equal the fame of Perseus and Heracles; the blood of both flowed in his veins, and just as legend traced their descent from Zeus, so he, too, had a feeling that in some way he was descended from Ammon. In any case, he undertook this expedition with the deliberate purpose of obtaining more precise information on this subject—or at any rate to say that he had obtained it.[53]

Alexander as Pharaoh was Son of Ra; his military and diplomatic successes had raised him to the height of any hero, Heracles included. Alexander seems to have gone to Siwa primarily to find out if he was in reality a son of Zeus, and although all biographers, except Arrian, mention that Alexander asked whether he was destined to rule over the whole earth, it was his possible divinity that was central to his mind.[54]

---

50. Cartledge, *Alexander*, 193.

51. The Greek word *pothos* is normally understood to imply intense religious desire. De Selincourt (Arrian, 151) translates it as eager longing.

52. Diod. 49.2; *Trogus* 11.11.

53. Arrian 3.3.1, 2.

54. Lane Fox, *Alexander*, 203–10.

His journey to Siwa is portrayed as an epic journey. Siwa is in fact 150 miles from the Mediterranean coast and, as Fakhry makes plain, was on a caravan route and had been consulted by Croesus and by various Greeks. It was *not* off the beaten track. In similar terrain and in the height of summer, Alexander's troops covered between 210 and 250 miles in pursuit of Darius. Yet Diodorus and Curtius tell of Alexander and his troops spending days marching through waterless desert and being rescued from dying of thirst by a miraculous rain cloud[55] while all except Trogus speak of Alexander being guided by crows or two talking snakes. The journey to Siwa lost nothing in the telling and helped his biographers emphasize the significance of Alexander's pilgrimage.

His Arrival and Greeting

On arrival at Siwa, Alexander encountered the priests of the shrine of Ammon–Zeus. Diodorus recounts how, when Alexander was conducted into the temple of Ammon, the one who held the position of prophet, an elderly man, came to him and said, "Rejoice, son; take this form of address as from the god also." He replied, "I accept father; for the future I shall be called thy son."[56] According to Curtius, "He [Alexander] was addressed as 'son' by the eldest of the priests, who claimed that the title was bestowed on him by his father Jupiter," a title Alexander accepted.[57] Plutarch offers the ingenious suggestion that the priest, desirous of a piece of courtesy, decided to address Alexander in Greek and intended to greet him with the words *ho paidion* (O my son). However, in his foreign pronunciation he used a sigma instead of a nu which turned the address into *ho paidios* (O son of Zeus) which mistake pleased Alexander very much and it became known that the oracle had called him so.[58] Arrian does not tell of the priest referring to Alexander's divine sonship, simply commenting that Alexander "put his question to the oracle and received (or so he said) the answer which his heart desired"[59] but Trogus tells his readers that:

> Alexander's mother, Olympias, had confessed to her husband, Philip, that it was not by him that she had conceived Alexander but by a huge serpent. Moreover, shortly before his death, Philip

55. Diod. 49.5; Curtius 4.15.
56. Diod. 50.51.
57. Curtius 4.25.
58. Plutarch 27.5.
59. Arrian 3.5.1.

had publicly declared that Alexander was not his son, and had
for that reason repudiated Olympias as guilty of adultery. So it
was that, wishing both to claim divine birth, and also to clear his
mother of infamy, Alexander sent men ahead to bribe the priests
to give the responses he wanted. When he entered the temple,
the priests immediately hailed him the son of Hammon and he,
delighted at his divine adoption, ordered that he be henceforth
regarded as the god's son.[60]

The issue of Alexander's sonship of Zeus was raised in a different way.
Clearly Alexander had the murder of Philip at the back of his mind when
he went to Siwa and, as suggested in Chapter 1, he might have been concerned with his possible complicity in the crime and hence his blood guilt.
According to Diodorus, Alexander asked the priest: "Have I punished all
those who were the murderers of my father or have some escaped me?" The
prophet shouted: "Silence! There is no mortal who can plot against the one
who begot him. All the murderers of Philip, however, have been punished,"
an account supported by Curtius and Trogus.[61]

Some Modern Responses to these Acclamations

On whatever basis, the story went out that Alexander had been hailed as
son of Zeus by the oracle of Ammon at Siwa. Modern biographers respond
to this in various ways. Tarn is clear that the greeting of Alexander as son
of Ammon-Ra was due to the use of his royal title as Pharaoh.[62] Wilchen,
while agreeing over this point, sees a different response from Alexander,
who did not expect this appellation but was converted to its message: "[A]ll
his lifelong Alexander clung to the mystic faith that he was the son of Zeus
Ammon . . . yet he never thought of introducing a political cult of himself as
son of Zeus."[63] Hamilton doubts whether the greeting was ever uttered but
points out that there is a world of difference between being a son of god and
being a god.[64]

Green is clear that Alexander deliberately chose a Greek oracle (for
such Green believes Siwa to be) and went there to obtain divine sanction
for the building of Alexandria and to be cleansed of blood guilt. Alexander's
desire to be acclaimed as son of Zeus was that this would free him from any

60. *Trogus* 11.5–11
61. Diod. 17.51.2, 3; Curtius 4.7.25; *Trogus* 11.11
62. Tarn, *Alexander*, 1:43.
63. Wilchen, *Alexander*, 127–28.
64. Hamilton, *Alexander*, 76.

suggestion of patricide. But although Green is skeptical about Alexander's motives, he has no such view as to the effect of the visit. "Whatever Alexander heard at Siwa," he writes, "it struck him with the force of a revelation, and left a permanent mark on his career."[65] "Whatever Alexander's attitude before the visit," writes Bosworth, "the consultation of the oracle made a profound and lasting impression upon him." It is evident that he regarded Ammon, the oracular deity of Siwa, as the local Libyan manifestation of Zeus. Bosworth is clear that Alexander was acclaimed as son of Zeus whatever developments may have followed, for he says: "This key fact, underlined by Callisthenes, is repeated in almost all the later sources and cannot be dismissed"[66] while Worthington writes: "What is common to all accounts is that after the consultation Alexander called himself Son of Zeus."[67] Hammond comments that the one thing we know for certain is that the visit to Siwa made a very deep impression on Alexander. Hammond also believes that it was the assiduous attention paid to Zeus-Ammon by Alexander that led his soldiers to infer that at Siwa he had been told he was indeed the son of Zeus-Ammon.[68]

Perhaps the most comprehensive of modern biographies is that of Lane Fox. He holds that in the god Ammon the traditions of three people had long been combined; Ammon was the father of Pharaoh, a local Libyan deity and appropriated by the Greeks as a local manifestation of Zeus. The oracle at Siwa had a worldwide reputation and Alexander went there as he approached the heights of a fabulous career. One result was the establishment of a little known cult, of which Lane Fox writes:

> Nearly 900 years later, in A.D. 529, the natives of a small oasis near Siwah were still paying worship to Alexander and Zeus—Ammon, although Christianity had been the recognized religion of their empire for the past two hundred years. The Roman emperor, Justinian, saw fit to intervene and ban their malpractice, putting an end, it might seem, to the history of a young man's impudent boast. But that same myth had driven a Macedonian to India and the eastern edges of the world and then remained firm, where it first became public, as a focus of loyalty for nine successive centuries in a rapidly changing world. When millions, now as then, still pin their faith on a subsequent son of god, it is not for the historian to explain away the belief that helped Alexander onwards. It is salutary, rather, to remember

65. Green, *Alexander,* 272–75.

66. Bosworth, *Conquest,* 282–83.

67. Worthington, *Alexander,* 89.

68. Hammond, *Alexander,* 127.

that claims to be the begotten son of god have been made before, upheld by companions and ended, so men said, in boos from angry mutineers.[69]

According to Plutarch, Alexander encountered the philosopher Psammon in Egypt; a meeting he recounted as follows:

> Among the sayings of one Psammon, a philosopher, whom he heard in Egypt, he most approved of this, that all men are governed by God, because in everything, that which is chief and commands is divine. But what he pronounced himself upon this subject was even more like a philosopher, for he said, God was the common father of us all, but more particularly of the best of us.[70]

This story is not repeated by other biographers, nor is Psammon mentioned by other writers. The similarity of the names Psammon and Ammon is striking and suggests that the story is more myth than history and most modern biographers of Alexander dismiss it. But is this just? Tarn, supported by Fuller, points out that this on the face of it is a plain statement that all men are brothers, and, if true, is the earliest known, at least in the western world. Tarn also points out that Psammon's statement is very similar to the teaching of Aristotle.[71] And in the *Moralia,* Plutarch quotes Eratosthenes (c. 275—194 BCE):

> For Alexander did not follow Aristotle's advice to treat the Greeks as if he were their leader, and other peoples as if he was their master. . . But he believed that he came as a heaven-sent governor for all, and as a mediator for the whole world. . . and he brought together in one body all men everywhere, uniting and mixing in one great loving-cup, as it were, men's lives, their characters, their marriages, their very habits of life.[72]

Summary of Alexander's Visit to Egypt

The following points are beyond dispute:

1. Alexander was in a state of euphoria after his welcome in Egypt.

69. Lane Fox, *Alexander,* 218.

70. Plutarch, 27.6

71. Tarn, *Alexander,* 1:435–6; Fuller, *Generalship,* 106.

72. *Moralia,* 329.6

2. He was certainly recognized as, and probably crowned as, Pharaoh.

3. He founded the important city of Alexandria.

4. Koine Greek began to become the language of Egypt after his visit.

5. He visited Siwa.

6. What happened to him there affected him for the rest of his life.

7. After this visit he began to describe himself and be described as the son of Ammon/Zeus.

The following points are strongly indicated by the narratives, if not established beyond dispute:

i. He was hailed as son of Zeus.

ii. He was assured that Philip's murderers were all punished.

iii. He was assured, as he had been at Delphi and Gordium, that he was destined to rule Asia.

THE RULE OF ASIA—SUCCESS AND PROBLEMS

The Egyptian idyll ended and Alexander moved to fight with the Great King, Darius III of Persia. At Gaugamela, 200 miles north of Babylon, he engaged him in a decisive battle, the vast Persian army melted away and Alexander was lord of Persia. The ancient city of Babylon, the Persian capital of Susa and the summer capital of Persepolis opened their gates to his all-conquering army, the latter to be partially burned as a reprisal for the burning of Athens by Xerxes. This act completed the Pan-Hellenic crusade; Persia was defeated, cowed and humbled by Alexander. He was only twenty-five years old and had been king of Macedon for just five years. And although another eight years of military campaigns lay ahead of him, his main problems now became political.

Though Gaugamela was militarily decisive, politically it was inconclusive. Darius had escaped and, though shorn of most of his power, was still Great King of Persia. Secondly, Alexander now had to administer his conquest effectively, for if he was to seek and eliminate Darius, he would have to secure his communications which must grow ever longer as his rival withdrew towards Afghanistan. But was he to do any such thing? He had invaded Persia to punish its raids into Greece and its interference with Greek internal affairs. Had he not succeeded to the satisfaction of all? He had collected hoards of bullion and treasure and established so fearsome a reputation for his troops as would guarantee that the Greeks were left in peace by the Persians for many a long year. The Greek cities in Asia Minor were free from Persian rule; Egypt was no longer in thrall to Persia and had accepted Alexander as Pharaoh. There was a strong case, made by many Macedonians, for going home.[73]

But opposed to this was Alexander's belief in his destiny. At Siwa he was given an unequivocal answer, for he was told that he would be granted victory in all his wars and possession of the whole world.[74] *It was his destiny to rule the lands he had conquered.* So he himself must become Great King and rule the Persian Empire. And if he was to do so, he had to work out how it was to be done. His army of less than fifty thousand troops could not hope to control this vast area and therefore Macedonian governors were not an option. Something new was required or perhaps the adaptation of something old.

The Persian satrap system was indeed old and it was tried and tested. A Satrap was a Persian grandee, who was given control of a large area by mandate of the Great King.[75] He had a military force to assist him but the commander of this small army was appointed by and directly loyal to the Great King. Rebellion was made well-nigh impossible and the system was so obviously sensible that Alexander adopted it. According to Arrian, directly after Gaugamela Alexander headed for Babylon and appointed Mazaeus (a Persian) to the governorship of the city, (while) Apollodorus of Amphipolis (a Macedonian) was put in command of the troops there. . .[76] He was following the pattern set by the Great Kings before him, save that the troops allotted to the satrap were under Macedonian commanders.

After the capture of Babylon, Alexander captured Susa and Persepolis and then moved in pursuit of Darius. If Alexander could not capture him, he had a rival and his claim to be Great King would be based on force alone. But when he did find Darius, he had been deposed and mortally wounded by his commanders; and most reports say that Alexander arrived too late to converse with him.[77] One of Darius commanders, Bessus, was now accepted by a small faction as Great King and in due course Alexander would have to hunt him down.

However, the morale of Alexander's army was shaken by this turn of events. Quite clearly the invasion was to continue and the Macedonians knew that they were not going home in the immediate future. Some, no

73. Green, *Alexander,* 297–99.

74. Curtius 4.7.27; Diod. 17.51.3; Plutarch 27.4; *Trogus* 11.11.10.

75. Cartledge, *Alexander,* 41–43.

76. Arrian 3.16.9.

77. Arrian 3.22: Diod. 17.73.2; Curtius 5.13.25.

doubt, were happy with this continuation of military service but many longed to see their families, to marry and settle down. At the same time they loved their commander and would follow him almost anywhere. This was partly because he was perpetually victorious; troops love a successful general. But also he belonged to them, shared their trials and hardships and lead from the front. The tale of his refusing to drink from the water being carried back to those fainting by the wayside until all had reached the river would inspire any soldier.[78] So the army stayed loyal to Alexander for the time being, though clearly tensions were increasing.

But the very success of the Macedonians seemed to cause their beloved commander to distance himself from them by his increasing adoption of Persian friends, Persian customs and Persian dress. This was perhaps inevitable. The administration of the Persian Empire on Persian lines meant a Persian speaking civil service and Alexander largely took over the system which had belonged to Darius.[79] This created immediate tension; for Macedonians were accustomed to their own ceremonies or, rather, the lack of them. They expected to call their king by his name Alexander and to greet him with a soldier's salute. His commands in battle may have been obeyed without question, but away from military action he was subject to the army council. He was king of their small country that was accustomed to a royal family which stood on little ceremony.

Persians on the other hand behaved differently. Though their king was not a god, he was the instrument of the gods and was treated with elaborate ceremony. He did not sit down to dine with army officer and get drunk with them but dined in solemn state. He did not ride a horse into the forefront of battle but stood in a sacred chariot directing events. He did not wear armor but robes befitting to his state. If Alexander was to keep Persian respect, he had to conform to Persian expectations. So there must have been a strange duality in Alexander's court and one that worried both sides. The Macedonians did not like to see their king and friend being treated with all this ceremony and feared that they might be expected to conform to it themselves.

Changes and Macedonian Reaction

The first sign of the new times was the acquisition by Alexander of a Persian eunuch. According to Curtius, a high ranking official of Darius court, Nabarzanes, surrendered to Alexander bringing lavish gifts "including Bagoas, an exceptionally good looking eunuch in the very flower of his youth.

78. Curtius 7.5.9–13; Plutarch 42.4.
79. Hammond, *Alexander,* 163.

Darius had had a sexual relationship with him and Alexander was to do so as well."[80] Macedonian kings were not expected to act like that!

Then Alexander began to change his dress. Though he refused to wear trousers or overcoat, he did wear a striped tunic, a girdle and the head ribbon or diadem, this last always worn by the Great King. He went further, access to his royal person was directed by a staff under a Greek comptroller called Chares; the royal concubines were reinstated and Alexander's court was in effect "Persianized."[81] If his troops were a long way from Macedon, they seemed much further from court life at Pella. Curtius expresses what must have been the reaction of many when he writes: "It was at this point that Alexander relinquished control of his appetites. His self-restraint and continence, supreme qualities at the height of good fortune, degenerated into arrogance and dissipation. The traditional ways of his people, the healthy, sober discipline and unassuming demeanor of the Macedonian kings he considered beneath his eminent position."[82] There were those who were so worried at what they saw as the loss national identity that they plotted unsuccessfully to kill Alexander, engaging in a conspiracy that led to the assassination of Parmenio, his second in command.[83]

Worse was to follow. A demoted Macedonian commander called Cleitus rowed with Alexander during a drinking bout and the king, completely losing his self-control, ran him through with a javelin.[84] For someone to have insulted Darius in the way that Cleitus undoubtedly insulted Alexander would have regarded himself lucky to die with a straightforward spear thrust; impaling would certainly have been his lot. But to the Macedonians, Alexander had crossed another line, for Cleitus and Parmenio had died without trial. Alexander then piled Pelion on Ossa by marrying, not a Greek or Macedonian woman, but an Afghan princess[85] and, at about the same time, by beginning the training of 30,000 local boys as recruits for his army. The Macedonians must have seethed.

The Prostration Affair

Anger bubbled over when Alexander asked to be greeted with prostration. According to Herodotus, "when one man meets another in the way (in

---

80. Curtius, 6.5.23.

81. Green, *Alexander*, 334–36; Lane Fox, *Alexander*, 277.

82. Curtius 6.6.1, 2.

83. Tarn, *Alexander*, 1:65; Worthington, *Alexander*, 124.

84. Arrian 4.8.4–8; Plutarch 50.1–6; Curtius 8.43.

85. Arrian 4.19.5.

Persia), the humbler bows down and does obeisance to the other."[86] All Persian prostrated themselves before the king and Alexander, bent on achieving the cohesion he had sought within his empire since his meeting with Psammon, tried to introduce this custom among his Macedonians. According to Arrian and Plutarch, he did this at a dinner of senior Macedonians. A loving cup was sent round and each person, having drunk, prostrated themselves before Alexander and received from him the kiss of friendship. This series of actions was intended to remove any suggestion of self-abasement on the part of the Macedonians.[87]

But it seems there was an important precedent for refusal. According to Herodotus, Spartan ambassadors many years before had refused to prostrate themselves to the Great King, even if it meant their death, explaining that where they came from it was not customary to offer prostration to mortals.[88] Alexander's war correspondent Callisthenes followed the example of the Spartans, refused prostration and probably paid for his stubbornness with his life. The experiment was a failure. As Heckel puts it: "The Macedonians are believed to have refused partly because it was a barbarian custom but mainly because they saw it as the increasing self-aggrandizement of Alexander."[89]

Perhaps it also failed because of a misconception. "In Greece," writes Lane Fox, "*proskynesis* is paid only to the gods"[90] and there were certainly those who saw its introduction as an attempt by Alexander at self-deification. Among modern writers opinions are divided. Wilchen is clear that it was no such thing, writing: "We must decidedly reject the view that he meant indirectly to force his recognition as a god . . . his purpose was to express the equal position of the Persians with the Macedonians and Greeks by means of this court ceremonial."[91] He has the support of Bosworth: "the *proskynesis* was not an act of worship"[92] and Heckel: "it is certainly wrong to regard Alexander's experiment with *proskynesis* as a prelude to ruler cult. It was instead an unsuccessful attempt to blend Macedonian and Persian court practices."[93] This opinion is disputed by Tarn who argues that Alexander *must* have known how Greeks and Macedonians regarded *proskynesis*

---

86. Herod. 1.134.

87. Arrian 22.12, 13; Plutarch 54.3, 4; Green, *Alexander,* 375–76.

88. Herod. 7.136.

89. Heckel, *Conquest,* 107; Bosworth, *Alexander,* 117–18.

90. Lane Fox, *Alexander,* 322.

91. Wilchen, *Alexander,* 168–69.

92. Bosworth, *Alexander,* 284.

93. Heckel, *Conquest,* 7.

and points out that: "if he knew this, I do not see how the scene could mean anything but a preparation for his recognition as a god."[94] The *proskynesis* is seen by Worthington as an ill judged attempt by Alexander to be accepted as divine.[95]

Reference to the primary texts raises an interesting point; only one refers to Alexander's action as having any bearing on self-deification. Arrian refers only to Alexander's increasing arrogance and Plutarch to the great disgrace of the prostration; Diodorus does not mention the story at all and Trogus declares the idea a piece of vanity, which was subsequently rejected.[96] Curtius alone takes it as a sign of self-deification, seeing it as a depraved idea, conceived because Alexander wished to be believed, not just called, the son of Jupiter, as if it were possible for him to have as much control over men's minds as their tongues.[97] So the suggestion that Alexander introduced prostration to deify himself hangs upon Curtius *interpretation* of an event; he is not presenting his readers with new facts but simply giving an opinion, which is rendered dubious by a comment about the death of Darius: "the king [i.e. Darius] who a short time ago had ridden in a chariot and received divine honors from his people. . ."[98] Curtius seemed unaware that the Persian king was not a god and hence *did not* receive divine honors. And since his very mode of expression suggests that he is not prepared to accept the idea that Alexander was seeking cohesion by his action, his view may be set to one side.

Curtius claims that Cleitus was murdered by Alexander because he ridiculed the oracle of Jupiter who Alexander claimed as his father[99] and this is a clear indication that the question of Alexander being a son of god had offended and still offended Macedonian sensibilities. But the attempt to introduce prostration had nothing to do with divinity and though Curtius (writing at the time of the Roman Emperor Caligula) may have thought it did, he was clearly wrong.

Alexander was facing a nearly impossible task. Governing the Persian empire with the use of the existing Persian civil service meant being regularly in a situation where he was required to appear either as a Persian king or as a colonial ruler. Many Macedonians would have liked Alexander to be the latter but this would have alienated the Persians and made Alexander's

94. Tarn, *Alexander*, 2:361–62.
95. Worthington, *Alexander*, 143.
96. Arrian 4.13: Plutarch 54.5; *Trogus* 12.7.1.
97. Curtius 8.5.5.
98. Curtius 5.12.16.
99. Curtius 8.1.42.

policy of fusing the cultures impossible. When he attempted a compromise and adopted some Persian customs, it still upset the Macedonians. It ended in failure and the flashpoint was the prostration. It is entirely false to see this as an attempt by Alexander to encourage acceptance of his sonship of Ammon–Zeus. As has been clearly shown, the Great King was not a god or even a son of god and so the attempted introduction of the prostration was a political attempt at fusion.

Three key episodes are crucial in considering the question of Alexander's divinity, and each is hotly disputed, both in the ancient and the modern literature. The first is his visit to the Siwa oasis in Libya in the winter of 332/1; the second, the attempted imposition of the Persian custom of obeisance at Bactra in 327; and the third, the order allegedly issued by Alexander from Susa in 324 commanding the Greeks to deify him.[100]

After the death of Cleitus, Alexander invaded India where he faced his first defeat. Having endured a campaign lasting seven years in which they had marched over four thousand miles, his troops refused to go further and forced Alexander to return to Persia.[101] He arrived to find that in his absence, the administration there had become corrupt and he had to take stringent measures to restore the rule of law. But it was a different Alexander now. Years of superhuman exertion had taken their toll as had the serious wounds that he had sustained. It has been argued that his debilitation was exacerbated by heavy drinking.[102] His personal bravery remained beyond dispute but his judgment was perhaps impaired; his march through the desert of Gedrosia was probably a serious mistake.[103] Above all the colossal weight of responsibility was starting to crush him. However, fire burned within him still and he was now to embark on his greatest struggle; the attempt to fuse the cultures of Greece and Persia.

First he paid off the debts of his troops; an action naturally very well received[104] and then held a mass wedding of his senior troops to Persian women, which was rather less popular.[105] But when he was joined by the 30,000 troops recruited originally in Afghanistan, he announced that his oldest troops were to be sent home. These veterans, many of whom were over sixty years old, saw this retirement as a deliberate attempt on the part

100. Cartledge, *Alexander*, 221.

101. Arrian 5.25.2.

102. Curtius, 9.9.27; Lane Fox, *Alexander*, 309.

103. Diod., 17.105.6.

104. Arrian 7.5.4; Plutarch 70.3.

105. Plutarch 7.4.2; *Deipn.* 12.538–39.

of their commander to put his Persian subjects above them and mutinied.[106] Alexander's reaction to this revolt reveals clearly his extraordinary mastery of his troops. Without a bodyguard, he walked into the midst of them, indicated the ringleaders, who were led away for execution, walked out unharmed, dismissed the whole army from his service and retired to his tent. His troops responded by spontaneously rushing to his tent and begging for forgiveness, which they received in full measure.[107] Such an incident has no parallel in the history of war and was perhaps Alexander's most remarkable achievement.

But if his relationship with the Greeks of his army were improved, those with the Greeks and Macedonians at home were not. Ten years before he had led the invasion of Asia in a punitive expedition; now he was seeking to fuse Persia and Greece into one empire. To the Greeks he was no more than king of Macedon and war leader of the Greeks while to the Persians he was the Great King. As war leader he had exceeded his powers by sending the veterans home. The problems confronting him at the time of the prostration affair returned to trouble him again; he was fish to one and fowl to the other. And as he grappled with the problem, he suffered a devastating loss; Hephaestion, his lifelong and greatest friend died. Hephaestion had been his boyhood friend, Patroclus to Alexander's Achilles, he had been his Grand Vizier, his cavalry commander and (it was rumored) his lover. Alexander was distraught. But, when the first pangs of grief were over, he devoted himself to Hephaestion's funeral and his memorial[108] and this included the possible deification of his friend.

How to Become a God in Greece

The acceptance of someone as a god was not as dramatic to the ancient Greeks as it sounds to Christians or Muslims two thousand years later. Victory in the Peloponnesian War (431—404) had belonged to Sparta and they owed their victory principally to Lysander. Spartan reaction to the victor was characteristically restrained but this self control was not shared by exiles returning to the island of Samos, where people set up altars, sang paeans and renamed their annual religious festival Lysandrea after their new patron god. Lysander exploited this adulation and set up twelve bronze statues at Delphi, one of which depicted him being crowned with the wreath

---

106. Lane Fox, *Alexander,* 424; Green, *Alexander,* 454–55.

107. Arrian 7.9–12; Diod. 17.108.

108. Arrian 7.14.1–14.

of victory by Poseidon and showed that he must be regarded as a god.[109] Lysander's example was followed by Philip II of Macedon who, having named the city of Philippi after himself, had thirteen bronze statues cast (twelve for the Olympians and the thirteenth of himself) to be carried in procession for his daughter's wedding. It seems clear that this was also an attempt at self-deification.[110]

These are the two most pertinent cases of the deifications of mortals in that both Lysander and Philip claimed descent from Heracles and both had proved outstandingly successful generals. They therefore fitted into the Greek pattern of being heroes in the classical style of Heracles, son of Zeus, who as a liberator of the oppressed and one capable of mighty deeds, was received in death by the gods as one of themselves. Alexander the Great, who also claimed descent from Zeus both through his father and mother, had far greater military achievements to his credit and had received far more adulation than either Lysander or Philip and could reasonably expect similar exaltation.

Alexander seems to have had three reasons for seeking formal deification at this moment, the first political, the second mystical and the third human.

Political

Alexander's first attempt at fusion of the cultures had foundered over the issue of the prostration that the Macedonians had refused to perform because it was a gesture only performed to the gods. Alexander had abandoned the experiment. But on this, his second attempt, he was determined to succeed. If his deification was the only way of receiving the prostration and thus achieving a greater sense of fusion, deified he would be. Equally, as war leader he had no right to send the veterans home and give them grants of land in Greece, but as a god he had every right. Heckel is clear that it is perhaps in the context of the Exiles Decree that Alexander's request for divine honours may best be understood. There was great political sense in Alexander becoming a god.[111]

---

109. Cartledge, *Alexander,* 218.

110. Ibid. *Alexander,* 218–20.

111. Heckel, *Alexander,* 147; Stoneman, *Alexander,* 81–83, Wilchen, *Alexander.* 210–16.

Mystical

As already made plain, Alexander's experience at Siwa eight years before had been a religious event of the highest order. Unquestionably he was considered by some to be a son of Zeus, as is made plain just before the murder of Cleitus.[112] Unquestionably his endless military successes inflated his ego. As Wilchen puts it, "it is a mistaken view of Alexander's character to bar out his inner religious experience and to assume that the demand [to be recognized as son of Zeus] was a purely political move."[113]

Human

In addition to arranging a massive funeral for Hephaestion, Alexander sought his deification. He sent a message, not to Delphi or Dodona or even nearby Didyma but to Siwa, to ask that Hephaestion might be worshipped as a god. He received the reply that he could be worshipped as a hero or demi-god, a reply that pleased Alexander very much.[114] But it is obvious that if Hephaestion (his loyal subordinate) could be formally recognized as a hero, then he, Alexander, could be formally acknowledged as a god; as the son of Zeus, already accepted by the oracle at Siwa seven years before. The approval of hero status for Hephaestion by the oracle Siwa paved the way for Alexander's full deification.[115]

So in 324, shortly before his death, Alexander demanded that the Greeks recognize him as an "invincible god."[116] It was a matter for the Greeks and the Greeks alone; Alexander was already a god in Egypt and did not need to be one in Persia. Exactly how his request was transmitted to Greece is not clear but it received a predictable and cynical reaction. We are told that: "The orators Pytheas and Lycurgus waxed sarcastic at Alexander's expense, (but) Demades warned the Athenians not to lose the earth by guarding the heavens. . ." while Demothenes, after opposing the proposal, is said to have remarked, "Let Alexander be the son of Zeus, and of Poseidon too, if he wants to be." Elsewhere in Greece was heard only the ironical utterance of the Spartan Damis who said, in true Laconic style, "Since Alexander wants to be a god, let him be a god."[117]

112. Curtius, 8.1.42

113. Wilchen, *Alexander,* 212.

114. Diod. 17.115.6; Plutarch 72.2, 3.

115. Heckel, *Alexander,* 168.

116. Mosse, *Alexander,* 83.

117. Hamilton, *Alexander,* 9: Ael. 31, 94; *Moralia* 219.

Such sarcasm may have been expected. But, as Stoneman writes, "the jokes concealed the remarkable change in political life that this decree produced. Hitherto no man had become a god in his lifetime. After Alexander, it became practically routine for the Hellenistic kings to adopt divine honors." This view is supported by Bosworth: "beginning as a Heraclid and descendants of heroes, he [Alexander] had become the son of Zeus and competitor of heroes. Finally he had become a god manifest on earth . . . The precedent for the worship of a living man was firmly established. . ."[118]

CONCLUSION

Alexander has been shown in this chapter as a most remarkable individual, a superb general, an astute politician, a philosopher and botanist as well as a man possessed of a restless and inquiring spirit. He transformed the world in which he lived in a remarkable way. The legends that adhered to his name were legion. Tales of his supernatural birth are recorded in Appendix 1. "It is my belief that there was in those days no nation," wrote Arrian, "no city, no single individual (who was) beyond the reach of Alexander's name; never in all the world was there another like him."[119] It is my own conviction that he transformed the title Son of God in a dramatic and enduring way, uniting the two strands shown in Chapter 1 and adding a third.

First, he believed he was descended from the sons of god from the legendary past of Greece. Second, he became Pharaoh and hence son of Ra. But thirdly he received divine affirmation of the title at Siwa, when the prophet—priest greeted with the words "Hail, son of Ammon." As son of god he continued his fabulous career and concluded it by becoming not only a son of god, but a god himself. It is impossible to avoid the conclusion that no person named as a son of god in an area where tales of such an extraordinary life continued to circulate could have avoided comparison with Alexander the Great.

118. Stoneman, *Alexander*, 81; Bosworth, *Alexander*, 290.
119. Arrian 7.30.

3

The Title Son of God in Canonical and Extra-Canonical Jewish Writings

Chapter 1 referred to the three main cultures in the area between the river Danube, the upper reaches of the river Nile, the Adriatic Sea and Hindu Kush as Persian, Egyptian and Greek. However, there was a fourth one, smaller but distinctive and this was Jewish. The descendants of Abraham and followers of the Law propounded by Moses were fiercely independent and monotheistic, insisting that they, and no one else, were in an extra–special relationship with the one true God. After 586 BCE they lost their national independence and for much of the next 600 years became essentially a priestly state or group of states, centered on the temple at Jerusalem and subject to one or other of the great empires of the period. Into these states Jesus of Nazareth was born and there he grew up, exercised his ministry and was executed and it was there that his followers began their historic mission to tell the world that he was not dead but alive and was the most significant of men. At some stage they began to refer to him as Son of God.

The researcher into this subject confronts an immediate problem. The Church at Nicaea in 325 CE pronounced that Jesus was the only begotten Son of God and was of one substance with God the Father. From this position the Church has never departed; rather it has reinforced this pronouncement with millions of pages of teaching and apologetic. The researcher finds that although there is enormous writing about what was meant by Jesus being called Son of God, there is very little about the use of that title itself *except* when it refers to Jesus. How, where, when and why Jesus was referred to as Son of God in the early Church will be discussed in Chapter 4. The

Jewish use of Son of God before it was used of Jesus is the subject of this chapter.

The point is crucial. For followers of the dead and resurrected Jesus to refer to him as a prophet or a rabbi when speaking to Jews who might be potential converts to Christianity was natural enough. Every Jew knew what a rabbi and a prophet was. To refer to Jesus as a messiah was more controversial, but Jews understood what was meant by the name. Messiah, rabbi and prophet were all terms in regular use in first century Jewish vocabulary. But it is very doubtful whether this was true of the term Son of God. *Indeed, there seems to be no example of the regular use of this term as descriptive of a person in Jewish literature.* That is not to say it was never used; in the Hebrew Scriptures, in the so-called Apocrypha and other Pseudepigraphical writings and in the Dead Sea Scrolls there are occasions when there is reference to a son of God. The main aim of Chapter 3 will be to look for occasions when the title Son of God is used and to assess its significance in each case. It will also be to look for areas where the concept of sonship of God is explored. A secondary aim will be to provide the necessary background to Chapter 4 of the book, which looks at the appellation Son of God as applied to Jesus in the New Testament. Chapter 3 will break down into four sections: Son of God in the Hebrew Scriptures; Son of God in the Apocrypha and Pseudepigrapha; Son of God in the Dead Sea Scrolls and Son of God in Philo and Josephus.

THE HEBREW SCRIPTURES

In his article, "The Son of God in the Old Testament," de Boer says that the data of the Old Testament can be organized under four headings: (1) the son as a divine being; (2) the son as king; (3) the son as the people of Israel; and (4) theophoric[1] personal names. This provides such an excellent framework for examining Hebrew Scripture references to the appellation Son of God that it will be followed in this book, though the order de Boer used will be varied. If the title Son of God was current among the Jews in the first century CE as a result of their reading of their scriptures, it must have resulted from the texts linked under one or more of de Boer's headings. Each must therefore be looked at in turn and its value assessed.

---

1. A theophoric name is based on the cult name of a god and implies that the person so named is a member of the cult; Matthews, Names, Personal, Greek in *OCD*, ad loc.

A Theophoric Personal Name

The name "father," ascribed to YHWH, appears in various personal names; the Hebrew word *ab* [father] is the basis of such names as Joab, Abiya and Abihu and implies some special relationship with YHWH. However, though the name Joshua [Greek—Jesus] probably means YHWH is Salvation,[2] it was not an unusual name for a Jew, "Jesus, called Justus"[3] being an example. Therefore, to suggest that being called Joshua or Jesus implied divine sonship must be discounted.

The Son as the People of Israel

De Boer starts his introduction to this section by referring to the Book of Malachi: "Have we not one father," says the prophet, "has not one god created us?" asks the prophet.[4] This, according to de Boer, is not referring to the physical relationship of child to father but to honor and obedience on the part of individuals and groups who are bound to the god of the people in whose society they are living. But he goes on to say: "By far the greatest number of passages with the expression 'the son of god' belongs to (this) group, a group which includes all the texts from the prophetic writings."[5] So Jeremiah has God saying to Israel: "Return, O faithless children, for I am your master"[6] and later: "I thought you would call me, my Father," while Isaiah makes the Israelites say: "Yet, O Lord, you are our Father." In the Pentateuch can be read: "you are children of the LORD your God"[7] and later: "is not he (i.e. God) your father?"[8] Moses says to Pharaoh: "thus says the LORD "Israel is my first born son."[9] The relationship of Israel and the Israelites to God is frequently seen as that of a son or children to a father.

But could an Israelite be accounted a Son of God on the strength of this usage? Surely the answer must be no. Clearly the father—son usage is that of relationship. The language makes this very plain. The tone of the passages makes it even clearer; God stands in a relationship to Israel as a father stands in relationship to his son. When the Deuteronomist says of Israel: "O

2. Simpson, "Joshua," 53.

3. Col 4:11.

4. Mal 2:10.

5. De Boer, "The Son of God," 19.

6. Jer 3:14–19.

7. Deut 14:1.

8. Deut 32:6.

9. Exod 4:22.

foolish and senseless people! Is not he [the LORD] your father, who created you, who made you and established you?"[10] this is surely allegorical and not literal. What can be said of the title Son of God under this heading is that it makes clear to the reader that the language of sonship was in use in Palestine in the first century CE.

The Son of God as a Divine Being

In Job 1:6 and 2:1 a heavenly court is described with the words, "one day the heavenly beings came to present themselves before the LORD . . ." The heavenly beings so described are the *bin-elohim* in Hebrew, which may be rendered sons of Elohim or sons of God in English but which the writers of the Septuagint translated into Greek as *hoi angeloi tou theo* [the angels of god].[11] Though the Targum follows this translation, the authors of the Peshitta and the Vulgate use "Sons of God" to translate this passage, while the writers of the Targum prefer "angels" and Jerome and Augustine both translate the phrase as *angeli dei.*[12] These heavenly beings appear again at the creation of the universe, "when the morning stars sang together and all the heavenly beings shouted for joy."[13] Again the Hebrew gives us "sons of god" in this passage which the Septuagint represents as "all my angels." The inescapable conclusion is that the author of Job sees the sons of God as angelic beings.

The Psalmist has a similar view. "For who in the skies can be compared to the LORD?" he writes and continues, "Who among the heavenly beings (Hebrew—sons of God) is like the LORD? A God feared in the council of the holy ones."[14] Elsewhere he says, "Ascribe to the LORD, O heavenly beings (Hebrew—sons of God), ascribe to the LORD glory and strength."[15] But to the Psalmist, the sons of God are also perhaps gods; lesser gods than YHWH but gods nonetheless. "All gods bow down before him (i.e., YHWH)," the Psalmist proclaims, "for you, O LORD are most high over all the earth; you are exalted far above all gods."[16] He reintroduces the concept of the heavenly court: "God has taken his place in the divine council; in the

---

10. Deut 32:6.

11. Rahlfs, *Septuaginta,* 342 and others.

12. Dhorme, *Job,* 5.

13. Job 38:7.

14. Ps 89:67.

15. Ps 29:1.

16. Ps 97:7.

midst of the gods he holds judgment."[17] He goes on to describe the lesser gods as sons of god: "I say you are gods, children of the Most High, all of you; nevertheless, you shall die like mortals, and fall like any prince."[18] It seems clear that there is a metaphysical divide to be considered. The Sons of God are individuals of the order god; they are divine and they belong to the world of God in much the same way as a prophet belonged to the sons of the prophets.[19] They are separate from the world of men. In some sense they are gods,[20] a view reinforced by the Psalmist. But there is no suggestion whatsoever that they are conceived by YHWH in the way that Heracles or Perseus were conceived by Zeus.

Reference must be made to the author of the books of Kings: "I saw the LORD sitting on his throne, with all the host of heaven standing behind him to the right and to the left of him. And the LORD said, 'Who will entice Ahab . . ?' (and) a spirit came forward and stood before the LORD, saying 'I will entice him'"[21] Clearly this is parallel to the picture in the prologue of Job and the attendant beings (here referred to as spirits) are there to do God's bidding.[22] In the true translation, they are God's messengers and they exist to carry out his wishes. They are free agents, however; Gen 6.2 has the sons of God take wives from among the daughters of men, apparently without YHWH's instruction or permission.

It is clear that the sons of god discussed under this heading are angelic beings or lesser gods, those who form the court of heaven and whose role is to praise YHWH and do his bidding. It might be postulated that one of these might have been sent to earth to become Jesus of Nazareth, and this possibility is mentioned in Chapter 4. However the author of Hebrews seems to refute the idea in his first chapter.[23] The existence of angelic beings, often described as sons of god in the Hebrew Scriptures, seems not to have been offered by the early Church as a reason for Jesus of Nazareth being given the title Son of God.

The First Book of Samuel ends with the death of King Saul and the first chapters of the Second Book are devoted to the rise of David, son of Jesse, to be king of all Israel[24] and the selection of Jerusalem as capital of the

17. Ps 82:1.

18. Ps 82:6–7.

19. 2 Kgs 2:5.

20. Driver and Gray, *Job*, 9–10.

21. 1 Kgs 22:19b, 21.

22. Gordis, *Job*, 12.

23. Heb 1:5–14.

24. I Sam 5:3.

united kingdom of Israel and Judah. Chapter 6 sees David bringing the Ark of the Covenant into Jerusalem, thereby making it a religious center, and Chapter 7 shows David planning to build a temple for the Ark. It is part of this Chapter that provides the key quotation for this section.

When David believes that he should build a house for the Ark of the Covenant, the prophet Nathan initially believes that YHWH approves.[25] But YHWH instructs Nathan to tell David that he is not to be the one to build a temple. Then YHWH says to David:

> When your days are fulfilled and you lie down with your ancestors, I will raise up your offspring after you, who shall come forth from your body, and I will establish his kingdom. He shall build a house for my name, and I will establish the throne of his kingdom forever. *I will be a father to him and he shall be a son to me* (my italics).[26]

YHWH goes on to promise that this king will forever be the recipient of YHWH's steadfast love. The Psalmist uses similar language of the occupant of the throne of Israel. "He shall cry out to me," he says, echoing 2 Samuel, "You are my Father, my God, and the Rock of my Salvation" and follows by repeating the promise that God's steadfast love will never be withdrawn from him.[27] In Psalm 2, he declares: "I will tell of the decree of the LORD: he said to me, 'You are my son; today I have begotten you.'" Here are references to a king of Israel being divine, and here clearly is an example of a human being referred to as a son of god.

But where does this come from and where is it going? Weiser, commenting on this verse, claims that the idea of sonship in the Hebrew Scripture follows prototypes of the Ancient Orient, appearing in Jerusalem as a result of Canaanite practice. Further, he is certain that the relationship of God as father to the king as son is not a physical one but one of adoption. He goes on: "It is understandable that the Old Testament rejected the idea of the physical divine sonship of the king as incompatible with its spiritual notion of God. In fact, the psalmist, too, excludes the idea of a physical begetting by adding the word 'today' and by using the ancient formula of adoption 'you are my son.'"[28]

Collins, supporting the idea that the David's son will be adopted by God, claims that the language used for such an adoption is modeled on the

25. 2 Sam 7:2–14.

26 203 2 Sam 7:7.

27. Ps 89:26–29.

28. Weiser, *Psalms,* 87.

grant of land made by a king to a loyal vassal.[29] The establishment of the house of David is legitimatized in this way, the king receiving his land and his authority by virtue of his adoption. The idea is formulaic and not very far from the practice of the Egyptians (see Chapter 1) who, to confirm the authority of their Pharaoh, called him Son of Ra.

But does the quotation refer to Solomon or to some future figure? Here the evidence of the Chronicler, writing in the second century BCE, is of assistance, for he makes a significant change to the Second Book of Samuel. He writes of God saying to David: "I will raise up your offspring after you, *one of your own sons* (my italics); I will establish his kingdom."[30] The reference to Solomon is clear. However, Smith sees the word offspring as referring to the dynasty and not simply to Solomon as an individual and Driver supports him by suggesting that though the reference is clearly to Solomon, the latter is in fact representative of the dynasty as a whole.[31]

Solomon, then, on the basis of the verses quoted above, might be regarded as the adopted son of God and have divine status and this status might also be possessed by his successors. Such a concept is at once powerful and far-reaching. *But the extraordinary thing is that future generations did not follow it up.* When the kingdoms of Israel and Judah divided, Rehoboam does not claim that the secession of Israel is sinful because he is a son of God;[32] when Jehoshaphat of Judah agrees to campaign with Ahab of Israel, he accepts parity with the latter;[33] when Jerusalem is under threat from Babylon, King Zedekiah does not claim divine protection because he is a son of God[34] and when the Jerusalem is re-established under Persian authority, there is acceptance that the Jewish faith can survive without a king. The suggestion that Solomon and his line will continue because they are sons of God did not form part of the Jewish faith. Indeed the reverse was perhaps the case for the writers of the Book of Jubilees in the second century BCE make a change when they repeat the writing of 2 Samuel, resulting in: "And I shall be a father to them (i.e., the children of Israel), and they shall be sons to me."[35] The title Son of God as an appellation of the king of Israel is not established.

29. Collins, "Mark and his Readers," 39.

30. 1 Chr 17:11.

31. Smith, *Samuel*, 300; Driver, *Hebrew Text*, 276.

32. 1 Kgs 12:12–19.

33. 1 Kgs 22:4.

34. 2 Kgs 25:1–7.

35. 2 Sam 7:14a; Jubilees 1:24–25.

THE APOCRYPHA AND PSEUDEPIGRAPHA

The researcher into the appellation son of God in the Apocrypha and Pseudepigrapha will be immediately struck by the very few times that the title is mentioned. Byrne offers seven quotations,[36] Schweitzer and Lohse offer four[37] and the index to Charlesworth's two volume *The Old Testament Pseudepigrapha* offers a meager seventeen. In a body of literature of over eight hundred thousand words this can scarcely be accounted a significant number of mentions. But this number is effectively reduced still further, for it is found that nearly all of these mentions are from literature emanating from the end of the first century CE and therefore are almost certainly influenced by, if not inspired by, the early Christian faith.

As an example of this influence, there are five verses in the *Odes of Solomon* which include some reference to a son of god (e.g., "So the Virgin became a mother with great mercies and she labored and bore the Son. . .")[38] but the *Odes* was probably written about 100 CE.[39] Indeed, with the exception of 1 Enoch (see below) there seem to be only three references to Son of God that may be reasonably deemed to be free of the influence of Christianity in the whole Apocrypha and Pseudepigrapha. The *Wisdom of Solomon* mentions three times that Wisdom is the child of the Lord[40] clearly influenced by a quotation from *Proverbs,* "The Lord created me at the beginning of his work,"[41] and is intended to be figurative rather than literal. The writer of *The Sibylline Oracles* refers to the Jews when he prophecies that the sons of the great God will live peacefully around the Temple,[42] a quotation which Charlesworth attributes to the second century BCE.[43] *Joseph and Aseneth* twice refers to Joseph (son of Jacob) as son of God[44] but Charlesworth, who assigns a date to *Joseph and Aseneth* between 100 BCE and 100 CE, is clear that all that is implied is that Joseph is superior to the son of Pharaoh. The meager supply of references seems to have become virtually nonexistent. However 1 Enoch, at first sight, offers better material.[45]

36. Byrne, "Sons of God," 164, 174, 176, 177, 209, 261.

37. Schweizer and Lohse, "Son of God," 339.

38. Odes 19:7, 8; Charlesworth, *The Old Testament Pseudepigrapha*, 2.752.

39. Ibid. 2.726.

40. *Wis* 2:13, 16, 18.

41. Prov 8:22.

42. *Oracles* 3.732.

43. Charlesworth, *The Old Testament Pseudepigrapha*, 1.358.

44. *Joseph* 2:209, 223.

45. The question as to whether the use of the title Messiah in the Pseudepigrapha may be interpreted as referring to a Son of God is fully examined in Appendix 2 and the

1 Enoch

1 Enoch is a collection of apocalyptic texts that were composed between the fourth century BCE and the turn of the era.[46] The first part of the book is concerned with a version of the Fall as portrayed in Gen. 6.1–4 which tells the reader that the sons of God had intercourse with human women who bore children by them and who were the heroes and warriors of old. This short passage in Genesis forms the introduction to the story of the Flood; God sees corruption everywhere and determines to drown all that he has made.[47] The connection between the activities of the sons of God and the great evil that God finds upon the earth is simply that the two stories are juxtaposed in the text. However, in I Enoch the Sons of God of Genesis are often called the Watchers, their descent from heaven triggers evil and the result of their action is that the four archangels, called the Holy Ones,[48] intervene and Enoch is commissioned to reprimand the sons of heaven.

Three things are clear in 1 Enoch: the terms "sons of god," "watchers," and "angels" are synonymous terms; they are always used in the plural and are clearly heavenly beings; the appellation Son of God is never used in Enoch to refer to a single transcendent being. The progeny of watchers and human women are great giants, who begin to kill men and drink their blood.[49] Whereas in Greek legend the product of gods and humans were on the whole good and referred to as the sons of god (e.g., Heracles), and whereas in Genesis the offspring of angels and humans are referred to as heroes,[50] in 1 Enoch they are seen as wicked beings. The sons of God in 1 Enoch do not provide a model for a human Son of God.

THE DEAD SEA SCROLLS

[the spirit of God] dwelt on him, he fell down before the throne . . . O [K]ing, you are angry forever and your years . . . your vision and all. For ever you . . . [the gre]at ones. An oppression will come to the earth . . . a great massacre in the provinces . . . the king of Assyria [and E]gypt . . . he will be great on earth . . . will make and all will serve . . . The son of God he will be proclaimed

---

opinion expressed there is that it may not.

46. Nickelsburg and VanderKam, *1 Enoch*, vii.

47. Gen 6:5–7.

48. 1 Enoch 9:2.

49. 1 Enoch 7:2–3.

50. Gen 6:4.

(or proclaim himself) and the son of the Most High they will call him. Like the sparks of the vision, so will be their kingdom. They will reign for years on earth and they will trample all.[51]

Surnamed "the Son of God fragment" by Vermes, 4Q246 is an apocalyptic passage that contains the words son of God and son of the Most High and it seems as though these phrases could offer a basis for Son of God as an appellation used by the Jews in the first century CE. But there is a major problem in inferring this, for it is unclear whether reference is being made to a magnificent and godly figure (such as a messiah) or to a blasphemer (who would use the title for self-aggrandizement). Milik indeed believes that this Son of God could be that malign figure, Alexander Balas of the Seleucid empire while other writers suggest he might be an Antichrist or an angelic being.[52] However Fitzmyer ˈexamines the thesis that the reference could be to a future messiah, which, if true, identifies the messiah as a son of God. Since his conclusions on this crucial issue are relevant to this book, they need rehearsing.[53]

Fitzmyer first notes that the word "messiah" is not used in the text and considers that "Son of God" refers to a coming Jewish ruler, who will probably be a member of the Hasmonean dynasty. Though he will sit on David's throne, this does not mean that he will necessarily be a messiah. He points out that "though the king on the Davidic throne is often said to be God's son (e.g., 2 Sam 7.14; Ps 2.7, 8), these titles are not used there of a messianic figure." *In Christian writings of the New Testament they are used of him who is the Messiah, but that is an entirely different matter* (my italics). He goes on to echo Hengel by saying that however anyone wishes to interpret this text, it makes it clear that the title Son of God was not completely alien to Palestinian Judaism.[54] His arguments are important for they both highlight the danger of using the Christian concept of Messiah as a starting point for the discussion and show that the appellation Son of God has a limited use in the Dead Sea Scrolls.[55]

---

51. Vermes, *DSS* 4Q246, 618

52. Milik, *"Les Modeles,"* 38; Vermes, *DSS* 4Q246, 617.

53. Fitzmyer "4Q246," 4.

54. Hengel, *The Son of God,* 45.

55. Fitzmyer, "4Q246," 6. See Appendix 2.

Josephus and Philo

The two most important contemporary writers on Jewish society in the century that saw the life of Jesus of Nazareth were unquestionably Philo and Josephus. The former, writing in Alexandria, was a philosopher and moralist, who sought to establish links between Jewish and Greek philosophy; the latter, writing in Rome, had been first a Jewish commander against the Romans and then an ambassador for the Romans during the war of 66—70 CE. As a pensioner of the emperor Vespasian he wrote a history of the Jewish War and then a history of Israel. It should be noted that both Philo and Josephus wrote in Greek.

Josephus

Josephus is to be mainly remarked in this book for the two things he did *not* write. In *The War of the Jews*, which covers the first half of the first century, he does not mention Jesus of Nazareth and neither in this work nor in *The Antiquities of the Jews* does he use the appellation Son of God.[56] The former omission has already drawn comment in Chapter 2; the latter is revealed in the following two significant passages. When Josephus retells the story of David and the LORD's refusal to allow him to build the temple, the Jewish historian makes no reference to the account in the Second Book of Samuel where God says, "I will be a father to him, and he shall be a son to me."[57] And when Josephus does mention Jesus of Nazareth at the end of *The Antiquities* he does not describe him as being called Son of God by his followers.[58] Josephus is silent on divine sonship.

Philo

Philo was born two or three decades earlier than Josephus and wrote in the tradition of the wisdom literature of the scriptures. Though he does comment that only good and outstanding men are called "god's sons" by Moses[59] his main theology seems to be directed towards God as creator. Adapting the Platonic concept of God as the demiurge who created the universe, and styling him as Father, he asserts that the mother of the world is divine

---

56. Schweitzer, "Jesus," 35; see also Chapter 4.

57. 2 Sam 7:14.

58. *Ant* 18.3.63.65.

59. *Quaest in Gen* 1.92

reason and identifies this figure with the Biblical concept of Wisdom.[60] He therefore refers to the visible world as the son of God and, as Hengel points out, he is remarkably restrained in transferring the designation son of God to *men*. Indeed, so reticent is he that Radice's article in *The Cambridge Companion to Philo*[61] does not contain one reference to such an appellation. The two great Jewish writers of the first century in the Common Era show no evidence that a human son of God is expected or that the title is one of great significance.

CONCLUSION

The body of literature considered in this chapter is vast, encompassing the whole of the Hebrew Scriptures, the Apocrypha and Pseudepigrapha as well as the works of Josephus and Philo, a total of over three million words. It was compiled over eight centuries and covers history from the creation of the world to the period that saw the coming of the Christian faith. It contains history, prophecy, poetry, philosophy and the apocalyptic and it was compiled in Hebrew, Aramaic and Greek. It is the whole library of early Jewish literature.

In this huge body of literature, there are references to sons of God and occasionally a Son of God. These sons of God are normally the angelic or divine beings that make up the court of heaven (Job 1 & 2). When Son of God is used in the singular, the references are generally to Israel as son of God and are clearly metaphorical (e.g., Exod. 4.22). References to an individual as a son of God are sparse but when they do appear they are connected with the Davidic kingship (e.g., Ps. 2.7). Two references stand out: "I will be a father to him and he shall be a son to me"[62] and the quotation from DSS 4Q246 "The son of God he will be proclaimed . . ."[63] Each sounds futuristic and each, perhaps taken out of context, can be quoted as pertinent to justify its use as referring to a human being as yet unborn. It is well perhaps to again cite Fitzmyer when he makes it clear that the title Son of God was not completely alien to Palestinian Judaism.[64]

However, as will be seen, Jesus of Nazareth was known to posterity as the only begotten Son of God, and this was perhaps his most enduring and significant title. So important was this title that the Church was to split over

60. Prov 8:22–24; *Ebr.* 30–31; Hengel, *The Son of God,* 51–53.

61. Kamesar, *Companion to Philo.*

62. 2 Sam 7:14a.

63. Vermes, "4Q246," 61.

64. Fitzmyer, "4Q246," 17.

its usage in the fourth century in the Arian controversy. But as this chapter has indicated, *there are surely not enough references to the title Son of God in Jewish literature to account for such a significant use of the appellation, or to constitute a point of origin or departure for such use.* As this book examines the way the followers of Jesus wrote about him and the frequent references to him as Son of God, it will become clear that the title originated in Macedonia and in Greece, though once it had become an established appellation for Jesus, Jewish literature was used to justify its use to the Jews. The origins of the widespread custom of referring to Jesus of Nazareth as Son of God are discussed in the next chapter.

4

Son of God in the New Testament

PREAMBLE

Chapter 3 examined the use of the appellation Son of God in Jewish literature that was written before the cult of Jesus was established and found that though the title was seldom used of a single human being, it was occasionally used of Solomon, probably of his successors and perhaps of a Maccabean leader. But it clearly established that there was not nearly enough use of the appellation to justify it becoming the major title of Jesus. Chapter 4 deals with the New Testament itself and looks at the emergence and use of the title Son of God as it appears there.

It is generally understood that Christianity, the worship of Jesus Christ as a divinity, is the largest religion in the world to which over one billion people adhere. The origins of Christianity are to be found in The Holy Bible, which is the most widely produced book in literature and revered by many Christians as the inspired word of God. Jesus of Nazareth and his followers are a predominant theme in Western art and Jesus himself is probably the person most written about in the history of the planet; every aspect of his life is covered in book, film, painting and sculpture. The literature about Jesus' life, personality and activity is vast and, therefore, I have been forced to focus my research on a very narrow area and accept the view of the majority of scholars on a number of issues without further investigation. This book must be strictly confined to examining the *title* Son of God and this chapter must equally be concerned with its *use* in the New Testament and do so within the confines of what is history, avoiding theological inferences supplied by later generations.

In Chapter 2, as the story of Alexander the Great was unfolded, it became clear that though there had been at least eighteen contemporary biographies of Alexander written by people involved in his campaigns, not one of these biographies had survived. The student of Alexander has to manage with the writings of Trogus, Diodorus, Plutarch, Curtius and Arrian, which deal with Alexander's life in great detail, as well as references to Alexander made by historians such as Cassius Dio and Livy. Trogus, Diodorus and Plutarch have all written authoratively on a number of significant historical figures of which Alexander is but one, while Curtius and Arrian, whose main works concentrate on Alexander, are noted historians. None of the five conceal from their readers that Alexander was a flawed character, capable of cruelty and murder, though they also portray him as a man of exceptional generosity and excellence. Though all but Arrian hold that he was acclaimed as son of Zeus–Ammon at Siwa, not one of the five belonged to an Alexander cult or is known to have worshipped him.

When the Gospels (canonical or apocryphal) of Jesus are examined, an entirely different situation is found. These, the only surviving "lives" of Jesus, are written by people who, because they hold him to be in some sense divine, omit any reference to moral failure on his part. All the writers of the early Christian literature are members of the Jesus cult; all may be described as Christians. Some of them wrote epistles to other Christians and others wrote what have come to be called Gospels (i.e. stories of the good news about Jesus).[1] The latter, though they have the form of a biographical account, are found on examination to be no such thing. They are stories of Jesus, which exhort or justify faith in him as the one who mediates between God and man, but they lack historical support. So in answer to the question, did Jesus claim to be the Son of God, Dunn says that Christian understanding of this possible claim by Jesus is in fact the result of decades of Christian development.[2] None of the stories that appear in the Gospels are corroborated by writers outside the Christian cult, and this is particularly true of the only significant contemporary Jewish historian.

1. Beare, *Records,* 19.
2. Dunn, *Evidence,* 30.

JOSEPHUS

Josephus was between thirty and forty years younger than Jesus.[3] He was by turn an Essene, a priest in the Jerusalem temple, a visitor to Rome and the commander of a rebel contingent of Jews in their rebellion against Rome in 66 CE. When he was captured, he became an ambassador for the Romans to the rebels and then a pensioner of the Emperor Vespasian and his sons, writing a book entitled *On the Jewish War* about the Jews and their activities, leading up to the crushing of their rebellion in 70 CE. The book deals with many people and happenings in Jerusalem, including much copy on Pontius Pilate *but there is no mention of Jesus of Nazareth whatsoever*. While it can be argued that the crucifixion of Jesus was omitted because it showed neither Jewish nor Roman authorities in a good light, or because Jesus was not of sufficient importance to merit comment, Josephus is as silent on the subject as Pliny the Elder or any other historian who might possibly have referred to the life and death of Jesus of Nazareth. Josephus does devote 150 words to Jesus in his *Antiquity of the Jews*,[4] written 30 years after *On the Jewish War*, but there is deep suspicion among some commentators that these words have been subtly altered by Christian interpolators.[5] The student of Jesus of Nazareth has, therefore, only the biased evidence of those who belonged to the Jesus cult and it is to an examination of this material that the book must now turn.

METHODOLOGY

Essentially there are three types of writing in the New Testament; the Gospels and Acts, the Revelation of St. John the Divine and twenty-one Epistles. Of these last, it is generally accepted that four are of undisputed Pauline origin (Romans, 1 and 2 Corinthians and Galatians), three (1 Thessalonians, Philippians and Philemon) are probably of Pauline origin and two (2 Thessalonians and Colossians) may be by Paul. The Pastoral Letters (1 and 2 Timothy and Titus) and Ephesians are generally accepted as being Deutero-Pauline. There are also seven Catholic Epistles (James, Jude, 1 and 2 Peter, 1, 2, and 3 John, and the Epistle to the Hebrews). It is important to emphasize the authorship of some epistles, for when readers study 1 Corinthians and read of the resurrection; they know that this is Paul's version of events and

---

3. The full life of Josephus is well told by Williamson in his old but highly readable *The World of Josephus*.

4. *Ant.* 18.3.63.

5. Wells, *Historical Evidence,* 18.

make of it what they will. Paul's letters are mainly written to encourage faith, to rebuke sin and to give rulings to Pauline communities on certain issues.[6] The Gospels and the Acts of the Apostles are more complex. As already seen, these have the form of historical biography while being in fact vehicles for counteracting error and encouraging belief in Jesus and his mission. Some scholars go so far as to embrace the Gospels as divinely inspired truth and insist that every word in them is historically accurate. When contradictions emerge, these have to be explained away. So, in the healing of the Gerasene (Gadarene) demoniac(s),[7] Mark speaks of a man with an unclean spirit, while Matthew speaks of two demoniacs. Were there one or two demoniacs? To this day there are writers who insist that there must have been two such healings as the only way to preserve the absolute truth of both narratives.[8]

Most students allow some latitude for the Gospel writers to make errors or to tell their stories with a differing emphasis. Once this latitude is granted, all manner of possibilities emerge. For example, in the writing of A. N. Wilson[9] the theory is put forward that St. Paul was none other than Malchus, the servant of the High Priest who had his ear cut off in Gethsemane!

There is no need for this book to examine such extremes. The view will be taken that the writers of the Gospels wrote narratives constructed out of traditional materials with literary art and theological motives.[10] A conventional approach will be taken to the way source critics handle the Synoptic Problem and explain the interdependence of the first three Gospel narratives, a subject exhaustively examined by Streeter,[11] and more recently by such writers as Kloppenborg, Sanders and Davies and Goodacre.[12] Belief in the primacy of Mark, accepted by most scholars since Schweitzer's groundbreaking *The Quest of the Historical Jesus,* will not be challenged, nor will the existence of some other source, conventionally known as Q, which it is believed, was used alongside Mark, as a primary source by Matthew and Luke.[13] Some of the events in the story of the life of Jesus as given by Mark will be accepted as based on historical happenings, with the understanding

6. Barrett, *Paul,* 1–20.

7. Mark 5:1–20; Matt 8:28–34.

8. The author heard a vehement assertion of the two stories idea in All Souls, Langham Place in 2001.

9. Wilson, *Jesus,* 78–97.

10. Johnson, *The Real Jesus,* 4.

11. Streeter, *The Four Gospels.*

12. Kloppenborg, *The Formation of "Q"*; Sanders and Davies, *Studying*; Goodacre, *The Synoptic Problem.*

13. Manson, *The Saying of Jesus,* 15–20; Kloppenborg *The Formation of Q,* 8–40; Sanders and Davies, *Studying,* 112–19.

that these are embroidered and occasionally altered by Matthew and Luke. Again, a conventional approach is taken to form criticism, it being accepted that there was a strong oral tradition which affected the writing of the Gospels and that there was no significant order in which these stories were relayed to the Gospel writers. Bultmann famously said: "I do indeed think that we can know almost nothing concerning the life and personality of Jesus, since the early Christian sources show no interest in either, are moreover fragmentary and often legendary; and other sources do not exist."[14]

In brief, modern scholars cannot be sure what Jesus said or did. Certainty exists only in knowing what the early church believed was said or done by Jesus when a written work about him was produced. So, if a date of around 70 CE is accepted as the emergence of the written Gospel of Mark, all the student can know for certain is that there was a school of Christianity which existed immediately before 70 CE which believed and taught (for example) that Jesus did such things as walk on water.[15]

REDACTION AND NARRATIVE CRITICISM

In *The Gospels and Jesus*, Stanton refers to redaction criticism as "The Evangelists as authors" and narrative criticism as "The Gospels as stories."[16] Both redaction and narrative criticism signal a switch from concentration on the basic material available to the evangelists, to interest in the evangelists themselves and what they made of this material. Stanton cites the important article by Bornkamm to show how Matthew transformed the story of the stilling of the storm from its use in Mark.[17] The student is encouraged to look, not so much for what may actually have happened by the Sea of Galilee, as the *use* Mark and Matthew made of it.

This naturally affects the *order* in which the incidents are portrayed. The writers of the Synoptic Gospels, for example, tell of the casting of the money-changers out of the temple immediately after the Triumphal Entry into Jerusalem, an event soon to be followed by Jesus death.[18] John transfers the incident to the beginning of the ministry of Jesus[19] immediately following his first miracle when he turned the water into wine. Such a rearrangement of incidents in the life of Jesus indicates that the authors were

14. Bultmann, *Jesus and the Word*, 8.

15. Mark 6:45–52; Matt 14:22–33; John 6:15–21.

16. Stanton, *The Gospels,* 29–36.

17. Ibid., 30; Borkamm, "The Stilling of the Storm"; Matt 8:23–27; Mark 4:35–41.

18. Matt 21:10–17; Mark 11:15–19: Luke 19:45–48.

19. John 2:13–22.

using their lives of Jesus to make different points. The evangelists seem to be arranging their material to show significant events in Jesus' life according to their own motifs and surely one of these was Jesus as the Son of God.

THE SON OF GOD MOTIF

This is especially true of the Gospel of Mark, which opens, in most versions, with the words: "The beginning of the good news of Jesus Christ, the Son of God."[20] Jesus is then affirmed as Son of God by a voice from heaven.[21] He engages with unclean spirits who acknowledge him as the Son of God.[22] He goes up a mountain to pray and again a voice speaks from heaven and proclaims him Son of God.[23] He is questioned about this title by the High Priest[24] and finally is affirmed as Son of God by the very centurion who was in charge of the squad who crucified him. The motif of the Gospel is surely to set Jesus forward as the Son of God.

If this thesis is sustainable and the early 70s CE accepted as the date of the completion of the existing Gospel of Mark, it follows that the idea of Jesus as the Son of God was finding favor with Christians at this time. However, there was a problem in the title gaining universal acceptance, for there were perhaps those who argued that this was a title not used by Jesus. Mark's response was to introduce an air of secrecy into his Gospel and tells his readers (for example) that "Whenever the unclean spirits saw him (i.e. Jesus), they fell down before him and shouted: 'You are the Son of God.' But he sternly ordered them not to make him known."[25] This secrecy motif allows the reader of Mark to understand that though the crowd did not understand the meaning of the demoniac's strange cries, the spirits recognized the source of his authority.[26] Since Chapter 3 has demonstrated that Son of God was neither a title of the expected Messiah nor of any significant Jewish figure before it began to be applied to Jesus, the title must have come into use among Christians in the period between 30–70 CE and in the secrecy motif Mark has provided a reason why it came into use later rather than earlier. To see how the title emerged it is necessary to look at the history of the early church.

20. Mark 1:1.
21. Mark 1:11
22. Mark 3:11; 5:7.
23. Mark 9:7.
24. Mark 14:61.
25. Mark 3:11–12.
26. Hooker, *Mark,* 110.

THE LIFE OF THE EARLY CHURCH

If it is impossible to create an historical account of the life of Jesus of Nazareth, it is quite possible to write a history of the early Church, provided that the basic framework of the Acts of the Apostles is not seriously disputed.[27] Few would in fact doubt the story that Jesus died in Jerusalem (almost certainly in the fourth decade of the millennium) and that his followers initially remained in Jerusalem before spreading throughout Palestine and as far as Antioch. Key figures in the emerging church are accepted as being James (the brother of Jesus), Simon Peter (also called Cephas), John the Evangelist and Paul. It is certainly Paul who provides the student with much evidence about the existence and history of the early church, for he wrote many letters to the emerging Christian communities and a number of these letters have survived.

Paul is described in Acts as making a missionary tour to Cyprus and Asia Minor before attending the Council of Jerusalem.[28] He is reported to have travelled again in Asia Minor and visited Ephesus before crossing the Aegean Sea to visit Macedonia and Greece. He is said to have gone again to Jerusalem and then returned to Ephesus where he spent over two years.[29] Acts says that he finally made a valedictory visit to Greece before journeying to Jerusalem to face imprisonment, trial, a journey to Rome and death.

It is possible to date some of Paul's activities fairly accurately from a date that emerges in the Acts of the Apostles. Paul is said to have stayed in Corinth for 18 months during his first visit to Greece and this coincided with a time when Gallio was the Roman proconsul of Achaia.[30] According to an inscription at Delphi, Gallio was in Corinth from 51–52 CE and since it seems probable that Paul wrote to the Thessalonians while on his way to Corinth,[31] the date of this writing may reasonably be dated around 50 CE.[32] This in turn means that Paul's stay in Ephesus on his second visit may be dated about 54–55 CE and it was during his two years there that it is supposed by many that he wrote letters to the Galatians, Corinthians, Philippians and Philemon and probably to the Colossians and Romans.[33]

---

27. Hengel *Acts*, 35–39; Barrett, *Acts*, xxxv–xl.
28. Acts 15.
29. Acts 19:10.
30. Acts 18:11–12.
31. Dunn, *St. Paul*, 20; Barrett, *Acts*, 279.
32. Fee, *The Thessalonian Epistles*, 3–5.
33. Barrett, *Romans*, 3–5; Stuhlmacher, *Paul's Letter*, 5–6; Cranfield, *Romans*, xi.

Ephesians and the Pastoral Epistles are generally believed to be written after Paul's death, an event that probably occurred about 65 CE.[34]

SON OF GOD IN PAUL

The Epistles to the Thessalonians

The term Son of God is not used in these Epistles. Both begin with the same salutation: "Paul, Silvanus and Timothy, to the church of the Thessalonians in God the Father and the Lord Jesus Christ, grace to you and peace."[35] This salutation, as will be found, begins almost all Pauline letters and its use both of God the Father and the Lord Jesus Christ is significant. Increasingly in the New Testament God is referred to as Father and a combination of Lord, Jesus and Christ becomes a Pauline appellation for Jesus.

The Epistles from Ephesus

Galatians

Paul begins by repeating an extended salutation of 2 Thessalonians: "Grace to you and peace from God the Father and the Lord Jesus Christ"[36] and goes on to say, "God . . . was pleased to reveal his Son to me." The filial relationship of Jesus to God is thus established and reinforced by the statement, God sent the Spirit of his Son into our hearts, crying "Abba! Father!"[37] The word *abba* is Aramaic and means Father, and both Chrysostom and Theodoret, who came from Syria, agree that children from there call their fathers *abba*. According to Jeffrey, *abba* is used of God only very rarely and uncertainly in Jewish Palestinian documents, this usage being an innovation of Jesus, to whom God was always "my father." God the Father of the Letters to the Thessalonians has become a more personal God in the letter to the Galatians.

34. Muddiman, *Ephesians*, 34–36; Aageson, *Paul,* 3–5.

35. 1 Thess 1:1; 2 Thess 1:1.

36. 2 Thess 1:2; Gal 1:3.

37. 2. Thess 4:6.

1 Corinthians

Again Paul repeats his conventional salutation: "Grace and peace to you from God our Father and the Lord Jesus Christ"[38] and goes on to say "God is faithful; by him you were called into the fellowship of his Son, Jesus Christ our Lord."[39] As in Galatians, Jesus is referred to as God's son.

2 Corinthians

This time the formula of Paul's conventional greeting is repeated near the end of the letter: "The God and Father of the Lord Jesus. . ."[40] But Paul develops his naming of Jesus by using the actual title Son of God: "For the Son of God, Jesus Christ, whom we proclaimed among you. . ."[41] This is almost certainly the earliest time that the appellation Son of God is used in the New Testament.

Romans

Although Paul includes his conventional salutation,[42] he begins this epistle:

> Paul, a servant of Jesus Christ, called to be an apostle, set apart for the gospel of God, which he promised beforehand through his prophets in the holy scriptures, the gospel concerning his Son, who was descended from David according to the flesh and was declared to be the Son of God with power according to the spirit of holiness by resurrection from the dead, Jesus Christ our Lord.[43]

Here, in a document dated about 56 CE, biblical scholars are provided with the first unequivocal declaration that Jesus is the Son of God and it comes from no lesser person than Paul. The actual statement is supported by other comments which might easily have been found in any of the letters written in Ephesus: "For God, whom I serve with my spirit by announcing

---

38. 1 Cor 1:3.

39. 1 Cor 1:9.

40. 2 Cor 11:31.

41. 2 Cor 2:19.

42. Rom 1:7.

43. Rom 1:1–4.

the Gospel of his Son is witness without ceasing," and "We were reconciled to God through the death of his Son."[44]

Schweizer suggests that Son of God in Romans is a functional concept, i.e., it refers to one who carries out the function of God's Son, by exercising sovereignty over God's people[45]. He goes on to contrast this with Greek-speaking Judaism (such as he sees in the Gospel of John), which produces a concept of the Son so exalted that he is distanced from humanity. It may be questioned as to whether this theory fully takes account of the background to the title Son of God. Alexander the Great, as has been seen in Chapter 2, was declared to be son of Ammon at Siwa and this was most certainly not because he exercised authority over God's people, but rather on account of his divine parentage. I see no reason at all to doubt that Paul was using the appellation Son of God in the same spirit.

It is highly significant that Paul speaks of Jesus as being descended from David according to the flesh. As has been seen in Chapter 1, sons of gods had earthly as well as divine fathers, and it does not seem that Paul has a problem in accepting Jesus as both son of Joseph and son of God. The myths of the virgin birth have perhaps yet to emerge.

Other Epistles

All the other epistles in the New Testament are judged to be written later than Romans (with the probable exception of Philippians and Philemon) and all but two offer little or no mention of the Son of God. The Pastoral Epistles, James, 1 Peter and Jude do not mention the appellation at all, though they do use the expression God our Father and the Lord Jesus Christ quite frequently. 2 Peter uses the title Son of God once, probably quoting from Matthew or Mark.[46] Ephesians offers: "The gifts he gave were that some would be apostles, some prophets, some evangelists, some pastors and teachers to equip the saints for the work of the ministry for building up the body of Christ until all come to the unity of faith and the knowledge of the Son of God . . ."[47] Colossians says: "He (God) has rescued us from the power of darkness and transferred us into the kingdom of his beloved Son."[48] The author of Colossians develops the significance of the Son in the next eleven verses, offering him a mighty role, for he is the head of the

44. Rom 5:10.
45. Schweizer, *Jesus*, 81.
46. 2 Pet 1:17.
47. Eph 4:12–13.
48. Col 1:13.

body, the church; he is the beginning, the firstborn from the dead, so that he might have the first place in everything.[49] The cosmic significance of Jesus is also developed in Revelation. Two books in the New Testament, apart from the Gospels, do make frequent and significant use of the title Son of God and they are the Epistle to the Hebrews and the First Epistle of John. The former will be examined after the Synoptic Gospels and the latter after the Gospel of John.

THE SON OF GOD IN THE SYNOPTIC GOSPELS AND ACTS

In the literature of the New Testament examined so far, the title Son of God has been used without explanation or definition and its origin has not been identified. Why Paul starts to call Jesus Son of God at this period in his mission is not explained; the title simply starts to appear in his writing. But when the reader looks at the Synoptic Gospels, an explanation is offered by showing how the appellation was applied to Jesus in a variety of circumstances. In the Synoptic Gospels, Jesus is addressed as Son of God, referred to as Son of God and (probably) says he is the Son of God. Since the hypothesis of this book is that the title Son of God was adopted by the Church as the result of interaction with Greek culture and religion, the date that the Gospels were written is important and how they provided a life of Jesus needs to be examined. As it is not possible to launch a full investigation of the dating of the Gospels, a consensus of scholars will have to suffice.

In her *The Gospel according to St. Mark*, Hooker[50] suggests that Mark is usually dated between 65 and 75 CE, though she makes it clear that opinions differ in fixing a more precise date within this general period. Further, there is almost universal agreement that the Gospel of Mark predates those of Matthew and Luke by about ten years[51]. So it will be accepted that Mark was written in around 70 CE and Matthew, Luke and Acts between 80 and 90. The appreciation of the person of Jesus and the names by which he was called are therefore those of the eighth decade of the first century CE.

---

49. Col 1:18

50. Hooker, *Mark*, 8.

51. Streeter, *The Four Gospels*, 223–71 and others. B. H. Streeter in his book, written in 1924, examines this subject exhaustively and though there have been disagreements with his findings, most scholars concur with his general theme.

The Son of God in the Gospel of Mark

On eight occasions Mark specifically uses the title Son of God and Telford is clear that most scholars agree that for Mark it is the most important title ever given to Jesus.[52] The eight are:

Editorial

Mark begins his narrative with the words "A beginning of the Good News of Jesus Christ, the Son of God."[53] Most manuscripts contain the words Son of God but a significant number omit them. Opinions as to whether there was a scribal omission caused by a scribe or an addition by someone so moved by the content of Mark that he added Son of God are divided. My own opinion is that, even if the latter explanation is true, the case of the use of "Son of God" is appropriate. The good news in Mark is surely about Jesus, the Son of God.

A Voice Sounds from Heaven

In two significant places within the Gospel narratives, a voice sounds from heaven. The first is on the banks of the river Jordan, where Jesus goes to be baptized by John the Baptist. As Jesus emerges from the water a voice sounds from heaven with the words, "You are my beloved son." The second is on a mountain where Jesus is transfigured before Peter, James and John and a voice sounds from the covering cloud: "This is my beloved son." Luke similarly repeats the statement, though he replaces the word beloved with chosen.[54]

Comment on the Voice from Heaven

Clearly the reader is expected to see the two events as crucial moments in Jesus' life and equally clearly the second is redolent of associations with Mount Sinai. "Where Mark is concerned," writes Telford,[55] "the Old Testament has clearly been a formative influence both on the evangelist and on

---

52. Telford, *Theology*, 38.
53. Mark 1:1.
54. Luke 9:35.
55. Telford, *Mark*, 209.

his tradition. Here are Moses and Elijah,[56] here is the cloud,[57] here is the voice of God[58] and here is the dazzling whiteness of clothes.[59] The parallels are manifold."

There is another parallel to the events at the River Jordan, and that is what happened at Siwa as described in Chapter 2. Alexander the Great, like Jesus, went to seek a prophet of God to gain self-understanding, and like Jesus, he was named a son of a divinity. Again like Jesus, Alexander went out into the desert after the experience and (according to Plutarch) immediately developed, through his encounter with Psammon, the concept of world harmony that became his life's mission.

Demons and Demoniacs address Jesus as Son of God

Twice the divine sonship of Jesus is recognized by the forces of evil, for the reader is told that unclean spirits cried out with the words, "You are the Son of God," while in a parallel passage, Luke describes the evil forces as demons.[60] Later, when Jesus and his disciples arrive on the eastern shore of the Lake of Galilee, they are accosted by a demoniac who shouts out aloud, "What have you to do with me, Jesus, Son of the Most High God?" Matthew amends the story by saying that there were two demoniacs.[61]

This book accepts that Jesus was primarily a wandering Jewish exorcist and prophet and that both these stories are almost certainly founded upon real historical incidents. The responses of the demons as described in Mark may, however, be seen as reflecting the theology of the seventh decade.

The Parable of the Vineyard—Son in Allegory

In this parable or allegory, a man leases his vineyard to tenants and goes away for a time. He sends servants to claim some of the produce but the tenants beat them up or kill them. Finally he has only one person left to send, his son, but him they kill as well, inviting the wrath of the owner and their

---

56. Mark 9:4.
57. Mark 9:7; Exod 19:18.
58. Exod 20.
59. Mark 9:3; Exod 35:30.
60. Mark 3:10–11; Luke 4:41.
61. Mark 5:7; Luke 8:28; Matt 8:29.

own dispossession.[62] This son is referred to as beloved by Mark and Luke but simply as a son by Matthew.[63]

This seems as though a parable has been turned into an allegory and as an allegory it lacks coherence. The original parable is about stewardship—if the master is away, the tenants must care for his property and be ready for his return. The addition of the beloved son leads to confusion. The killing of the son for the motive of gain would in reality be the act of imbeciles; for surely the tenants had no power to withstand the wrath of the avenging father. The Son of God motif has been added to an existing story and confused it, though there can be no doubt that it adds support to Mark's theme that Jesus is, in fact, the Son of God.[64]

Jesus Claims the Title—The Interrogation of Jesus

When Jesus has been arrested he is brought before the Sanhedrin and asked by the High Priest if he is the Son of God, Jesus replies "I am" which is, on the face of it, an unequivocal acceptance of the title.[65] Jesus' reply is followed by a reference to a passage in Daniel, "you will see the Son of Man seated at the right hand of the Power and coming with the clouds of heaven."[66] Kim sees this passage as accepting that the two titles Son of God and Son of Man are co-terminus, but it is a difficult argument to sustain in light of the way Matthew and Luke tell the story.[67]

Both Matthew and Luke give different accounts of the exchange. According to Matthew[68]: "Then the High Priest said to him, 'I put you under oath before the living God, tell us if you are the Messiah, the Son of God,' and Jesus replies, 'You have said so.'" According to Luke, they all then ask, "Are you, then, the Son of God?" and Jesus is reported as replying "If I tell you, you will not believe."[69] Notwithstanding the variations, both Matthew and Luke follow Jesus responses by recording the identical words about the Son of Man that are used by Mark.

Is there any reason to believe that there were witnesses who remembered that Jesus claimed that he was the both the Messiah and the Son of

---

62. Mark 12:1–9; Matt 21:33–41; Luke 20:9–19.

63. Mark 12:6; Luke 20:13; Matt 21:37.

64. Hooker, *Mark*, 273–77.

65. Mark, 14:61–62.

66. Dan 7:13.

67. Kim, "The Anarthous *Uios Theou*."

68. Matt 26:63–64.

69. Luke 22:67–70.

God? For such a belief to be substantiated, these people must have had access to the Sanhedrin and then kept the secret close for over thirty years. But here is excellent reason to believe that Mark inserted the story into the Gospel that bears his name, for it is entirely consistent with the Son of God motif. To the enquiring High Priest, the true nature of Jesus ministry is declared. And it is not surprising to find that Matthew and Luke find such a bald assertion troubling. Matthew prefers "The words are yours," which is a usual response in Jewish literature to an awkward question[70] and Luke gives the evasive reply "If I tell you, you will not believe."

Centurion (and Soldiers)

The story of the Centurion has already been told in the Preamble where it was noted that the actual statement that he made was literally truly this man was a son of a god. Matthew gives an almost identical appellation, though he makes it come from others beside the centurion.[71] Luke, as has already been shown, avoids the suggestion of divinity in favor of a declaration of the righteousness of Jesus: "Beyond all doubt, this man was innocent." Again, it seems possible that Luke is seeking to limit the forthright declaration that Jesus was Son of God.

Conclusion to the Son of God in Mark

The Son of God motif is complete. After an editorial comment by Mark, the appellation Son of God comes first from heaven itself, for thus it was that God had spoken to Moses, to Elijah and to Job[72] and thus it must be that God speaks to Jesus. The appellation comes then from the forces of evil; the powers of darkness recognize their foe. It then comes, if obliquely, from Jesus himself, first in the form of a parable and then in response to the high priest before the Sanhedrin. Lastly it comes from a Roman centurion, a bastion of authority and order, who pronounces that the dead Jesus is a son of a god. To declare the divine sonship of Jesus is surely revealed as Marks chief aim in writing.

---

70. Vermes, *Jesus*, 145–49.

71. Matt 27:54.

72. Exod 19:3; 1 Kgs 19:13; Job 38:1.

THE SON OF GOD IN Q

The Temptations (Matthew and Luke)

Following his baptism at the hands of John the Baptist, Jesus goes into the desert where Matthew and Luke say that the devil offers him three temptations. On the first occasion the devil asks Jesus to show his divine power by turning stones into bread, with the words "If you are the Son of God." In the second temptation in Matthew (the third temptation in Luke), the devil suggests that Jesus prove his divinity by jumping off the pinnacle of the temple and again begins the temptation with the words, "If you are the Son of God." In both these temptations the definite article is missing from the word son, though is used for God; a son of God is an accurate translation. The third (or, in Luke, the second) temptation does not begin with the words, "If you are the Son of God." Instead: the devil is described as taking Jesus to a very high mountain, and showing him all the kingdoms of the world and their splendor; and saying to him, "All these I will give you, if you will fall down and worship me."[73]

There are many suggestions as to the meaning of the temptations, as to why there were three and the purpose of each of them.[74] I will suggest in Chapter 7 that whereas the temptations about the stones into bread and the casting down from the pinnacle of the temple were centered upon the historic figures of Moses and Elijah, that about the dominion of the kingdoms of the world was centered upon Alexander the Great.

THE SON OF GOD IN MATTHEW

The Birth Story according to Matthew

Matthew asserts that Joseph was not the father of Jesus for, having traced the family of Joseph from Abraham using the formulaic word which the REV translates as "was the father of" (e.g., Abraham was the father of Isaac),[75] he ends his genealogy with, "Jacob was the father of Joseph the husband of Mary of whom Jesus was born, who is called the Messiah."[76] Later, Matthew explains that before Joseph and Mary had intercourse, she was found to

---

73. Matt 4:8–9; paralleled by Luke 4:5–6.

74. Fenton, *Matthew*, 62–64; Schweizer, *Matthew* 56–59; Leaney, *Luke*, 115.

75. Matt 1:2.

76. Matt 1:16.

be with child from the Holy Spirit,[77] a state of affairs emphasized by the appearance of an angel to Joseph and by Matthew quoting from the LXX translation of Isaiah 8:8: "Look, the virgin shall conceive and bear a son"[78] to show that the event had been foretold. However, it must be noted that, though Jesus birth was by operation of the Holy Spirit, there is no explicit statement that he is the Son of God in the narrative, though this must surely be implied.

Son of God as recognized by Jesus' Apostles

In the Gospels of Matthew and Mark, the Feeding of the Five Thousand is followed by the story of the Walking on the Water.[79] Mark's account simply tells of the disciples being terrified by the approach of Jesus walking on the water and the wind ceasing when he got into the boat with them. Matthew makes two additions; first Peter tries to walk on water and fails while when the boat reaches land the disciple acclaim Jesus as Son of God. There is a striking resemblance between this affirmation and that of the Centurion at the Crucifixion.[80] Matthew's account of the acclamation of Jesus in the story of the Walking on the Water by the apostles owes at least something to the story of the Centurion or vice versa.

The Confession of Peter

Shortly before Jesus sets out for Jerusalem, he asks his disciples who people believe him to be. His disciples report that he is said to be John the Baptist, Elijah or perhaps one of the prophets of old. But Jesus then asks them who they, the disciples, believe him to be and (according to Matthew) Peter says that he is the Christ, the Son of the Living God.[81] However when the same story is told by Mark and Luke; the former says that Peter declares Jesus to be the Christ[82] and the latter, that he is the Messiah of God.[83] It is difficult to avoid the conclusion that Matthew has inserted the affirmation by Peter that

---

77. Matt 1:18.
78. Matt 1:23.
79. Matt.14:23–33; Mark 6:45–52.
80. Matt 27:54.
81. John 16:15–16.
82. Mark 8:29.
83. Luke 9:20.

Jesus is the Son of God as a way of emphasizing Mark's use of Christ rather than as an historical account.[84]

Son of God as a Means of Mockery

In Matthew's story of the crucifixion, the crowds mock Jesus by repeating the words of Satan in Chapter 4, "If you are a son of God."[85] Three verses later the chief priests and scribes and elders make a more sinister comment: "let God deliver him now, if he wants him, for he said that he was son of a god." Here again Matthew departs from Mark and Luke and may be creating a story for doctrinal reasons.[86]

THE SON OF GOD IN LUKE AND IN ACTS

Adam as a son of God

In Luke's genealogy of Jesus, Adam is described as son of God.[87] This statement is of no value to the argument of this book; Adam is the father of mankind and hence all people on earth are descended from him, whether they are a son of God or not.

The Birth Story according to Luke

Luke approaches the subject of the birth of Jesus in a way that is totally different from that of Matthew. The theme for miraculous birth is conceptualized first with reference to John the Baptist. Only after Elizabeth is in her sixth month of pregnancy does an angel appear to Mary, foretelling the birth of Jesus "who will be great, and will be called the Son of the Most High."[88] When Mary protests that her virginity makes this impossible, the angel says to her: "The Holy Spirit will come upon you, and the power of the Most High will over shadow you, therefore the child to be born will be holy; he will be called Son of God."[89]

---

84. Fenton, *Matthew*, 268; but see also Schweizer, *Matthew*, 340.
85. Matt 27:40.
86. Fenton, *Matthew*, 439.
87. Luke 3:38.
88. Luke 1:32.
89. Luke 1:35; Leaney, *Luke*, 82–84.

This pair of constructions is remarkable not so much for what they say but for what they do not say. Jesus is described as having an abnormal birth, something that is also said of Plato, Alexander the Great and Augustus[90] and this birth is said to make him a son of god. (The birth stories are told of Jesus in spite of the fact that both Matthew and Luke had been to great lengths to show that Joseph was descended from David.)[91] But both Gospels also insist that there can be no question of a dual parentage of both god and man. Matthew comments that Joseph took Mary to be his wife "but had no marital relations with her until she had borne a son" while in Luke Joseph takes Mary "to whom he was engaged" with him to Bethlehem, the use of the term betrothed making it plain that the marriage between them had not been consummated. Jesus, it is made crystal clear, is not the son of Joseph, nor is he the son of a dual conception by Joseph and God.[92]

But, though there can be no doubt that both Matthew and Luke see the birth in Bethlehem as being the entry of a special son of God into the world, the argument is not developed. Matthew never uses the words Son of God during the birth narrative of his Gospel and though Luke does use a divine title in his, the definite articles are missing and the translation of the last two words of verse 1:53 is effectively a son of a god.[93] Furthermore in verse 32 Jesus is destined to be a son of the Most High so surely he is to be *a* son of God; there being no suggestion that he is to be the only Son. In both Matthew and Luke the birth stories parallel other miraculous birth stories but though the Gospels produce accounts that are unquestionably more beautiful than the accounts of, say, Trogus of Alexander the Great, they no more make Jesus divine than Trogus makes a divinity of Alexander.[94]

That being said the stories were to acquire more value and emphasis for humankind than any other religious event in human history. They are the substance of the Christmas story, which it is estimated, is now celebrated in one way or another by two billion people. The story of the Son of God being born of a virgin in a stable in Bethlehem, however historically justified, is the reason why billions of people exalt the name of Jesus today.

90. Cartlidge and Dungan, *Documents for Study,* 129–37.

91. Matt 1:1–17; Luke 3:23–38.

92. Schweizer, *Matthew,* 32–35.

93. The absence of the definite articles is explored further in Appendix 3.

94. See Chapter 2.

Saul's Confession

After his conversion and temporary blinding on the Damascus Road, Saul has his sight restored at the hands of Ananias and "immediately began to proclaim Jesus in the synagogues, saying 'He is the Son of God' and by proving that Jesus was the Messiah."[95] This is the only use of son of God in Acts and is possibly formulaic.[96] As has already been shown in his writings, Saul or Paul only started using the title Son of God in the mid-50s. It is significant that this, the only mention of the Son of God in Acts, is attributed to the lips of Paul.

The Epistle to the Hebrews

There is considerable debate among scholars as to whether this interesting work is an epistle at all and much time could be spent in assessing its true character.[97] However, this book is concerned not with the form of the document but with its date. Hebrews describes Jesus as the Son [of God] ten times, a number equaled by Matthew and exceeded only by John. Son of God is a predominating theme in Hebrews and so it is important to establish whether Hebrews predates the Gospel narratives, follows them or is contemporary with them.

Questions as to who wrote Hebrews and to whom they wrote it have exercised generations of biblical scholars, who agree only on the view that it was not written by Paul. In the days when detective work of authorship was fashionable, some scholars found a candidate for the author of Hebrews in the person of Apollos. Hunter was one who espoused this idea and he was followed by Montefiore, who suggested that Hebrews was written to the Christians at Corinth by Apollos from Ephesus.[98] This theory would, if true, suggest that Hebrews was written as early as 52—54 CE. While an interesting idea, most modern scholarship does not take this hypothesis seriously.

Therefore, since it is not known where it was written, by whom it was written and to whom it was written, it is not easy to do more than guess at the date of the writing. Bruce is clear that there can be no certainty as to whom the Epistle was addressed, but says that the addressees appear to be a group of Jewish Christians who had never seen or heard Jesus in person,

---

95. Acts 9:10–22.
96. Barrett, *Acts,* 139.
97. Wilson, *Hebrews,* 17.
98. Hunter, *Introducing the New Testament,* 52–3: Montefiore, *Hebrews,* 23–24.

but learned of him (as the writer of the epistle also did) from some who had themselves listened to him.[99] He goes on to say that Hebrews was quoted by Clement of Rome (96 CE), was possibly written in the lifetime of Timothy[100] and concludes that AD 70 is a probable date of writing. Ellingworth, however, denies that either destination or readership can be fully attested but suggests that a pre-70 date is quite possible because the author of Hebrews uses the present tense in describing religious acts in the temple which implies that it was still in use at the time of writing. For example, Hebrews states that: "Every high priest chosen from among mortals is. . ."[101] Ellingworth also comments that because Hebrews was written in a time of persecution, it may well have been written during the Neronian persecution of the 60s CE.[102] Moffatt conclusively establishes that Clement quotes Hebrews[103] and concludes that cannot have been written later than about AD 85 though Telford suggests that a later date is possible.[104] Robinson favors the idea that the Epistle to the Hebrews emerged from the Alexandrian school in around 70 CE[105] while Westcott is clear from the internal evidence that Hebrews was written in the late 60s.[106] This is also the date agreed by Wilson, who expresses the personal view that the addressees were Roman and the date of the epistle is about 67—70 CE.[107]

It is reasonable, therefore, to postulate that Hebrews was written around 70 CE, since this date seems to have the support of the majority of commentators. The effect of this reasoning is far-reaching for it means that Hebrews either predates the Gospels or was written at the same time as Mark and, therefore, competes with the latter to be the first book of the New Testament to fully explore the meaning of Jesus as Son of God.

Aims of the Epistle to the Hebrews

The epistle opens with the following statement, "Long ago God spoke to our ancestors in many and various ways by the prophets, but in the last days he

---

99. Bruce, *Hebrews*, 4–9.

100. Heb 13:23.

101. Heb 5:1; see also 7:5 and 8:3, etc.

102. Ellingworth, *Hebrews*, 3–21.

103. Moffatt, *Hebrews*, xiii—xv.

104. Telford, *Theology of Mark*, 198.

105. Robinson, *Hebrews*.

106. Wescott, *Hebrews*.

107. Wilson, *Hebrews*, 12–16.

has spoken to us by a Son."[108] The writer to the Hebrews justifies his use of the title Son of God by reference to the Hebrew Scriptures and demonstrates that the Son is superior to angels. He quotes Psalm 2: "For to which of the angels did God ever say, 'You are my Son, today I have begotten you'" and follows with a quotation from 2 Samuel 7.14, "I will be his Father and he will be my Son." Three verses later the author attributes verse 8 of Psalm 45 as an address to the Son: "Your throne, O God, is forever and ever, and the righteous scepter is the scepter of your kingdom."

Chapter 3 of this book explored the thesis that the title Son of God emerged from the Hebrew Scriptures and found the case for believing this to be weak. Dodd is clear that though the term Son of God is not infrequently found in Jewish writings, it invariably has a metaphorical significance.[109] However, the writer to the Hebrews uses what material he has at his disposal and makes the best case he can to show where and when the coming of the Son of God is prophesied in the Hebrew Scriptures. But though he makes an excellent case, *he is justifying the use of an existing title.* Son of God was far too prominent and significant a title in the budding Christian churches for the writer to the Hebrews to successfully establish that it came from a few ambivalent verses of the Hebrew Scriptures.

The writer then goes on to show that the use of the title makes Christ superior to Moses: "Now Moses was faithful in all God's house as a servant. . . Christ, however, was faithful over God's house as a son." The writer also declares that Christ is superior to Melchizedek, whose name means the King of Righteousness and who has neither father, mother nor genealogy but, resembling the Son of God he remains a priest forever.[110] Christ is shown to be a superior priest to Melchizedek for he is a son of God.

The writer now *uses* the title to demonstrate the superiority of Christ over those two significant biblical figures, Moses and Melchizedek. The choice of Moses needs no explanation, for, as the great law-giver and one who spoke to God face to face, he is arguably the greatest of the children of Israel. But the author to Hebrews is clear that he is nonetheless a servant, compared with Jesus who is a son of the household. The significance of Melchizedek does need explaining, and the writer does this by pointing out that the patriarch Abraham offered him tithes.[111] The priesthood of Melchizedek is nonetheless inferior to that of Jesus, whose high priesthood

---

108. Heb 1:1–2.

109. Dodd, *Interpretation*, 252.

110. Heb 7:3.

111. Heb 7:4.

is the central theme of the Christology of Hebrews.[112] Though Melchizedek resembles the Son of God, Jesus by being the Son of God is greater than any other member of the Jewish race.

The writer warns that: "those who have once been enlightened (but now) . . . have fallen away are crucifying again the Son of God."[113] He goes on to say that: "Anyone who has violated the Law of Moses dies without mercy . . . how much worse punishment will be deserved by those who have spurned the Son of God."[114]

Telford points out that for Mark and Hebrews their supreme point of contact lies in their mutual "Son of God" Christology. Whereas for Mark this is the supreme title, but is subject to secrecy, for the author of Hebrews, Jesus is risen, ascended and seated at God's right hand.[115] For both, however, the title has now become an appellation that raises Jesus of Nazareth to a figure of unparalleled significance. The crucifixion becomes an event of immense importance for it was the crucifixion of the Son of God.

The Significance of Hebrews for the Title Son of God

Assuming a date of around 70 CE for the writing of Hebrews, it is clear that Son of God was an appellation for Jesus, which was a cause of both significance and concern to Christians and unbelievers of the period. The writer gives the background to the title, establishing it as justified from the Hebrew Scriptures and goes on to show the significance of the title as demonstrating the superiority of Jesus over the greatest biblical figures. In the process of doing this, he raises at the crucifixion to an event of cosmic significance.

But all that being said, the argument the writer to the Hebrews presents is exactly parallel to that in Chapter 3 and already commented upon. The writer accepts the title Son of God as appropriate to Jesus of Nazareth but does not explain its origin. Further, the use of Scripture is unconvincing. To take one example, having used the classic text from 2 Samuel[116] which is certainly a reference to the Son of God, the writer then quotes from Deuteronomy[117] and Psalm 45, which contain no reference to the Son of God at all.

---

112. Telford, *Theology of Mark*, 203.

113. Heb 6:6.

114. Heb 10:29.

115. Telford, *Interpretation of Mark*, 203.

116. 2 Sam 7:14.

117. The quotation is from the Septuagint, the reading from the Masoretic text is different.

To restate my argument, it is clear that the appellation can be found in the Hebrew Scriptures but its use there is minimal.

THE GOSPEL OF JOHN

Irenaeus's comment that John, the son of Zebedee, lived to a great age in Ephesus and there wrote the Gospel, created a tradition which suggests that the Gospel of John was written towards the end of the first century CE. Though people who wrote before Irenaeus do not mention this tradition, there is no reason to doubt its veracity. Papyrus fragment P52 (also referred to as the Rylands papyrus), which is dated around 130 CE contains a few verses of John 18, and this must mean that the original cannot have been dated much later than 100 CE.[118] On the other hand, it is probable that the author had read some, if not all, the Synoptic Gospels[119] which implies that the Gospel of John must have been written after 85 CE. Therefore, a date of 90 –100 for the writing of the Gospel seems likely to be accurate[120]. A very different date is suggested by Robinson in his "The Priority of John," but an examination of his efforts to re-date the New Testament is beyond the scope of this book.

The framework of John is different from that of the Synoptic Gospels. To take some examples, in John the call of Peter and Andrew takes place at the Jordan whereas in the Synoptic Gospel it takes place by the Sea of Galilee.[121] In John, this is followed by a brief visit to Cana for a wedding, where Jesus turns water into wine, and a visit to Jerusalem during which the tables of the money-changers were overturned.[122] In the Synoptic Gospels, the visit to Jerusalem is postponed until shortly before the death of Jesus. In John, the Last Supper has no bread or wine, but instead has a lengthy discourse of four chapters.

The Prologue of John

Having started from the premise that the Word was God, John declares that it became flesh and lived among us and that we have seen his glory, the glory as of a father's only son. Three verses later, the unique nature of the Jesus

118. Brown, *John*, lxxxii.
119. Ibid. 14–16; Sanders and Mastin, *John*, 8–12.
120. Brown, *John*, lxxxiv; Barrett *John*, 109; Bruce, *John*, 6–12.
121. John 1:40–42; Mark 1:16–18.
122. John 2:1–18.

event is declared: "No one has ever seen God; God's only Son (or the Father's only son), he who is nearest to the Father's heart, has made him known."[123]

John seems not to betray any interest in, or apparent knowledge of, the virgin birth as described in Matthew and Luke (unless a variant reading of John 1.13, can not only be accepted as the true reading but also accepted as implying an abnormal birth.) After all, a miraculous conception would mean that Jesus became a son of God from the moment of conception. John lifts sonship to an altogether higher plain, and adheres to the concept of pre-existence.[124] The use of "only begotten" adds a new dimension to the title Son of God, for it introduces the concept of the Son within a relationship. In John, as distinct from the Synoptic Gospels, Jesus is seen as being the Son of God because God is his Father and he becomes the only begotten of the Father, his Father's only Son. This is an entirely new departure.

Human Use of Son of God

As in the Synoptic Gospels, so in John, Jesus is recognized as Son of God at the River Jordan by John the Baptist. In the Gospel of John, the Baptist himself testifies to the voice from heaven and recognizes in Jesus the Son of God.[125] The encounter with the Baptist is followed by the calling of future apostles and one of them, called Nathanael, remarks "Rabbi, you are the Son of God! You are the King of Israel."[126] Much later in the Gospel, Martha says to Jesus: "I believe that you are the Messiah, the Son of God."[127]

These remarks of John the Baptist, Nathanael and Martha are perhaps the only times in the whole New Testament when an ordinary person calls Jesus Son of God (unless the comment by Peter in Matt 16.16 is taken seriously). Gone are the writings of questionable formulaic voices from heaven—Satan, demons, the mockery of the Chief Priests and the legendary comment of a centurion; these are straightforward assertions by John, Nathanael and Martha. Interestingly, Nathanael links the Son of God with Jesus as King of Israel, while Martha links it to the more usual title of Messiah.

---

123. John 1:18.
124. Dodd, *Interpretation*, 260.
125. John 1:34.
126. John 1:49.
127. John 11:27.

Jesus Teaches about his Relationship with the Father

Dunn points out that whereas the synoptic gospellers call God "Father" 42 times and "the Father" a further 5 times, John refers to God as "Father" 100 times and "the Father" a further 73.[128] He asserts that John is not recording history but speaking theologically and the theology that he is using is that of the Church at the end of the first century CE. What the author of John is doing is reflecting, not on a historically attested Jesus, but on the theological realities of his day.

So, in his conversation with Nicodemus in Chapter 3, Jesus affirms that those who do not believe in the name of the only Son of God are already condemned, whereas "whoever believes in the Son has eternal life." In Chapter 5 Jesus develops the relationship between himself and his Heavenly Father: "Indeed, just as the Father raises the dead and gives them life, so also the Son gives life to whomever he wishes and the dead will hear the voice of the Son of God, and those who hear him will live." In Chapter 10 Jesus exalts himself to equality with God, saying "The Father and I are one," and finally asserts that he is God's Son. In the long discourse of Chapters 14—17, Jesus speaks almost exclusively of the relationship between the Father and the Son, the word "Father" being used forty five times and "the Son" less than ten. To John, Jesus is the Son of God because he exists in a loving and filial relationship with God the Father.

Is the appellation "King of the Jews" Blasphemy or Treason? (Luke and John)

It has been noted that Nathanael said to Jesus: "Rabbi, you are the Son of God! You are the King of Israel." During Jesus' triumphal entry into Jerusalem the crowds quote from Psalm 118, verse 26 and say, "Blessed is the one who comes in the name of the Lord—the King of Israel."[129] It must be remarked that the King of Israel is no part of the LXX text. Matthew and Mark in reporting the same incident stick to a straight quotation, but Luke when he writes about it inserts (according to some MSS): "Blessed is he who comes as king in the name of the Lord,"[130] without explaining why. These two references to the King of Israel in John do not fully prepare the reader for what is to follow.

128. Dunn, *Evidence*, 44.
129. John 12:13.
130. Luke 19:38.

It is attested in Chapters 18 and 19 of Johns gospel that after Jesus has been arrested, he is led to Pilate who, understanding that Jesus offence was a matter of Jewish law, suggests that the Jewish authorities deal with him. The Jews insist that Pilate try the case because they claim that Jesus crime requires the death penalty. Pilate then summons Jesus and asks him surprisingly, "Are you the King of the Jews," to which question Jesus, by returning evasive answers, seems to convince Pilate that he is innocent of the charges against him. But an enraged Jewish mob, led by the chief priests, demand that Jesus be crucified, saying, "We have a law, and according to that law he ought to die because he claimed to be the Son of God." But in spite of this interjection, the charge against Jesus continually spoken by Pilate is that Jesus claimed to be a king, culminating in the sign set up over the Cross, "Jesus of Nazareth (literally the Nazarene), the King of the Jews," a message that Pilate would not amend .

In Matthew's story of the crucifixion, the crowds mock Jesus by suggesting that, "If you are a son of God, come down from the cross" and the chief priests and scribes and elders comment; "let God deliver him now, if he wants him, for he said that he was son of a god."[131] But in Luke it is the soldiers who mock Jesus with the words, "If you are the King of the Jews, save yourself," while an inscription is set up (by whom is uncertain) which says, "This is the King of the Jews."[132]

There seems to be an identity between being the Son of God and being the King of the Jews. To this there must be a serious objection. Luke records the bringing of Jesus before Herod[133] and though the latter would seem to be the one person who might have objected to the title "King of the Jews" being ascribed to anyone but himself, this appellation is not mentioned at his court. It seems that it was to Pilate that the charge of claiming to be King of the Jews was treason and hence to a Roman was a capital offence. One reason for this, to be explored in Chapter 6, probably lies in the aggressive claim to divine sonship by Domitian, who was Emperor of Rome when the Gospel of John was written. Pilate may well have justified the execution of Jesus by accepting that to say one was a Son of God was to claim sovereignty, which was the sole perquisite of the emperor.

131. Matt 27:40–43.
132. Luke 23:36–38.
133. Luke 23:6–16.

The End of Johns Narrative

Assuming that Chapter 21 is an appendix to the main narrative,[134] John provides an end to his main narrative by saying that it "is written that you may believe that Jesus is the Christ, the Son of God."[135] In one sense, this provides the perfect ending to the four Gospels; the four having begun with Mark's: "The beginning of the good news of Jesus Christ, the Son of God"[136] and ending with John's, "This is written that you may believe that Jesus is the Christ, "the Son of God."[137] The use of the title Son of God is mainly presented in the Gospel of John as being the one sent by the Father.[138] The verbs in Greek for "sent" are used over forty times in the Gospel, suggesting the Son is a delegate to speak his Fathers words and do his Father's deeds. The Father has also given him authority over humankind.[139] He has perhaps become more divine than human, a characteristic that is found in the Epistles of John.

THE REVELATION OF ST JOHN THE DIVINE

This apocalyptic document is said to be written by John but in fact no one knows for certain who the author was. Dionysius of Alexandria pointed out as early as the third century CE that the John of Revelation is not the author of the Gospel of John,[140] though this point of view is now rather surprisingly challenged by Beale.[141] The authorship, therefore, is no help in ascertaining the date of the writing of Revelation to which subject Beale devotes twenty-three pages of the Introduction to his Commentary.[142] Revelation was clearly known to Papias of Hierapolis[143] and so it must have been written before 120 CE. Essentially there is dispute between those who favor an early date and those who prefer a later one. An argument of the former is based in part on the reference to the seven kings[144] which, assuming these refer

---

134. Barrett, *John*, 479.
135. John 20:31.
136. John 1:1.
137. John 20:31.
138. Dodd, *Interpretation*, 254.
139. John 5:27.
140. Preston and Hanson, *Revelation*, 23.
141. Beale, *Book of Revelation*, 34–36.
142. Ibid., 4–27.
143. Knight, *Revelation*, 18.
144. Rev 17:9.

to Roman Emperors, means Revelation must have been written during the reign of the seventh emperor, Galba, who ruled briefly in 68—69. A date of about 90 CE seems in fact much more compelling for it sets the writing of the book in the time of Domitian's persecution.[145] The date of the writing of Revelation, therefore, fits into the same period as the writing of the Gospel of John and the Epistles of John.

Revelation uses the term Son of God only once,[146] where it is used in the apocalyptic language that characterizes this work. In the rest of Revelation key titles that refer to Jesus are the Lamb, the Messiah and the Son of Man.[147] Son of Man in particular has an important place among the angels, which appear in many texts throughout the book. As in Colossians, Ephesians and Philippians, so in Revelation, Jesus is being raised to a person of cosmic significance and is seen as ruler in earth and heaven. Whether named as such or not, he is clearly revealed as a figure worthy of the appellation Son of God.

THE EPISTLES OF JOHN

The title "Son of God" is used six times in 1 John as well as another six times in which Jesus is referred to as Son. Perhaps the most profound uses of the appellation are in John: Chapter 5, verse 5, "Who is it that conquers the world but the one who believes that Jesus is the Son of God" and in verse 11, "Whoever has the Son has life; whoever does not have the Son of God does not have life." Clearly for John, the title Son of God has assumed the beginnings of creedal significance. As Lieu puts it:

> The author wants his believers to experience life through the Son of God, he is even more insistent that Jesus must be acknowledged as this Son and, apparently, that as such he entered the sphere of human existence (flesh) that believers share. . . The call to acknowledge Jesus as the Christ or the Son of God does not mean to identify him with a figure from a more widespread expectation; both Christ and Son of God (in the Johannine epistles) have been transformed from any earlier meaning to carry resonances distinctive to this specific understanding of Jesus advent.[148]

145. Preston and Hanson, *Revelation*, 23; Beale *Book of Revelation*, 5–19; Thompson, *Revelation*, 13–17; Knight, *Revelation*, 18–19.

146. Rev 2:18.

147. Rev 5:6; 12:10; 14:14

148. Lieu, *I, II and III John*, 21.

CONCLUSION

Perhaps twenty years elapsed between the death of Jesus and the writing of the first letter to the Thessalonians, an epistle in which the title Son of God was not mentioned. Within the following ten years, Son of God was used in the epistles written from Ephesus but its full significance was not explained. However, it is manifestly clear that in the furor of the seventh decade, when the Jews revolted and were subdued and Nero instituted a persecution of Christians which accounted for the lives of Peter and Paul, the appellation developed a widespread use. By the end of the decade, Hebrews was exploring the meaning of the title and Mark was making its use a major theme of his Gospel. In the following fifteen years the use of Son of God was cautiously developed, though Matthew differs from Luke as to how the appellation is used. In the last decade of the first century CE, John carried its use beyond the possibly historical settings of the Synoptic Gospels into a field of pure doctrine. As the next chapter will show, Jesus as the Son of God became a major Christian preoccupation.

In roughly fifty years, then, the appellation has been introduced, used, demonstrated, explained, developed and finally allowed to assume a major theological dimension. What must be noted is the way the appellation Son of God changed and developed over those fifty years. Exegetes, ancient and modern, often speak as though the title Son of God carried the same meaning throughout the New Testament. I have shown during this chapter that this is not so and have further demonstrated that the title was almost certainly not applied to Jesus during his lifetime. As suggested in the Introduction to this book, the title Son of God was not used until at least twenty years after Jesus died. It was the interface between the Christian message and Greek culture that inspired Paul and his companions to use a Greek appellation for their Lord and its use came to dominate Christianity.

But the title Son of God had undergone considerable change since Homer told of sexually exercised gods producing progeny on earth. The appellation was not just used of Perseus, Heracles and Theseus who inhabited the realm of myth and legend but also of Alexander who came from the more recent realm of history. If, as is postulated, Paul used the title as a way of showing the greatness of Jesus to Greek men and women, he must have been influenced by the great Macedonian.

5

Son of God in Extra-Canonical Writings to 165 CE

PREAMBLE

Chapter 5 deals with the use of the title Son of God as an appellation of Jesus of Nazareth in the writing of the early church. The literature involved is vast and research must be limited to the origin of the title and its development. It was established in Chapter 3 that there was not sufficient evidence in the Hebrew Scriptures to justify the use of the title Son of God as Jesus most significant appellation but it was shown in Chapter 4 that an attempt to do so was made by the writer of the Epistle to the Hebrews. Chapter 5 examines the use made by the early church of both Old and New Testaments and how much these scriptures may have affected the way the use of the title Son of God developed. Some ideas on this subject have already been explored but one is particularly pertinent to this chapter, namely eschatology.

The Eschatological Messiah and the Eternal Son of God

As Christianity entered the second century CE, one thing was certain to its followers above all others; the *parousia* was delayed![1] Reported prophecies ascribed to Jesus indicate that he shared the view that the hopes of Jewish apocalypticism had not been fulfilled and so these hopes naturally fell out of

1. Frend, *The Early Church*, 61.

favor with Christian evangelists. Such remarks as: "Truly I tell you: there are some of those standing here who will not taste of death before they see the kingdom of God come with power"[2] and "Verily I say unto you, this generation shall not pass away until all these things have been accomplished"[3] naturally caused concern. On the other hand, texts such as Luke 11.20, 17.20–21 and Matt 11.12, which indicated that in the person and ministry of Jesus the time of salvation had already come, became increasingly relevant.[4] Jesus the Messiah, an eschatological figure, who ushers in the *parousia* and who is to be identified with the apocalyptic Son of Man[5] becomes displaced by Jesus the Son of God who reigns forever in heaven. The growing emphasis in the Second Century of the use of the title Son of God can therefore be easily understood against the gradual erosion of a belief in the imminence of the *parousia* and a growing belief in a permanent Church.

Authority

According to tradition, the Jewish insurrection of 66—70 CE forced members of the founding church at Jerusalem to leave their city and flee to the area of Pella.[6] Brandon argues that this tradition cannot be an accurate one, for he holds that it was impossible for a mass migration of Christians to have taken place at the time suggested.[7] However, he does accept that for a period the Mother Church of Jerusalem vanishes from recorded history and this cannot but imply that from 70 CE there was no central church to which new churches could appeal for legitimacy or instruction. There could not be another Council of Jerusalem, such as the one portrayed in Acts 15, to resolve thorny problems in the life and beliefs of the Church. Further, by the year 100 CE, all those who had seen or heard Jesus were either dead or in their dotage. So as the Church entered the Second Century, it had to look elsewhere for authority. "As the living voice (of Jesus) receded into the past," wrote Carrington, "the surviving literature became supremely important. The written Gospels superseded the living voice of the actual disciples and disciples of disciples; the written Epistles took the living voice of the

---

2. Mark 9:1.

3. Mark 13:30 in the RV. The NRSV text is very colloquial.

4. Fiorenza, *Eschatology*, 276.

5. Werner, *Formulations*, 120.

6. Bruce, *The Church of Jerusalem*, 6; Carrington, *Early Church*, 250–51; *Hist. eccl.* 3.5.2–3.

7. Brandon, *Fall of Jerusalem*, 169–73.

apostolic founders."[8] But there was also continuing oral tradition, which extended into the second century and beyond, leading in time to a considerable literature which existed in parallel with the earliest writings.[9]

This immediately posed a question; how were people to judge which letters had authority and which stories contained the true teaching of Jesus and his followers? The answer was believed to lie in authorship; most Christians held that if a letter or gospel was written by an apostle (or one of Jesus' closest disciples) it carried authority, while if it was written pseudepigraphically it carried less authority or even none at all The question of authorship, therefore, was crucial but a consensus on the matter was not quickly achieved, and it was not until the fourth century that the canon of the New Testament was agreed.[10]

Early Christian writings not included in the New Testament are catalogued and recorded by Elliott in *The Apocryphal New Testament*. In this massive work of over 700 pages, Elliott points out that dating the writings is difficult because, as the church developed, it tended to marginalize works not regarded as canonical. Much early literature survives, some as part of much later documents, where it exists alongside works of a more doubtful origin. So the probably factual description in the Gospel of Peter of a crowd of ill-wishers taking Jesus for trial "who took the Lord and pushed him as they ran and said, 'Let us drag the Son of God along now that we have power over him'"[11] exists alongside the clearly mythological story of Hades reviling Satan for crucifying Jesus.[12] Readers have little knowledge of the origin of either story, of the author or even of the date; decision as to whether there is any historic truth contained in them tends to be subjective.

However, at the same time that much of the writings contained in *The Apocryphal New Testament* were being written, authors such as Ignatius and Justin Martyr were starting to explore what the Christ event meant to the Christian, the Jewish and the pagan world. Their more philosophical style frequently contrasts with the myths and fables that make up much of *The Apocryphal New Testament* and since the church saw fit to approve the works of Ignatius and Justin, the student has early copies of their writing and can establish their place and time of writing with a fair degree of accuracy. For example, readers know beyond reasonable doubt that Justin wrote

---

8. Carrington, *Early Church*, 468.

9. Elliott, *Apocryphal Jesus*, 1.

10. Sanders, *Literature and Canon*, 679–82.

11. *Gos. Pet.* 1.3:6

12. *Des. Inf.* 7 [23] 1.

in about 150 CE to defend Christianity against the charge of atheism.[13] An examination of both genres must follow.

New Testament Apocryphal and Pseudepigraphical Writings

Stories about Jesus in New Testament Apocryphal and Pseudepigraphal literature are essentially of two types; stories of the New Testament retold with significant additions (which I refer to as Amplifications) and substantially new stories (which I call Legends). However, the reader is left in almost total ignorance as to whether a particular writing results from oral tradition unincorporated in the New Testament or whether it is simply invented by one particular community or borrowed from another tradition and made into a story of Jesus.[14] The use of the title Son of God appears in both Amplifications and Legends and it is on passages where this appellation appears that this book will concentrate.

AMPLIFICATIONS

Birth Narratives

In the New Testament, stories of the birth of Jesus are to be found in Matthew and Luke, who, by showing that Jesus was born of a virgin, indicate that Jesus was indeed the Son of God.[15] The title Son of God is avoided in the birth stories of the Apocrypha and Pseudepigrapha of the New Testament, though the tales of Jesus birth told there impart a breadth of mystery. For example, the baby Jesus is delivered without any bleeding by Mary and immediately after his birth is able to walk, while the midwife who examines Mary to find out if she really has given birth suffers a withered hand.[16] Devotees of Christmas carols find in Pseudo-Matthew the origin of the tale of Jesus in a manger adored by ox and ass.[17] When Mary, Joseph and Jesus leave Bethlehem, they rest in a cave and are attacked by many dragons, but Jesus (only a few days old) commands them to hurt no one. "Do not be afraid," he says, "and do not consider me to be a child, for I am and always

13. Barnard, *Justin Martyr*, 10.

14. In the same way, the story of King David pouring water brought to him at great risk on to the ground as an offering to God may in fact have been borrowed from a similar story about Alexander the Great (see Chapter 2).

15. Matt 1:20; Luke 1:15.

16. *Prot. Jas.* 20; Elliott, *Apocryphal Jesus*, 10–14.

17. *Ps.-Mat.* 14; Elliott, *Apocryphal Jesus*, 15.

have been perfect; and all the beasts of the forest must needs be docile before me."[18]

The impression of Jesus given in these narratives is of a pre-existent
and mythological divine being, who, even as a baby, has immense power.
The story of Jesus and the dragons may have been influenced by the story
of Heracles, the son of Zeus, being assailed by snakes while yet a baby and
strangling them both.[19] The story of the adoration of the ox and ass is
clearly influenced by the Hebrew Scriptures.[20]

The Baptism of Jesus

In the *Pilate Cycle*, a collection of writings from the fifth century,[21] which
almost certainly incorporates early tradition, is found what purports to be
an account by John the Baptist of his preaching to people in Hell and describing the baptism of Jesus to them.[22] He says (according to the Greek
version of the story):

> I am John, the last of the prophets, who made straight the ways
> of the Son of God and preached repentance to the people for the
> forgiveness of sins. And the Son of God came to me, and when
> I saw him afar off, I said to the people: "Behold, the Lamb of
> God, who takes away the sin of the world." And with my hand I
> baptized him in the river Jordan, and I saw the Holy Spirit like
> a dove coming upon him and heard also the voice of God the
> Father speaking thus, "This is my beloved Son, in whom I am
> well pleased." And for this reason he sent me to you, to preach
> that the only begotten Son of God comes here.[23]

This story makes John the Baptist not only a witness to the events described in the Gospels but also an evangelist for the divine sonship of Jesus.
The reference from Isaiah (Chapter 40, verse 3) is altered to include the Son
of God, and John recognizes Jesus as such when he appears. And although
not specifically stated, there is more than a suggestion that the divine voice
was heard by John who repeated it to others; perhaps for that reason he

18. *Ps.-Mat.* 18

19. Stoneman, *Alexander*, 7.

20. Isa 1:3; Hab 3:2.

21. Elliott, *Apocryphal New Testament*, 165.

22. *Des. Inf.* 2 [18] 2.

23. Isa 40:3.

speaks of Jesus as Son of God with a freedom rarely seen in the mouths of people in the gospels. The significance of this is developed in Chapter 7.

A version of the story in Latin provides a greater emphasis of the use of the title Son of God by men.[24] In this version there is the addition of John crying out, in fulfillment of Isaiah:[25] "This is the light of the Father, the Son of God" and Simeon, continuing from Luke Chapter 2, verses 30–32, saying: "Glorify the Lord Jesus Christ, the Son of God; for when born I took him up, an infant in my hands in the temple."[26]

The Trial of Jesus

In the *Pilate Cycle*,[27] there is also an account of Jesus being brought before Pilate. Pilate asks the Jews (in fact the elders, priests and Levites) why Jesus should die and the Jews reply, "because he called himself the Son of God and a king." When Pilate offers to release Jesus to the Jews they repeat: "you are not Caesar's friend if you release this man, for he called himself the Son of God and a king."[28] During the crucifixion, the chief priests and the rulers scoff saying that if he is the Son of God, he is to come down from the cross. The soldiers and Pilate, however, stick to the secular charge that Jesus claimed to be the King of the Jews.[29]

In this quotation from the *Pilate Cycle*, the Jews accuse Jesus of both blasphemy (calling himself the Son of God) and treason (calling himself a king). Pilate and the soldiers, however, will only react to the treasonable accusation and neither publicly accept or deny that Jesus might be the Son of God. The idea that to refer to someone as the Son of God is a treasonable act is examined in Chapter Six and the Pilate Cycle emphasizes the relation between the two.

The Via Dolorosa

In the excavations in Akhmin in 1886–1887 a document was found containing the *Gospel of Peter*.[30] Though Elliott believes that the document

---

24. Elliott, *Apocryphal New Testament*, 191.
25. Isa 9:2.
26. *Des. Inf.* 2 [18] 1–2.
27. *Acts Pil.* 3 [2].
28. *Acts Pil.* 4 [3] 1.
29. *Acts Pil.* 9 [4] 1.
30. Elliott, *Apocryphal New Testament*, 150.

dates from the eighth century, most scholars claim that the *Gospel of Peter* originated in the second half of the second century, for there are references to it in the works of Eusebius.[31] A passage describes a crowd of ill-wishers taking Jesus for trial who took the Lord and pushed him as they ran and said, "Let us drag the Son of God along now that we have power over him." These people then torment Jesus with the purple robe, reed and crown and shout: "With this let us honor the Son of God."[32] This ironic use of the appellation has already been demonstrated in Chapter 4.

The Penitent Thief

The *Pilate Cycle* describes Enoch and Elijah in Paradise speaking with the thief who had been crucified with Jesus.[33] The thief tells them that he has been given a password to heaven, "Jesus Christ, the Son of God, who has been crucified, has sent me."[34] In part of the *Pilate Cycle* called the *Narrative of Joseph of Arimathea*, which Elliott believes to be a document from the Middle Ages,[35] the thief says to Jesus as they both hang on their crosses, "Jesus Christ, I know you are the Son of God." Here, in a legendary setting, an ordinary mortal acclaims Jesus as Son of God.

Resurrection

In the Gospel of Peter, the title Son of God is used by soldiers guarding the tomb who witnessed the appearance of Christ from the sepulcher. The Gospel tells the readers that when those were of the centurions company saw this (i.e. the empty tomb), they hurried by night to Pilate. . . and reported everything they had seen, being greatly agitated and saying, "In truth he was (the) Son of God," Pilate answered and went on, "I am clean from the blood of the Son of God; it was you (the Jews) who desired it."[36]

It needs to be noted that though the title Son of God is nearly always used in contexts derived from the New Testament stories, the emphasis on its use in the Apocryphal and Pseudepigraphal writings is far greater than in canonical literature. John the Baptist in the *Pilate Cycle* stresses Jesus divine

31. *Hist. eccl.* 1926, 3.3.2
32. *Gos. Pet.* 1.3:6–7.
33. Luke 23:39–43.
34. *Des. Inf.* 10.26.
35. Elliott, *Apocryphal New Testament*, 165.
36. *Gos. Pet.* 11.4:6.

sonship with far greater enthusiasm than he does in the New Testament. In the Gospel of Peter the soldiers guarding the tomb tell Pilate that Jesus is the Son of God and Pilate concurs. The title has clearly become much more important to Christians in the second century than seems to have been the case in the first. And, as will now be seen, this is also true of the legends surrounding Jesus that are recounted in the rest of the New Testament Apocrypha.

LEGENDS

There are innumerable stories from Late Antiquity purporting to come from the hands of the Apostles, but passages mentioning that Jesus is the Son of God are sparse. In the *Acts of Andrew* (probably written early in the third century and of limited historical value),[37] the writer speaks of Andrew casting out devils and asking the crowd to profess their faith and they reply, "We believe that Jesus Christ whom you preach is the Son of God." When Andrew visits Thessalonica, a citizen declares, "truly Christ whom Andrew preaches is the Son of God" and a youth declares, in words redolent of the declaration of Nicaea, that "Jesus is the Lord of heaven and earth, the Son of God Almighty, very God with the Holy Ghost, continuing for everlasting ages."[38] In the fourth century *Acts of Peter*, a senator called Marcellus believes with his whole heart in the name of Jesus Christ, the Son of God. In the fifth century *Acts of Thomas*, the apostle tells a baptizand approaching her first communion to take the body of Christ and the cup of the Son of God and, when in prison, he declares to an adoring crowd, "I am not the Son of God." Finally, in Late Antiquity, there are visions of heaven where an angel shows Paul around the city of Christ and explains that Christ, the Son of God, sits at the right hand of God.

A Hallmark of Christianity

In the retelling of the New Testament stories under my heading Amplifications, the appellation Son of God is used more frequently than in the canonical gospels. What is significant is that it is often put into the mouths of mortal people. It was remarked in Chapter 4 that when the appellation occurs in the Gospels, it comes in a voice from heaven, from demons or from humans who use it in irony. In the Apocrypha and Pseudepigrapha

37. Elliott, *Apocryphal New Testament*, 235–36.
38. Ibid. 276–78.

it occurs with reverence in the mouths of people, notably John the Baptist, Pilate and the penitent thief. Quite clearly Jesus, as the significance of his life and ministry developed in the minds of his followers, acquired a majesty that led his followers to use the appellation Son of God more frequently. In the section headed Legends there is clear evidence that stories of Jesus being the Son of God show signs that the title is assuming creedal significance. The crowd in the *Acts of Andrew* professes that Christ is the Son of God, Marcellus believes in the name of Jesus the Son of God and an unnamed youth declares that Jesus is the Son of God Almighty, very God with the Holy Ghost, continuing for everlasting ages. To confess that Jesus is the Son of God becomes *the* hallmark of Christianity.

However, it is difficult to see how either stories amplifying the New Testament or the legends enumerated above seriously progress the objectives of this book. The increasing number of legends surrounding Jesus shows that as the Son of God he was seen as a unique being but they do not seem to reflect on the origin of the title, with the significant exception of the letter of Abgar.

THE LETTER OF ABGAR

From the second century comes an exchange of letters described by Eusebius.[39] They purport to be between Jesus and the dying Abgar, a legendary monarch of Iraq, who, when the divinity of Jesus Christ became famous, writes to ask him to come and heal him:

> Abgar Uchama, the Toparch, to Jesus the good Saviour who has appeared in the district of Jerusalem, greeting! I have heard concerning you and your cures, you make the blind recover their sight, the lame walk, and you cleanse the lepers, and cast out unclean spirits and demons, and cure those who are tortured by long disease and you raise dead men. When I heard of all these things concerning you I decided that it is one of the two, *either you are God, and came down from heaven to do these things, or are a Son of God for doing these things* (my italics). For this reason I write to beg you to hasten to me and heal the suffering which I have.

Jesus replies that he will send a disciple to Abgar after he has been taken up and in redemption of his promise, Thaddeus is sent to Abgar, who asks him, "Are you of a truth a disciple of Jesus, the Son of God?"

---

39. *Hist. eccl.* 13.1–21; Elliott, *Apocryphal New Testament*, 541–42.

The theology of the statement in italics is striking and asks a fundamental question. Did Jesus come down from heaven, in which case he is a pre-existent divinity, or is he the Son of God because he does these miracles upon earth? This question is redolent of Greek religion. As seen in Chapter 1, such tension was seen in the life of Heracles who was born a son of God, but because of his good deeds was welcomed in death to become a god on Mount Olympus. Alexander the Great, when he visited Siwa after becoming Pharaoh, effectively asked the same question; was he a son of Ammon because of his deeds or because of birth (see Chapter 2). In the story of Abgar, the king knows Jesus to be a healer and sends for him as such, and in his reflection on the true meaning of Jesus appellation, he seems to be guided by Greek philosophy. And, as will be seen in Chapter 6, Augustus is revealed to be a true son of God, as much by his moral excellence as by his sonship of the deified Julius Caesar. But though the thinking behind the letter of Abgar is profound and reflects on why Jesus might have been called a Son of God, Abgar does not advance ideas on the origin of the title. He does, however, provide a fitting prologue to the discussion of the philosophical and theological concepts of Jesus as Son of God that emerges in the second century.

Philosophical and Theological Concepts

During the first half of the second century, there were a number of confrontations brought about by differing thoughts and beliefs that were to affect the growing network of Christian congregations. First, Christianity was a religion whose core belief had become quite separate from that of Judaism but, since its origins lay in the Jewish faith, there was argument and acrimony between the two religions. Secondly, there was increasing tension between Christianity and those who embraced the official religion of the Roman Empire and other pagan faiths. Both deserve attention.

A crucial change occurred to Judaism in the decade from 66 CE for, with the revolt of the Jews and the subsequent destruction of the temple, the Pharisaic movement triumphed. The Sadducees, with no temple to serve, began to vanish from history; the Zealots were completely crushed and the Essenes all but eliminated in the revolt. With the loss of their temple and an end to sacrificial worship, the Jewish faith could only center on prayer and on the study of scripture. The reading of the Torah in synagogues and the studying of ancient Jewish writings replaced temple worship. The early churches and synagogues began to resemble one another.[40] Christians developed their beliefs and practices partly as result of dialogue with syna-

40. Evans, *First Christian Theologians*, 141.

gogues and partly as a result of confrontation with them and this affected the Christian literature discussed in this section.

The ancient Roman religion does not seem to have satisfied the religious needs of all Romans in the second century CE and there was considerable interest in eastern religion such as Mithraism and even greater interest in the semi-religious philosophy of Plato.[41] Many Christians and Jews spent much valuable time in creating theories as to how Plato and others had stolen their spiritual and scientific concepts from Moses.[42] So what Christians and Jews may have called pagan ideas were being imported into the new Christian Church and Christian thinkers of the second century had access to a far larger array of material than might otherwise have been possible. The writers of the early church reflect this.

PHILOSOPHICAL AND THEOLOGICAL CONCEPTS OF THE APPELLATION SON OF GOD

The Early Church Fathers

Whereas Christian dialogue with Jews hinged upon the rival interpretations of a common set of books (the Hebrew Scriptures), dialogue with the Gentile faith imposed a quite different problem. There being no recognized ground for debate between Christian and non-Christian Gentiles, Christians sought to consolidate their own religious beliefs and practices before engaging with those of other religions.[43] Much of the early church writings, therefore, concerned the question of Christian authority and practice. Soon, however, there was a growing need for Christians to defend their faith against the slanders perpetrated by ill-wishers and so they began to promote the stature, character and significance of Jesus of Nazareth.[44] Inevitably, this involved a discussion of his relationship with his God, a significant model of which was his divine sonship, and the most significant person to evoke such a discussion was Ignatius of Antioch.

41. Chadwick, *Early Christian Thought*, 36.
42. Riley, "Mimesis," 95.
43. Brent, *Ignatius*, 23–26.
44. Chadwick, *Early Christian Thought*, 66–73.

Ignatius

Ignatius is mostly known for his progression from Antioch to Rome to be martyred in the arena at Rome in about 110 CE.[45] Though his great contribution to the advance of the Church lies in his advocacy of the authority of bishops,[46] he also writes on the importance of the incarnation of Jesus, for this to Ignatius implies that he was a divinity. The term Son of God, he asserts, shows that the Son shares his Fathers being.[47] Ignatius coins the striking phrase the "Christ God"[48] which, while an appellation not found in the New Testament, seems to conform closely enough to the understanding of Jesus to be found in it.[49]

For Ignatius, then, the incarnation means that Christ is God and he insists that Jesus was an enfleshed divine being, though he seems unclear as to whether he was an angel or actually God himself.[50] Ignatius speaks of the virginity of Mary and her giving birth according to the appointment of God. He says there is one Physician, who is both flesh and spirit, born and yet not born, who is God in man, true life in death, both of Mary and of God, the only begotten Son of God (who) endured the cross and submitted to death. To him, the title Son of God raises Jesus to the status of a god himself. Gone is the mortal itinerant preacher from Nazareth—Jesus is, in essence, divine.

The Apologists

It seems clear that the aim of Ignatius was more to consolidate the emerging Christian congregations than to engage with the wider world. But as time went on, a more offensive strategy to represent the Christian Church was required, to show the world that followers of Jesus were not just a body of sincere and holy people, but a religious body possessed of a revelation and philosophy that surpassed all other. Those who were responsible for this exercise were called Apologists and they emerged in the second century. Unquestionably, one of the greatest of these was Justin Martyr, concerned not only with the refutation of attacks against Christians but to show that philosophy is truth, reason a spiritual power and Christianity the fullness of

---

45. Ibid. 46.

46. Ehrman, *Apostolic Fathers*, 295–309.

47. Ign. *Eph.* 20.2.

48. Ign. *Smyrn.* 10.1.

49. Bromiley, *Historical Theology*, 4.

50. Wagner, *After the Apostles*, 146.

both. But before the writings of Justin are examined it is necessary to inspect the *Epistle to Diognetus*.

The Epistle to Diognetus

This epistle is known only by its recipient and (like the Epistle to the Hebrews) there is no knowledge of its origin, authorship and date. It seems to have been written in the early or middle second century and the writer is generally counted as one of the Apologists.[51] He uses the concept of Jesus as "Son of God" in two ways. Firstly, he understands that the title Son of God means that Jesus is God. In Chapter 7, the author describes God "as a king sending his own son, he sent him as a king; he sent him as a god; he sent him as a human to humans." Secondly, the writer develops the idea of the Divine Word or Logos, saying: "But the truly all–powerful God himself, creator of all and invisible, set up and established in their hearts the truth and the holy word from heaven" not as a heavenly intermediary, "but as the designer and maker of the universe."[52] As Bromiley puts it, the author succeeds in combining in simple statements thoughts of no little theological profundity: "the gospel as God's Word, Christ as Word, Christ as God and man, Christ as the message and method of God. . ."[53] As in the writings of Ignatius, the message of the author of the *Epistle to Diognetus* is that Jesus is divine.

Justin Martyr

Justin was born around 90 CE to a Greek family who lived in Palestine. Although he was probably acquainted with Galilee and Judaea, he knew little Hebrew and Aramaic and his acquaintance with Judaism was limited.[54] Justin gives a graphic account of the studies that led him to becoming a Christian, of which Platonism was the most important. Barnard says of him: "Justin Martyr represents a pioneer type of Greek Apologist. He is concerned not only with the refutation of attacks against Christians and Jewish objections; he is also concerned to show that philosophy, truth and reason are a spiritual power and Christianity is the fullness of both."[55]

---

51. Meecham, *Diognetus*, 38–64; Bromiley, *Historical Theology*, 10.

52. *Diogn.* 7:4.

53. Bromily, *Historical Theology*, 11.

54. Wagner, *After the Apostles*, 158.

55. Barnard, *Justin Martyr*, 4.

Justin is very clear that Jesus, whom he generally calls Christ, is the Son of God. He speaks of him as Son of the true God himself; worthy to be called the Son of God; first begotten; Son of God and first begotten.[56] In all, he uses the term Son of God over fifteen times, as well as describing Jesus as the Son (of God by implication) a further forty times.

But the crucial distinction of the Apologists, and particularly Justin, from earlier Christian literature is that they *start* from the precept that Jesus *is* the Son of God and go on to develop their ideas from that position. Whereas in the Synoptic Gospels the key issue is that Jesus is recognized as Son of God, Justin accepts the title as "given" and goes on to work out its long term implications in the following ways

Justin sees great significance in the virgin birth. "Jesus our Christ," he says, "(is) foretold as coming, born of a virgin, healing every disease and sickness, and raising the dead, and being hated, and unrecognized, and crucified, and dying, and rising again, and ascending into heaven, being, and being called, the Son of God."[57] As there was no need for circumcision or Sabbaths, feasts or sacrifices before Abraham, there was no need for them furthermore since, "Jesus Christ, the Son of God has been born without sin, of a virgin sprung from the stock of Abraham."[58] In the earlier times, the Logos appeared in different forms to reveal the supreme Deity's will, but in recent days, claimed Justin, the Logos became incarnate through being born of a virgin.[59]

However firmly Justin may have stated the case for the virgin birth, it remained a problem for Jews. In Chapters 66 and 67 of the *Dialogue with Trypho*, Justin and Trypho dispute the prophecy of Isaiah 7.10–17. Basing his stance on the Septuagint translation of Scripture, Justin asserts: "Now it is evident to all, that in the race of Abraham according to the flesh no one has been born, or is said to have been born (of a virgin), save this our Christ." But Trypho objects, first, by using the Hebrew version of Scripture and denying that there is any reference to virginity, and, second, by referring to the virgin conception of Perseus in Greek legend and reproving Justin for talking foolishly like the Greeks.[60] This last passage indicates that there were those who suspected that the concept of the son of God had a Greek origin. But as with the title Son of God, so with the virgin birth, *the mythological aspect of this event has gone and is replaced by a theological view.*

56. Titles given in *1 Apol.* and *Trypho* 116.

57. *1 Apol.* 31.

58. *Trypho* 33.

59. Wagner, *After the Apostles*, 163.

60. This dialogue takes place within *Trypho*, 66–70.

Justin does not just insist that Jesus is virgin born, he also describes him as "the first begotten of the unbegotten God,"[61] prophesied as coming in the Hebrew Scriptures. "For with what reason," he writes, "should we believe of a crucified man that He is the First-begotten of the Unbegotten God and Himself will pass judgment on the whole human race, unless we had found testimonies proclaimed about Him before He came and was made man."[62] Justin is here starting to explore not just the relationship between God the Father and the Son, but the process whereby it has come about. He seems to be suggesting that Jesus was recognised as unique and as such can be none other than the Son of God and this is further shown by his use of the word Logos.

Perhaps the most important contribution that Justin made to Christology was his use of the word "Logos." This word appears significantly at the beginning of the Gospel of John: "In the beginning the Word already was. The Word was in God's presence, and what God was, the Word was."[63] Justin used the word Logos to develop his ideas of the relationship between Father and Son. He says, "the Word who is the first birth (i.e. first born) of God, was produced without sexual union, and that He, Jesus Christ, our Teacher, was crucified and died, and rose again."[64] He goes on to say: "moreover the Son of God called Jesus, even if only a man by ordinary generation, yet, on account of his wisdom, is worthy to be called the Son of God; for all writers call God the Father of men and gods. And we assert that the Word of God was born of God in a peculiar manner, different from ordinary generation."[65] Justin hereby makes it plain that he accepts that the prologue to St. Johns Gospel is speaking of Jesus as Son of God when he refers to the Word being made flesh.[66] Jesus is at once the Word of God and the Son of God.

This identification enables Justin to bring people who died long before Jesus was born within the Christian fold. So he writes, "We have been taught that Christ is the first born of God, and we have declared above that He is the Word of whom every race of men were partakers; and those who lived reasonably are Christians; even though they have been thought to be atheists; as, among the Greeks Socrates and Heraclitus, and men like them; and among the barbarians Abraham, and Ananias, and Azarias, and Misael

---

61. *1 Apol.* 58; *Trypho* 116.3.
62. *1 Apol.* 53.
63. John 1:1.
64. *1 Apol.* 21.
65. Ibid. 32.
66. 1 John 1:14.

and Elias . . ."[67] Jesus Christ is here being exalted to be above time so that all people of sincere life and philosophy may be accounted his disciples. This enables him to claim that Socrates, among others, may be accounted a Christian! It also enables him to speak of Jesus transcending both race and space.

CONCLUSION

By the time of Justin's death in 165 CE, the title Son of God was firmly established as the major title of Jesus of Nazareth and it was seen as both adulatory and explanatory. In the increasing mythological language of the Apocrypha and Pseudepigrapha, Son of God has become a significant title as an appellation of Jesus and is used at important moments (e.g., Jesus, Son of God, comes here.)[68] In the world of the Apologists and theologians, Jesus has become the pre-existent Word or Logos, someone who is to be identified as the Son of God. Though one hundred and fifty years were to pass before the Council of Nicaea was to pronounce that the Son was of one substance with the Father, the title Son of God had secured for Jesus the ontological belief that he was as one with God, and was indeed a god incarnate.

But, crucially, this development takes the student far from the origin of the concept of the appellation. When Paul first used the title Son of God in his epistles (see Chapter 4), he was using it as a *mythological* title, linking Jesus by the appellation to legendary figures such as Heracles, Perseus and Theseus and encouraging his Gentile readers (for whom the word Christ had virtually no meaning) to see the international significance of the son of the carpenter of Nazareth. Greeks did not speculate as to the ontological importance of the divine birth of Heracles, they took him as figure worthy of adulation, celebrated him in verse and fable and sought to follow his example. Similarly, the people who lived in what had been his empire were more interested in what Alexander had done (be it fact or legend) than what his reputed divinity might theologically infer. And as in the case of Alexander, so in the case of Jesus, the most exciting and unlikely stories accumulated around him as people became interested in his life and told stories around the camp fires about him.

However, the influence of the Johannine prologue led to a totally different use for the title Son of God, for Justin Martyr linked the words Son of God and Divine Logos together to develop the concept of a God–man. Justin was not concerned with the origin of the title but with its implication for

67. 1 *Apol.* 46.
68. *Des. Inf.* 2 (18) 2.

his theology, as can be illustrated is in the use of the story of the virgin birth. Originally, as shown in Chapter 4, Mary was a shadowy figure in Mark, but in Matthew and Luke she emerges as the virgin mother of Jesus. I have argued that Mary's virginity was proclaimed to make it plain that the God of the Hebrew Scriptures had not engaged in sex with a Galilean girl and that Jesus was not the result of the sort of dual parentage ascribed to Heracles or Theseus. Whatever the reason for their origin, legends of the early church were rife with stories of Mary, Joseph and the birth and early childhood of Jesus. Jesus' greatness, indeed his divine sonship, are emphasized by legends of his mother. But Justin is not concerned with the legendary birth of Jesus but with philosophical implications of that birth and so he uses the virgin birth theologically. Whereas many people understand that because Jesus was born without sin, sex had no part in his conception; Justin believed that Jesus was without sin because he was *born* of a virgin.

This chapter has shown how stories of Jesus from the gospels have been amplified and changed, how other stories, many the result of oral tradition, have been added to them and how these stories show a deepening awareness of the significance of describing Jesus of Nazareth as Son of God, as well as emphasizing its use. This chapter has also shown how early theologians used the title philosophically and how this led to the conviction that to be Son of God meant that the person so described was in reality a part of God himself. But this examination of the literature of the early church has unearthed little of value towards a discovery of the origin of the title Son of God. The stories of the virgin birth have been amplified; as have the stories of the crucifixion and the resurrection but there has been little increase of evidence about the emergence of the title itself. Chapter 6 will be found to contain much better fare.

6

Son of God in the Roman Empire

PREAMBLE

Chapters 4 and 5 focused on writings relevant to the Early Church in the period from the end of the New Testament to the death of Justin Martyr in 165 CE. Occasional references were made in these chapters to the attitude of people within the Roman world towards the emperor. Chapter 6 will deal with the significance of the title "Son of God" as applied to emperors of Rome in the period when Christianity was emerging as a separate religion.

This subject covers a vast amount of material. One of the supreme political events in the first millennium CE was the establishment of a Roman empire, an empire, moreover, whose rulers claimed to be divine.[1] To fully understand the complexity of Rome, its political system and its religious practice, to say nothing of the key personalities of its history, is beyond the scope of this book. Yet reference to these matters must be made if the divine titles applied to the emperors are to be understood. What will be attempted is a sketch of the process that produced a sole ruler of the Roman empire and an examination of the process whereby he was referred to as a son of god. There will be further discussion as to whether the use of this title by emperors of Rome influenced or indeed provided a reason for granting the same title to Jesus of Nazareth. There will also be an examination of other titles given to Roman emperors that may seriously affect the topic. This chapter will focus mainly on the life and implications of the reign of

1. Sweet, *Emperor Worship*, 11–12.

Augustus, but will also look briefly at the reign of Claudius and will examine the religious attitude of Domitian, who made significant claims to divinity during his life.

For the early followers of the religion of Jesus of Nazareth, the fact that the emperor was referred to as a son of god was of the greatest significance, for, when they began to refer to Jesus in similar terms, they ran the risk of being accused of disrespect to the emperor. I have argued in Chapters 1 and 2 that the appellation Son of God came from Greece and that a probable paradigm for Jesus affirmation in that title lay in the apotheosis of Alexander the Great at Siwa. But although Alexander was much admired by the Roman Emperors, he had no serious cult in their empire. If followers of Jesus chose to use the title of Son of God for their leader because it had been an appellation of Alexander, they were presumably free to do so without prosecution. But to refer to Jesus as Son of God, when such a title was a perquisite of the emperor, was almost certainly another matter.

This issue is explored in the story of the crucifixion. According to the Gospel stories, Jesus was tried before Pontius Pilate and all four evangelists agree that the first question that Pilate put to Jesus was: "Are you the king of the Jews?"[2] But the unanimity of the evangelists vanishes when the student is asked to define what is to be understood by the title King of the Jews. Many writers, basing themselves on Chapter 23 of Luke, understand that verse 2 implies that Jesus was accused before Pilate of claiming to be the Messiah. According to Brandon, who sees Jesus as a para-Zealot, it would seem that the main charge (against Jesus) was that of the assumption of royal power as the "King of the Jews," with the subsidiary charge of inciting the people to revolt and not pay the Roman tribute. Brandon goes on to argue that Jesus was presented as the real leader of the insurrection and not Barabbas.[3]

But the trial before Pilate was arguably the *second* trial, for Jesus had previously been arraigned before members of the Sanhedrin, though whether this was a formal trial is uncertain.[4] And one of the indictments the Jewish establishment is said to have produced is that Jesus claimed to be the Son of God[5] and it was his apparent admission of this charge that the Chief Priest found conclusive. So the Jewish authorities say to Pilate: "We have a law and according to that law he ought to die because he claimed to be the Son of God." But when Pilate allows Jesus to be crucified, he sets up a notice

---

2. Blinzler, *Trial*, 189; Matt 27:11; Mark 15:2; Luke 23:3; John 18:33.

3. Brandon, *Trial*, 148–49.

4. Allen, "Why Pilate?" 82.

5. Matt 26:63; Mark 14:61–62; Luke 22:70.

over the cross in Latin, Greek and Hebrew: "Jesus of Nazareth, the King of the Jews." The charge is clearly one of high treason, which under Augustus *lex Iulia maiestasis* carries the penalty of death, probably by crucifixion.[6]

Pilate clearly believed that Jesus had described himself as Messiah and he understood this to be the treasonable offence of claiming to be the king of the Jews. But I argue that the claim that Jesus was Son of God exacerbated the charge, for this was a specific title of the Emperor and to claim not only to be a king but also a son of God must make the offence worse. It is therefore necessary to examine how the Roman empire understood their emperor to be a son of god.

Son of the Deified

The key event that underlies this chapter is easily described. Gaius Octavianus, whom the world later came to know as Augustus, was born on 28th September 63 BCE.[7] His widowed mother, Atia, married a nephew of Julius Caesar[8] and the latter, developing an interest in Octavianus[9], named him as his son and heir. When Julius Caesar died in 44 BCE, it was not long before he was officially granted a cult of his own and became a *divus* (a deified being). He was, according to Suetonius, numbered among the gods, not only by a formal decree, but also in the conviction of the common people,[10] Octavianus was then able to declare himself to be, and be declared by others to be, *filius divi* (son of the deified) soon after 40 BCE.[11] Hard proof that this happened exists in the writing on a gold coin, minted in 28 BCE and now in the British Museum, which bears the inscription IMP CAESAR DIVI F COS VI (Imperator Caesar, son of the deified, Consul for the Sixth Time).[12]

The appellation *divus* needs examining. Romans adopted as their most important gods those whom the Greeks called Olympians[13] and these they

---

6. Blinzler, *Trial*, 213.

7. *Div. Aug.* 5.

8. Shotter, *Augustus*, 18.

9. The future Augustus is normally referred to by his original name, Octavianus, until 27 BCE when the title Augustus was granted to him.

10. *Div. Jul.* 88.

11. Scheid, "Augustus," 17.

12. "Eder, "Augustus," 23–24: A color photograph of both sides of this important coin is shown facing p. 260 of Galinsky, *The Cambridge Companion to the Age of Augustus*.

13. E.g., the Greek Zeus became the Roman Jupiter.

referred to as *dei*.[14] But, when a human being was elevated to divine state, he or she was said to be deified and referred to as a *divus* (i.e. a human who has been granted divine status). Whether there was a real distinction between *deus* and *divus* is challenged by the Oxford Latin Dictionary, which sees no clear difference between the two.[15] And in any case, the distinction, if distinction there was, existed only in the western half of the empire, which spoke Latin. In the eastern part of the empire the difference did not exist, for *divus* and *deus* are both renderings of the Greek *theos*. Hence *divi filius* (son of the deified) and *dei filius* (son of god) would both be adequate translations of *uios theou*. During the long reign of Augustus, from the Battle of Actium in 31 BCE to his death on 9th August 14 CE at the age of 75, he was known in his eastern provinces as son of God (*uios theou*).[16]

But what did the title *divi filius* say of the person upon whom it was conferred? Thus far this book has examined the way the Pharaohs were called sons of the god Ra as part of their royal titles; how Alexander became son of Ammon as the result of a spiritual experience at Siwa and how Jesus began to be called Son of God as the only way his followers could assert his essential closeness to God in a Gentile setting. With Octavianus, however, the title seems to have been given to him by accident of adoption; he was the adopted son of Julius Caesar and when the latter was deified, he became automatically son of the deified. This appellation seems to reflect on Julius Caesar and to say little of Octavianus. To understand the full significance of the meaning of son of the deified to the Romans, it is necessary to have a brief overview of their religion.

Roman Religion

Ando opens his *Roman Religion* with a quotation from Valerius Maximus On Religion, written in the time of Tiberius Caesar: "Our ancestors desired that fixed and formal annual ceremonies be regulated by the knowledge of the *pontifices* (priests); that sanction for the good governance of affairs be marshaled by the observations of augurs. . . and that the expiation of portents be accomplished in accordance with the Etruscan discipline."[17] So Roman religion provided identity to its people; to be a Roman was to be a follower of the Roman gods.[18] Further, Cassius Dio quotes the mythical

14. Beard, North et al., *Priesthood*, 30.

15. *Oxford English Dictionary*, 534–35 and 566.

16. Kim, "Anarthous."

17. Valerius, "Memorable Doings," 1.11a–b; Ando, *Roman Religion*, 1.

18. Beard and Crawford, "Rome in the Late Republic," 25–26.

Maecenas counseling the young Octavianus:" If you truly desire to be immortal, do as I advise. . . reject and punish those who make some innovation in its (Roman) worship."[19] The stability of Roman society was based on the belief that the gods preferred the *status quo*.

Those who controlled the religious affairs of the Roman state were elected by the city council and divided into three colleges—the *pontifices*, the *augures* and the *decemviri sacris faciundis*—which were originally independent of one another, it being the rule that no one person could be head of more than one college. The key religious figure in Rome was the *pontifex maximus* (high priest) who was elected from members of the public[20]. However, just as no military acumen was required of the consuls who confronted Hannibal so disastrously, no spiritual zeal (in the modern sense) was required of the *pontifex maximus* and some candidates for this office were a religious disgrace.

Notably, Julius Caesar announced his candidacy for the office of *pontifex maximus* resorting to the most lavish bribery. He was successful and polled more than his two rivals put together.[21] But he was the man of whom his soldiers sang during a triumph in Rome: "*Urbani, servate uxores: moechum calvum adducimus* (Men of Rome protect your wives; we are bringing in the bald adulterer),"[22] and of whom Suetonius says: "no regard for religion ever turned him from any undertaking."[23] Neither lack of morality or spirituality prevented Julius Caesar becoming high priest.

When Octavianus came to rule Rome, he broke the law that prevented one person holding headship of more than one of the three colleges and, by becoming *pontifex maximus* in 17 BCE, was absolute head of the Roman religious establishment. All future emperors, until Constantine became a Christian in 313 CE, assumed the same powers. Authority in Roman religion, far from being a part of a democratic activity of citizens, now came under the control of the emperor's minions. It was the emperor, not the people, who decided whether to declare his predecessor a *divus*. For practical purposes, the emperor was now the be all and end all of Roman religion. But the question must be asked, what does the title emperor imply?

19. Dio 52.36.1–3; Beard, North, and Price, *Priesthood*, 214.
20. Beard, North, and Price, *Priesthood*, 18.
21. *Div. Jul.* 13.
22. *Div. Jul.* 49.
23. *Div. Jul.* 59.

The Rulers

Tacitus, writing in the second century CE begins his Annals: "Rome at the outset was a city state under the government of kings: liberty and consulate were the institutions of Lucius Brutus. Dictatorships were always a temporary expedient. Neither Cinna nor Sulla created a lasting despotism: Pompey and Crassus quickly forfeited their power to Caesar, and Lepidus and Anthony their sword to Augustus, who, under the style of 'Prince,' gathered beneath his empire a world worn out by civil broils."[24] So Rome was a monarchy until kings were evicted and the city, now run by a form of elective government, became a republic (*respublica*). The heads of state were two consuls (magistrates), who were annually elected from the rich upper classes (*nobiles*) and they governed the city jointly for one year. From the *nobiles* the governing body (the senate) was also formed by election, as were all those with civic responsibility, including the clergy and military commanders. In its early history, this democratic system served Rome well.[25]

But as Rome thrived, she expanded, clashed with the great powers of the day and the democratic Roman system proved inadequate. At the Battle of Cannae in 216 BCE a huge Roman citizen army, under the joint control of the two militarily incompetent consuls *who actually held command on alternate days,* was annihilated by a much smaller Carthaginian force under Hannibal.[26] Rome, in desperation, appointed Fabius Maximus (*Cunctator*) as dictator for a limited period[27] and thereby set a precedent that was to lead to the end of republican government. Professional and trained commanders became essential to the survival of the Republic, for it was no longer possible to rely on the military acumen of elected consuls. The Roman armies ceased to be citizen levies and became instead professional military forces, increasingly remote from their employers (the Senate) and under the actual control of their army commanders.[28] When the latter chose to enter politics, the control of their troops and not the views of the citizens of Rome proved decisive. It was Julius Caesar's defeat of Pompeius (*Magnus*) that made him undisputed master of Rome and united the city under his authority. But the victor had then to contemplate certain problems, *who* was he to hold this

---

24. *Annals*, 1.1.243.
25. Syme, *The Roman Revolution*, 10–27.
26. Polybius, *Hisotries*, 107; Fuller, *Decisive Battles*, 1:126.
27. Bradford, *Hannibal*, 93, 119.
28. Fuller, *Decisive Battles*, 1:170–72.

authority; *what* was to be his title; *by what* name would soldiers and citizens swear allegiance to him?[29]

Rome was still, in name at least, a republic and both constitutionally and emotionally opposed to the return of a king. So though Julius Caesar would frequently remark, "*Caesarem se, non regem esse* (I am Caesar and no king)," a deep suspicion grew in the minds of many Romans that a king was really what he intended to be. Julius Caesar wisely opted for the appellation "dictator" but, having chosen this title to allay the fears of the Senate, he promptly infuriated them by declaring himself dictator for life and receiving them without rising. Anger, fear and envy, as well as hope for the restoration of the Republic, obsessed many members of the senate and Julius Caesar was assassinated in 44 BCE.[30]

The Augustan Settlement

Civil war then broke out afresh and ten years were to pass before Octavianus defeated Mark Antony at Actium (2nd September 31 BCE). This victory as surely made the former sole ruler of Rome, as had Julius Caesar's defeat of Pompey at Pharsalus[31]. Octavianus owed this victory to his control of the legions and was thus faced with the same problem as had beset Julius Caesar. If he was to govern Rome and her empire, Octavianus had to satisfy the senate that he was not seeking supreme power, while in practice obtaining it. So successful was he at solving this problem that the so-called Augustan settlement survived for three centuries and the title *divi filius* became less a reference to his being son of his adoptive father and more a reflection of Octavianus himself. He was deified soon after his death in 14 CE.

Augustus Achievements: What Were They?

After his accession to power, Octavianus avoided the tainted title dictator and took to calling himself *Imperator*[32] *Caesar* a title to be held for life only and hence the antithesis of kingship.[33] He was continually elected consul

29. Syme, *The Roman Revolution*, 78–96.

30. *Div. Jul.* 76–78.

31. Syme, *The Roman Revolution*, 315.

32. The translation of *imperator* (originally the title given to victorious generals) as emperor is confusing to modern ears. Generations, who have heard it used of British monarchs in India and Napoleon Bonaparte, think of an emperor as a kind of super king. A better translation of *imperator* might be "conqueror."

33. Dio 51.73; 52:40.1; 53.17; Syme, *The Roman Revolution*, 113.

from 43 to 27 BCE, but then he resigned all his positions and officially restored power to the Senate, an act for which he received the title Augustus.[34] It was a masterstroke, for, as Dio points out,[35] this comprehensive resignation resulted in his being granted absolute supremacy by the senate and by the people of Rome.[36] In 23 BCE, he was granted powers that made him commander in chief of all Roman forces, a position assumed by his successors.[37] But as the word *Respublica* continued to be used of the Roman state, Augustus chose to be referred to as the *princeps* or leading citizen, a title that carried no apparent threat of usurping power.[38] In reality, however, he was all-powerful and though he chose not to force his will over the senate (preferring the process of bribery and patronage), he was to all intents and purposes a king, with enough authority to produce an effective and well working government. He was awarded the title *Pater Patriae* (father of my country) in 2 BCE by the senate and the equestrian order and the entire people of Rome.[39] He had succeeded in his aim of achieving supreme power without seeming to have done so and so earned the grateful affection of his people.

His (Augustus's) rule began as the triumph of a faction of a civil war: he made it his task to transcend faction.[40] Long running civil wars are among the greatest of human sufferings, as modern examples in the Democratic Republic of the Congo and Sudan clearly demonstrate. The struggles in which Julius Caesar, Pompey, Marcus Antonius and Octavianus himself played a part were quite horrific in terms of broken families, loss of life, disruption of trade and famine. Romans recognised the horrors of war by establishing the temple of Janus in Rome, whose doors stood open while there was war in the Roman world. Only twice in Rome's long history had they been closed before Augustus reign, but during it they were closed three times.[41] Augustus produced peace and sought to preserve it. Aware of the dangers of private armies, loyal to their commanders first and to Rome second, he reorganized the legions and, by personally paying the legionaries from the spoils of war, guaranteed their loyalty to the emperor as embodying the state.

34. *Res Gestae*, 34.
35. Dio 53.2.6—53.19.5.
36. Beard, North, and Price, *Priesthood,* 167.
37 Dio 53.32.26.
38. *Annals* 3.28; Shotter, *Augustus,* 24–25.
39. *Res Gestae*, 35; *Div. Aug.* 58.
40. Syme, *Augustus,* 51.
41. *Res Gestae*, 13; Dio 51.57; Syme, *Augustus,* 303.

Not just that, but he produced an ordered society. Augustus limited the power of the *nobiles* and created a civil service in which freedmen (freed slaves) played an important part and, since they were totally loyal to him, he reduced corruption. He reorganized the law courts and, by often presiding as a judge, was seen as the source of justice and the protector of the rights of Roman citizens. Though it is quite correct for a modern student to see that in the Republic of Augustus there was little democracy, the commoners (*plebs*) of Augustan Rome did not care. As they looked around them, walked their streets in peace, earned their living without interruption and grew old enough to see their grandchildren grow up, they eulogized Augustus whom they rightly saw as providing this idyll.[42]

The city (Rome), which was not built in a manner suitable to the grandeur of empire, was so much improved under his (Augustus's) administration, that he boasted, not without reason, that he found it of brick but left it of marble.[43] With the booty he acquired during his campaigns, Augustus rebuilt and renovated the Roman temples.[44] The people of Rome found themselves living in a city of beauty and elegance and gave thanks for the provider. And it was partly this spirit of awe at their new surroundings that led the people of Rome to embrace a religious revival.

Shotter expresses the opinion that religious revival was a necessary part of the Augustan Republic.[45] This comment offers a cynical approach to Augustan religious policy. However justified, this cynicism would not have been endorsed by the people of Rome. The theology of success, beloved of some evangelical preachers of today, is no new feature of the worship of a divinity. Those who had lived through the awful times of the civil war and found themselves in a time of (comparative) peace and undoubted prosperity blessed their gods, and blessed Augustus as well.

One of the mainstays of Augustan religious policy was discipline.[46] Suetonius tells how, when Augustus became *pontifex maximus*, he collected whatever prophetic writings of Greek or Latin origin were in circulation anonymously or under the names of authors of little repute, and burned more than two thousand of them, retaining only the Sibylline books and making a choice even among those; and he deposited them in two gilded

---

42. *Annals* 1.2.

43. *Div. Aug.* 28.3.

44. Suetonius provides a long list of the religious buildings he built in Rome, notably new temples to Mars, Apollo and Jupiter; *Div. Aug.* 28.29.

45. Shotter, *Augustus,* 47.

46. Dio 52.36.

cases under the pedestal of the Palatine Apollo.[47] This was not the action of a control freak but one who desired to see the religion of Rome as a cohesive, rather than a divisive, force. Augustus encouraged *pietas*, the living of the simple and holy life that sought to appease the anger which the gods had so clearly shown during the disruption of civil war. He paid attention to religious details and not only restored the Roman temples but also improved the priesthood. In modern times, Augustus might have become a saint!

Augustus reigned a long time (41 years) and his achievements were portrayed, and seen by many, as prodigious. The image he wished to portray was of a golden age, in which the Republic was restored, peace and stability achieved, law and order maintained and religion reorganized and revitalized. There may have some who thought that the Republic was no republic, that peace at home was achieved at the price of constant war abroad, that the law favored the rich and powerful and that Augustan *pietas* was a cynical ploy but they, in the main, held their peace. Gratitude to Augustus and for his achievements was unbounded.[48]

So it is not surprising that by the first century CE, Augustus had become a god on earth to many people. An early Coan (i.e. from the Island of Kos) decree begins: "Since the Emperor Caesar, son of god, god Sebastos has by his benefactions to all men outdone even the Olympian gods. . ."[49] The sudden outburst of cults of Augustus helped to ensure the perpetuation of his personal authority. But to be seen as a god did not suit his image and he continued to portray of himself *princeps*, the first among equals. Only on his death in 14 CE was Augustus actually deified, though long before this date he was seen as a god by many. And, it cannot be too highly stressed that throughout his long reign he was *filius dei* (son of the deified) in the Latin world and *uios theou* (son of a god) in the Greek world. This encouraged myths about his birth and youth.

The Birth of Augustus

As in the case of Alexander the Great, Augustus birth was said to be accompanied by signs and portents from heaven. "It will not be out place to add an account of the omens which occurred before he was born," writes Suetonius, "on the very day of his birth, and afterwards, from which it was possible to anticipate and perceive his future greatness and uninterrupted good fortune." Suetonius goes on to tell of how a portent was observed at

47. *Div. Aug.* 31.
48. Shotter, *Augustus,* 47.
49. Price, *Rituals,* 55.

Rome, which gave warning that nature was pregnant with a king for the Roman people, and how the senate forbade the raising of any male child that year but how the wives of the citizen saw that the law was disobeyed. He further tells of how Augustus father, Octavius, was publicly told that Augustus was to be a ruler of the world, because, when he poured wine over the altar, flames sprang up and that had only happened once before, when Alexander the Great did the same thing.[50] But of even more significance comes Suetonius' story of August's conception and birth:

> I have read the following story in the books of Asclepias of Mendes entitled *Theologumena*. When Atia (Augustus mother) had come in the middle of the night to the solemn service of Apollo, she had her litter set down in the temple and fell asleep, while the rest of the matrons also slept. On a sudden a serpent glided up to her and shortly went away. When she awoke, she purified herself, as if after the embraces of her husband, and at once there appeared on her body a mark in colours like a serpent, and she could never get rid of it; so that presently she ceased ever to go to the public baths. In the tenth month after that Augustus was born and was therefore regarded as the son of Apollo. Atia too, before she gave him birth, dreamed that her vitals were borne up to the stars and spread over the whole extent of land and sea, while Octavius dreamed that the sun rose from Atia's womb.[51]

The way Augustus affected the Title Son of God

Alexander, as has been shown, was a passionate individual with a deep awareness of his birth into a family with putative divine antecedents. His extraordinary ability as a military commander and as a philosopher resulted in his conquest of a vast empire before he was twenty-five years of age. But the key moment of his life was spiritual; the revelation of Siwa was to convince him that he was a son of god. It was a conviction shared by many of his friends and subjects. Augustus was totally different. A quiet, slightly withdrawn, exceptionally able diplomat and statesman, he so inspired the people of his empire by bringing peace and stability, that they became convinced that he was nothing less than divine. But being granted the title Son of God was almost accidental; he was the adopted son of the deified Julius Caesar.

50. *Div. Aug.* 94.1–3.
51. *Div. Aug.,* 97.4.

His life, as portrayed by his biographers, transformed the appellation from one
of accident of birth to one of spiritual meaning.

Augustus and Alexander the Great

Augustus, and indeed the Roman world in general, were fascinated by Alexander. After the death of Mark Antony, Octavianus visited Alexandria and had the sarcophagus and body of Alexander the Great brought forth from its shrine, and gazing on it, showed his respect by placing upon it a golden crown and strewing it with flowers. But when asked if he also wished to see the tomb of the Ptolemies, he remarked acidly: "My wish was to see a king, not corpses."[52] So it is not surprising that Augustus should seek comparison with the great Macedonian. The story of flames springing up on a Thracian altar should surprise no one.

But the birth story of Octavianus has an extreme closeness to the birth of Alexander. Olympias dreamed of a thunderbolt from heaven on the night before her wedding[53] while Atia dreamed that her vitals were borne up to heaven. Trogus tells of Olympias, on the night of Alexander's conception, dreaming of being entwined with a large snake,[54] while Plutarch describes Philip of Macedon peeping through his wife's door and seeing a large snake in her bed, a snake which the *Romance of Alexander* infers was a sign of the god Ammon—Ra.[55] Since Olympias was known to be involved in a snake cult and since snakes were divine creatures in Egypt (where Alexander was declared son of Ammon), the symbolism of snakes may not be surprising but to the people of Rome the idea of divine conception through a snake would be surprising indeed. How close the parallels may be drawn is perhaps open to discussion but it is seems extremely likely that the birth stories of Augustus were influenced by those of Alexander.

There is a further point that may well be more than mere coincidence. Octavianus visited Alexandria in 30 BCE and the first coin declaring him "son of the deified" was stuck in 28 BCE. The question must surely be asked, did the visit to the tomb of Alexander, son of the god Ammon, encourage Augustus to promote his image as a son of a god?

52. *Div. Aug.* 18; Dio 51.47.
53. Plutarch, 2.1.
54. *Trogus* 12.16.2.
55. Plutarch, 2.1–6; *Romance* 1.10.

Claudius (41–54)

Following the death of Augustus, Tiberius, his adopted son[56] reigned for 23 years (14–37 CE). He seems to have been an unattractive personality, although his tireless work for his empire in the early part of his reign is commented on by his biographers.[57] His importance for this book is that by senatorial decree of 17th September 14 CE, he was made *divi filius*, thereby ensuring that this appellation could be applied to successors of Augustus as reigning emperors. Caligula seems not to have used this title, displaying such psychotic delusions of grandeur that he sought to take his place among the Olympians themselves, establishing a special temple to his godhead, with priests and with victims of the choicest kind[58] and ordering the Jews to set up his statue, in the guise of Zeus, in the temple at Jerusalem. Before he could carry out this disastrous plan, he was assassinated.

Claudius, a nephew of Tiberius and uncle of Caligula, was almost the only member of the Julio-Claudian family still alive when Caligula was killed and was forced on the senate as the only possible candidate for the post of emperor by the army.. He seems to have suffered from both physical and mental disabilities[59] and this had prevented him from military service, so he continually stressed the fact that he was the brother of Germanicus and the son of Drusus, military heroes both. But after the successful invasion of Britain by Plautus in 43 CE, Claudius needed these connections no longer. At Volubilis, a town in modern day Morocco, an inscription from 44 CE was found describing Claudius as *divi filius* (son of the deified).

The significance of this inscription cannot be understated. Augustus became, as has been shown, *divi filius* because of the deification of his adoptive father, Julius Caesar and this appellation appeared in documents and on coins. Tiberius became *divi filius* for exactly the same reason, though he seems not to have used the title[60]. Claudius could not be described as son of deified in the same way; he was not the son of, or adopted as the heir of, an emperor. By using what was Augustus's favorite title, Claudius was restoring his great predecessor's rule.

---

56. Dio 55:13.2.
57. *Tiberius* 25–28; Levick, *Tiberius*, 224–25.
58. *Gaius Cal.* 22, 1–3: *War* 2.10.1–3.
59. *Div. Clau.* 10; Levick, *Claudius*, 12–16.
60. Levick, *Claudius*, 80–81.

The Significant Events of 70 CE

Claudius died in 54 CE and was deified immediately, probably because his stepson and heir, Nero, wished to be called son of the deified.[61] Nero's reign was disastrous and in 68 CE he was assassinated, thereby precipitating a crisis. For Augustus reorganisation of the empire had made it essential that a single dominant figure was required to govern the empire. Some form of dynasty had to be established and yet, surprisingly, not one of his successors had a son of the male line to succeed them. When the last of these (Nero) died, a new emperor had to appear and, inevitably perhaps, it was the victorious military commander who had put down the Jewish revolt, who succeeded to the throne. Vespasian became ruler of empire and reigned until 79 CE, to be succeeded by his sons Titus (79—81) and Domitian (81—96).[62]

The Flavian Emperors

This book is concerned with the appellation Son of God and this chapter has clearly established that Roman emperors of the Julio-Claudian family were indeed called sons of the deified. That this practice continued under the Flavians is made clear by the inscription of an early coin, now in the British Museum: IMP. T. CAES.DIVI VESP. F.AVG P.M. TR. P. P.P. COS. VIII (Imperator Titus Caesar, son of the Deified Vespasian, Augustus, Pontifex Maximus, holder of the Tribunician Power, Father of his Country, eight times Consul).[63] What will be investigated in the rest of this chapter is whether there are serious indications that other imperial stories and titles may have affected the portrayal of Jesus.

Vespasian's Healing Miracle

Suetonius describes the newly acclaimed emperor encountering a blind man who has dreamed that the god Serapis has promised that Vespasian could cure him if he would spit on his eyes. Reluctantly Vespasian does so in the presence of a large crowd and the man is healed.[64] However, Jesus is described in Mark (8.22–26) as performing an almost identical healing. Either Suetonius, Tacitus and Dio had all heard of the story of the healing told

---

61. *Nero* 8; Levick, *Nero*, 187.

62. *Div. Vesp.* 6.1–4.

63. Levick, *Vespasian*, xvii.

64. *Div. Vesp.* 7.2. Tacitus and Dio tell a similar story (*Histories* 8.81; Dio 65.8).

in the Gospel of Mark and ascribed it to Vespasian or Mark had heard of the act of Vespasian and ascribed it to Jesus. This subject is explored exhaustively by Eve in his article, "Spit in Your Eye: The Blind Man of Bethsaida and the Blind Man of Alexandria." Eve argues that the story of Vespasian healing a blind man would have been well known in Palestine in 70 CE and that it seems more than likely that Mark deliberately shaped the Blind Man of Bethsaida with the Blind Man of Alexandria in mind. Surely the healing miracle wrought by Vespasian influenced the writers of the Gospels and the healing miracle attributed to Jesus by Mark was redacted from a story about Vespasian.

Domitian: Three of his Titles

Domitian, the third of the Flavians, was unlike his father and brother in that he (like Claudius) had no military triumphs attached to his name. Perhaps for that reason, he seems to have been more concerned than his two predecessors with titles pertaining to his name. After the manner of Hellenistic kings, Domitian was referred to as *dominus* (English—master or lord) as well as receiving the titles savior and benefactor.[65]

According to Matthew and Mark, Jesus said to his disciples: "You know that among the Gentiles the recognised rulers lord it over their subjects, and their great ones make their authority felt." But Luke has Jesus say: "the kings of the Gentiles lord it over them and those in authority over them are called benefactors; not so with you."[66] Benefactor was not to be an appellation of Jesus. On the other hand savior is specifically used of Jesus in Acts 5.31, where God exalts Jesus at his right hand as leader and savior and the word is referred to by Luke in his birth narrative, when the angel says to the shepherds: "Today there has been born to you in the city of David a deliverer (savior)—the Messiah, the Lord."[67]

The three appellations, lord, savior and benefactor, appear in Luke and Acts and though lord is commonly used of Jesus by other writers in the New Testament, savior is not. Since Luke and Acts were almost certainly written when Domitian was emperor, a case for the writer being influenced by the names of Domitian must be plausible. But a far more significant passage must be analyzed.

---

65. Scott, *Imperial Cult*, 20, 97. In his *"Marks Incipit,"* Evans points out that in the Priene Inscription Augustus is referred to as savior and benefactor. (See Appendix 3).

66. Matt 20:25; Mark 10:42; Luke 22:25–26.

67. Luke 2:11.

Especially in the East, Domitian was celebrated as a god (*theos*). This led to the most extravagant of his autocratic titles. According to Dio, Domitian took most pride in being called "master" and "god." This appellation was not used merely in speech but also in written documents.[68] According to Suetonius: "he (Domitian) began issuing a circular letter in the name of his procurators, 'Our Master and our God (*deus*) bids that this be done.' And so the custom arose henceforth of addressing him in no other way, even in writing and conversation." Dominus may have meant nothing more than sir without any connotation of autocratic mastery, even though Augustus had rejected the use of such a title. But the use of the title god (*deus* rather than *divus*) created a precedent. As Jones says, the best an emperor could expect after death (up to then) was to be declared a *divus*, never a *deus*. . .[69] Domitian was clearly moving the goal posts.

Dominus can be a translated as "despot" but also as "lord" and there is every reason to suppose that Domitian was referred to as lord and god, a title that was to have far reaching consequences. For, in the Gospel of John, Thomas was absent from the locked room in which Jesus appears to his disciples and refuses to believe their statement: "We have seen the Lord."[70] "But when Jesus reappears a week later, Thomas acknowledges him with the words "My Lord and my God!"[71] Not only is this is the only time that Jesus is acknowledged as God in the New Testament by another person, it was probably written about 90 CE, when Domitian was emperor (see Chapter 4).

I am convinced that these are not coincidences; Luke and John are deliberately using the titles of the emperor Domitian as appellations of Jesus. Jesus is called savior because Domitian was called savior while, for reasons that cannot be established, he is said to have asked not to be called benefactor. Thomas is reported as using the special title of Domitian as an appellation of Jesus at a climactic moment of John's Gospel. There must be a correlation; Jesus *was* addressed with imperial titles. And if it is true of these titles, must it not also be true of the title "Son of God"?

It should be remarked that the title son of a god was not just used of Domitian because Vespasian had been deified. According to Philostratus, a magistrate was imprisoned at Tarentum because he had not added in the public prayers, when sacrificing, that Domitian was the son of Minerva.[72] The emperor had a predilection for Minerva whom he honored above most

68. Dio 67.7.7.
69. Jones, *Domitian*, 108.
70. John 20:25.
71. John 20:38.
72. *Vita Apoll.* 7.24.

of the gods. Her image appeared on coins struck during his reign and he had a *sacrarium* for her in his bedroom.[73] He seems to have believed he was indeed the son of the goddess Minerva and saw himself as the son of an Olympian. To Domitian, to be a son of god was not a reference to the deification of Vespasian nor yet an inherited appellation of Augustus; it was to be the actual son of a deity.

CONCLUSION

Three important points emerge from this chapter.

First, the title "son of the deified" was applied to the Augustus for the simple and straightforward reason that his adoptive father became the deified Julius Caesar. Son of the deified was subsequently used by his successors. The Greek rendering of the title was *uios theou* and hence, in the Greek speaking world, there was no difference between Son of the Deified and Son of God. The response of Pilate to the Jews[74] seems to make the point that to claim to be a son of God is usurping a title reserved for the emperor.

The frequent use of *divi filius* as an appellation of the emperor stands in contrast to the description of Alexander's son of Ammon. As seen in Chapter 2, there was considerable doubt as to how widespread was the use of this title for Alexander, because the extant primary sources that deal with the title were written three hundred years after the event. This was not so with Augustus and "Son of the Deified." Coins struck during his reign, together with an overwhelming number of biographical works assure the reader that Augustus was certainly *divi filius* and this chapter has shown that the title was conferred upon his successors. Jesus of Nazareth taught in a world where an emperor was described as a son of god.

Secondly, Augustus was a figure who could be portrayed as being possessed of such excellence that he dignified the title he received. In people's minds he was an individual worthy to be addressed as son of god. Though he refused to be actually deified in his life-time, many people believed him to be a living god before he died. The idea of a living human being a god became part of the culture of the Roman empire.[75]

Thirdly, it is clear that there was a deliberate use by Luke and John of imperial titles for Jesus of Nazareth. Thomas affirmation of Jesus in terms which Domitian specifically used for himself is unequivocal. The idea of Christ as king in chapter twenty-five of Matthew's Gospel probably derives

73. Scott, *Imperial Cult*, 167–181; Southern, *Domitian*, 121.

74. John 19:4–19.

75. Sweet, *Emperor Worship*, 69–70.

from the position of the Roman emperor. The vision of heaven in the twenty-first chapter of Revelation surely owes its imagery to the imperial court.

7

The Argument

Chapter 1 established that the kings of ancient Persia were not divine and hence the title Son of God was not an appellation of the Great King; that the kings of Egypt were considered to be sons of the god Ra and that in Ancient Greek mythology there were sons of various gods but only some were the kings. The difference between Greek and Egyptian use of Son of God is marked. Heracles is *begotten* of Zeus while the coronation of a person as Pharaoh made him a son of Ra by *adoption*.

SMALL EVIDENCE FOR THE TITLE SON OF GOD IN THE WRITINGS OF THE JEWS

Chapter 3 was devoted to examining the use of the title Son of God in canonical and non-canonical Jewish writings up to 100 CE. Though the chapter agreed with Fitzmyer that the title "Son of God" was not completely alien to Palestinian Judaism, it concluded with the following summary: "Jesus of Nazareth was known to posterity as the only begotten Son of God, and this was perhaps his most enduring and significant title. So important was this title that the Church was to split over its usage during the fourth century in the Arian controversy. There are surely not enough references of the title Son of God in Jewish literature to account for such a significant use of this appellation or to constitute a point of origin or departure for such use."

If the title Son of God as applied to Jesus did not come from the Jewish Scriptures, it must have come from elsewhere and I have argued that it came from Greece. However, Chapter 2 pointed out that the use of the title Son of

God underwent a change after the days of Homer and a main cause of this change was Alexander the Great.

As shown in Chapter 2, Alexander was a Macedonian who enjoyed the benefit of a Greek education. He was brought up on the works of Homer and had, in Aristotle, the personal tutelage of one of the greatest philosophers of all time. He believed, probably as a result of his mother's influence, that he was descended from the gods, Heracles being among his putative antecedents. He was therefore very susceptible to the idea of becoming a son of one of the gods.

His remarkable military campaign against Persia as head of an army comprised of Greeks and Macedonians resulted in his conquest of Egypt in 332 BCE where he was made Pharaoh and hailed as son of Ra. He then made his historic visit to the oracle at Siwa where he was almost certainly greeted by the religious leader of those at Siwa as son of Ammon, the Egyptian title for the god the Greeks knew as Zeus.[1] He was to hold to the title son of Ammon for the rest of his life and the idea that he was a son of a god was to prove the major force behind the remainder of his remarkable career. The shadow his personality cast over the world was immense and in the first century CE there was clearly a strand of Judaism that greatly admired him.[2]

But, as Appendix 1 points out, this shadow was not just to do with historical events; a huge number of mythical tales were told about him and they were embodied in what is called the *Romance*. According to Stoneman: "In the *Alexander Romance* the historical Alexander is almost entirely overlaid by another Alexander, a protean character who is able to embody some of the deepest fears and longings of the human condition."[3] He goes on: "It would hardly be an exaggeration to say that the legends of Alexander are as widely disseminated, and as influential on art and literature, as the Gospels."[4]

Alexander's legendary persona was something that no citizen of the Western World of the first century CE could have ignored and one with which every aspiring great man must expect comparison. The historical Alexander may have been Alexander the Great; the legendary Alexander was Alexander the Fabulous. The affect he was to have on the title Son of God proved enormous.

---

1. This matter is discussed exhaustively in Chapter 2.
2. *Ant.* 11.4.321–39.
3. Stoneman, *Romance*, 2.
4. From the Introduction of Stoneman, *Alexander Romance*, 2.

Alexander as a Primary Model for all to be called Son of God

Alexander was responsible for many ideas, concepts and examples but three are especially pertinent to this book.

First, he ensured that the title Son of God could be applied to a historical person as well as a mythical one. Theseus, Perseus and Heracles were mythical characters, described and discussed as such in the writings of Homer, Plutarch and Herodotus, but it is doubtful whether they were truly historical figures. The historicity of Alexander on the other hand cannot be doubted; his life and times are described and discussed at length by such historians as Diodorus Siculus, Curtius and Arrian.

Secondly, he conflated the Egyptian idea of Son of God with that of the Greeks and confirmed the title as spiritual as well as institutional. Having obtained control of a very willing Egypt by force of arms, Alexander was made Pharaoh at a temple on the Nile. This ceremony caused him to become a son of Ra (the Egyptian sun god) and so be regarded by the Egyptians as semi-divine. His subsequent visit to Siwa was as a pilgrim and supplicant to the shrine of Ammon, where he was welcomed as son of Zeus-Ammon. An intensely religious man, this was to be the supreme spiritual moment of his life and was to dominate him thereafter. His enthronement at Thebes and his affirmation at Siwa united the two strands of sonship of a god, and offered a prototype for Jesus of Nazareth and for the subsequent divinity of Roman emperors.[5]

Thirdly, his affirmation as a son of god is described by a number of historians who were not part of an Alexander Cult. Alexander's visit to Siwa and his acceptance as a son of Ammon are far better documented than, say, Julius Caesar's much quoted remark: "Veni, Vidi, Vici." Chapter 2 listed his five biographers, Diodorus Siculus, Trogus, Curtius, Plutarch and Arrian, and discussed the twenty sources written by contemporaries of Alexander. It was pointed out that though all five biographers were writers of renown, not one of them belonged to a cult of Alexander and that they gave a warts and all picture of their Macedonian subject. Four of them described Alexander's epiphany at Siwa as a factual occurrence. It is therefore difficult to believe that a person writing about someone proclaimed as Son of God in the Middle East during the first century CE could have avoided comparison of their subject with Alexander the Great.

5. See ch. 2.

Jewish opinion of Alexander

But would this have been true of the Jews? There is clear evidence that Jewish opinion on Alexander was divided. There are a number of hostile references to Alexander in the Book of Daniel. He is described as "a he goat. . . skimming over the whole earth without touching the ground";[6] as "a king of a country strong as iron which will shatter and crush all others";[7] and, less flatteringly, "as a beast, fearsome and grisly and exceedingly strong, with great iron teeth."[8] The First Book of Maccabees describes him as "one who traversed the earth to its remotest bounds and plundered countless nations and whose pride knew no limit."[9] It is clear that there were many Jews who regarded Alexander with disfavor.

On the other hand, there is convincing evidence that a section of Jewish society regarded Alexander with adulation, though how large this section was is impossible to estimate. Josephus recounts a striking anecdote about Alexander's supposed visit to Jerusalem in 332 BCE.[10] He tells of how the Jewish Chief Priest denied Alexander's request for troops to help in his conquest of Persia and how Alexander responded by leading his troops in warlike array towards Jerusalem. Advised in a vision, the Chief Priest took the entire temple staff, fully vested, out of Jerusalem to meet him, a gesture that so impressed Alexander that he formally saluted the Chief Priest. Then, surrounded by this entourage, Alexander *entered the temple and sacrificed* (the only known occasion for a gentile to have been said to have done so). When the Chief Priest asked that the Jews be absolved from tribute every seven years, Alexander granted all they desired: and when they entreated him that he would permit the Jews in Babylon and Media to enjoy their own laws also, he willingly promised to do hereafter what they desired, a tale expanded in rabbinic literature, notably in *The Book of the Gests of Alexander of Macedon (1962)*. While there are many who doubt the truth of this account, the story cannot but indicate that a section of first century Jewish society regarded Alexander as a figure of great goodness and importance. The writers of the New Testament could well have been part of this section.

6. Dan 8:5, 21.

7. Dan 2:40.

8. Dan 7:8; Barr, *Daniel,* 597.

9. 1 Macc 1:3.

10. *Ant.* 11.8.329–39.

The Roman Emperors as Sons of a God

Chapter 6 tells the story of how Julius Caesar was murdered by members of the Roman senate in 44 BCE and how he was afterwards deified. It also describes how his adopted son Octavianus (the later Augustus) was known as son of the deified (Latin—*divi*) and that, though there was probably a distinction in Latin between *deus* and *divus*, this distinction did not exist in Greek. *Divi filius* (son of the deified) and *dei filius* (son of god) were both rendered as *uios theou* (son of god) in the eastern half of the Roman empire.

The chapter goes on to make two further important points. The first is that the title *divi filius* originally signified nothing more than that Augustus was the son of a man who had been deified, but his conduct during his reign was such that he transformed it into a title of immense and excellent significance. The second was that *divi filius* became the appellation of all future Roman emperors up to the time of Constantine. During the whole century that saw the birth of Christianity, there was a Roman emperor who was known as a son of God. This must surely have had a huge effect on the title Son of God as applied to Jesus, a point that will be examined later in this Chapter.

Jesus as Son of God in the New Testament

The Introduction to this book set out the thesis that devotees of Jesus referred to him initially as the Messiah, but that, as their movement spread to Greece, Jesus began to be referred to as the Son of God. This idea was expanded in Chapter 4, where it was established that very little is actually known of the life of Jesus, but that some who were his followers in life became his followers in death, speaking in the Jewish temple and synagogues of the significance of Jesus to the whole Jewish movement. Chapter 4 also followed the career of Paul and showed how he referred to Jesus as Son of God from the fifth/sixth decade of the first century CE, most significantly in the letter to the Romans.

The remainder of Chapter 4 was devoted to examining the effect that this title had on the Christian movement. It examined the way the Epistle to the Hebrews attempted to reconcile the title Son of God with the Hebrew Scriptures and how it sought to demonstrate the superiority of Jesus over such figures as Moses and Melchizedek. It looked at the apocalyptic use made of the title in the Revelation of St. John the Divine and how the appellation developed into something of near creedal significance in the Epistles of John. But it was shown how it was in the writing of the Gospels that the title assumed its most important use. It was argued that if Jesus was widely referred to as Son of God in the later decades of the first century CE, people who were to read the story of his life naturally expected to learn how he was so acclaimed and how he presented himself as such during his life. And if that life was lost to history, stories of Jesus as Son of God had to be created or borrowed from some other source to handle the absence.

THE GOSPEL NARRATIVES

The Gospels are not histories; this point of view has been argued in Chapter 4. The opinion was expressed that the Jesus Seminar provided an excellent summary of a liberal understanding of the gospel narratives when it began with the assumption that the Gospels are not accurate histories but are narratives constructed out of literary art and theological motives.[11] Knowledge of the Jesus of history is limited but exists. Morton Smith has suggested that the external framework of Jesus life—the what, when and where—is reasonably certain.[12] Harvey states the following facts as beyond reasonable doubt: "That Jesus was known in both Galilee and Jerusalem; that he was a teacher; that he carried out cures of various illnesses, particular demon possession, and that these were widely regarded as miraculous; that he was involved with fellow Jews over questions of the law of Moses; and that he was crucified in the governorship of Pontius Pilate."[13]

Sanders provides an even longer series of postulations, creating what he believes is the bedrock of belief in the history of Jesus.[14] He adds to Harvey's list by saying that Jesus was baptized by John the Baptist, had a group of disciples and, of crucial importance, after his death Jesus' followers continued as an identifiable movement.

I find this understanding of the gospels convincing and argue that they have provided a brief outline of a historical figure, amplified by a variety of stories told about him. Where these stories came from, how they were arranged and how applied depended upon the motivations of the writers. So it is necessary to look at the stories themselves.

11. Johnson, *The Real Jesus*, 4.

12. Smith, *Magician*, 17.

13. Harvey, *Constraints*, 6.

14. Sanders, *Jesus and Judaism*, 11.

STORIES ABOUT JESUS OF NAZARETH

I suggest that the stories told about Jesus in the gospel narratives are of five types.

First are those based on real incidents in the life of Jesus and recalled by those present. An example is the lowering of the paralytic through the roof of a house.[15] This story has all the hallmarks of an incident that originated from the group that knew Jesus and were present when it happened. It is at once a likely occurrence but without the great significance that would cause it to have been invented. The purpose in telling the story is to reveal the power of Jesus to forgive sins.

Second are those that are probably based on real incidents in the life of Jesus, but ones that have been seriously altered, both in scale and in detail. An example of this is the story of the Gadarene swine.[16] There is no reason to doubt that an incident occurred in which a berserk man was exorcised and some pigs, panicked by his cries, rushed into the water and drowned. That there is dispute as to the place (Matthew generally reads Gadarenes; Mark and Luke generally read Gerasenes) and whether there were one demoniac or two can surely be put down to a variant of oral tradition but the sheer scale of Mark's story (the whole herd is said to have numbered about 2000), the recognition of Jesus as son of god by the demons and their subsequent request to be allowed to transfer to the swine are serious variations. According to Ellis, the story is told both to demonstrate the power of Messianic redemption and to show that Gentiles, like the Jews, reject it.[17] To emphasize the tale, the size of the herd of pigs must assume preposterous proportions.

The third type are those from Jewish sources and applied to Jesus. An excellent example is the story of the Rich Man and Lazarus.[18] This has many hallmarks of a Jewish story and ill accords with the normal Christian motif in which redemption is the result of faith. The rich man's only crime is to have wealth, repentance is not possible and the rabbinic belief that heaven is in sight of Hades is a significant part of the story. The idea of a dead soul being carried by angels probably comes from a Targum as does the concept of Abraham's bosom.[19] It seems likely though it is speculation to suppose that Luke includes the story because of its last clause: "If they do

15. Mark 2:1–5; Luke 5:17–20.
16. Matt 8:28–34; Mark 5:1–13; Luke 8:26–36.
17. Ellis, *Luke,* 130.
18. Luke 16:19–31.
19. Plummer, *Luke,* 393–94.

not listen to Moses and the prophets they will pay no heed even if someone should rise from the dead."

A fourth type is concerned with stories that are derived from pagan sources and applied to Jesus. An example of this type is the story of the turning of the water into wine. Originally a mythical tale about Dionysus,[20] this story is altered to involve Jesus and become the first miracle that he performed. As Lincoln puts it: "The Dionysian stories were known in Palestine and the acts of Dionysius were emulated by rulers (including Alexander the Great) to demonstrate their power over life. Martial in his Epigrams describes Domitian as surpassing Bacchus."[21] Lincoln concludes: "Whether there is any incident in the life of Jesus which gave rise to this story is exceedingly hard to know."

Finally there are stories without any historical background that are created by the author. An example must surely be the famous remark of the Roman centurion: "This man must have been a son of God." As discussed in the Preamble, this cannot have been a historical incident but one invented by Mark to make his point that Jesus is recognised as Son of God by a bastion of Roman society.[22]

It follows that, unless a story may be held to be of the first type, a highly significant quantity of material has been inserted into the narrative tale of Jesus, giving adequate opportunity for stories of Alexander or Augustus, among others, to affect the perception of the man of Nazareth as Son of God. One way this could be brought to bear was by attribution.

Attribution

In 1951 I heard the Conservative M.P., R. A. Butler, quoting Winston Churchill's speech demonstrating the incompetence of the then Labor Government. "We are an island made of coal, surrounded by a sea full of fish," the great man had (apparently) said to the House of Commons, "O genius of a bureaucracy that can create a shortage of both at the same time!" And yet ten years later I heard the ex Labor MP, Ian Mikardo, attribute the identical words to Aneurin Bevan, who had also (apparently) used them in an address to Parliament! Where Butler and Mikardo had heard the comment we shall probably never know but they had attributed it to their hero. Good stories are often attributed to great people! (An example of this has already been seen in Chapter 2.)

20. John 2:1–13; Marsh, *John*, 149; Lincoln, *John*, 132–34.
21. Martial *Epigrams* 4, 8.26.
22. Hooker, *Mark*, 378.

But the anecdote makes a deeper point. Both Butler and Mikardo could have made the witticism themselves. But they chose instead to attribute it to a noted orator who was much admired in their political party. The attribution had a dual effect; the enhancement of Churchill or Bevan as a wit and an increase of the impact of the story itself. An example of the latter point is seen when Augustus was asked, after he had seen the sarcophagus of Alexander, if he also wished to see the tomb of the Ptolemys. He remarked acidly: "My wish was to see a king, not corpses!"[23] This comment is remembered, not just because it is remarkable in itself, but because Augustus made it and so it enhances both Alexander and Augustus in the eyes of those who read it. Not only does a famous person attract good stories, but a good story, put into the mouth of a great person, enhances both person and story. Some accounts of Jesus were clearly modeled on other people.

This can easily be overdone. The story of the water into wine at Cana-in-Galilee was almost certainly a Dionysian myth which was modified to be placed in the Gospel of John and commentaries expand on the possibilities. Some writers, however, see more far reaching influences at work and produce over-extended models that are difficult to defend.

For example, in his "The Homeric Epics and the Gospel of Mark," D. R. MacDonald explores the concept that Homer's *Odyssey* provided a paradigm for the second evangelist. "In this book," he wrote on page 3, "I argue that the key to Mark's composition has less to do with its genre than with its imitation of specific texts of a different genre: Mark *wrote a prose epic* (my italics) modeled largely after the *Odyssey* and the ending of the *Iliad.*" MacDonald's idea is stimulating and interesting, but, in my view, is robbed of most of its value by overuse. To quote one of many examples, he parallels the preparations for the Last Supper with preparations for the cannibalistic Feast of the Laestrygonians![24] An interesting argument is largely destroyed by what many may consider to be bizarre overuse.

The Portrayal of Jesus

So the Jesus portrayed in the gospels is a composite figure, comprised of the framework of a real person and embellished with stories surrounding him. Some of these stories are based on genuine reminiscences about Jesus himself while many are taken from tales of other people and, suitably altered, applied to Jesus. The reported teachings of Jesus are similar. Some are

23. *Div. Aug.* 18; Dio 51:47.

24. Mark 13:14–16; *Odys.* 10.100–116; MacDonald "The Homeric Epics and the Gospel of Mark," 12.

almost certainly based upon memories of those actually delivered by Jesus while others equally certainly were taken from teachings of other people, altered and put into the mouth of Jesus. Since the use of the appellation Son of God belongs to these stories, attention must be paid to the background, style and content of passages where it occurs. My thesis is that many incidents and teachings surrounding the question of Jesus being the Son of God were modelled on those of Alexander the Great and the early Roman emperors, or were directly influenced by them. Their qualifications for this role are set out earlier in this chapter.

DIRECT INFLUENCES OF ALEXANDER THE GREAT ON THE LEGEND OF JESUS OF NAZARETH

The Concept of Declaring an Individual to be a Son of God

The Homeric sons of the gods were conceived by action of their divine fathers and stories about their begetting were told about them from the time of their childhood. Alexander was brought up to believe that he was descended from at least two of these demi-gods, but there is no evidence at all that when he invaded Persia in 334 BCE he had any idea that he was such a one. It was in Egypt that his perception changed, for the Pharaohs became sons of Ra on their coronation and it was his becoming Pharaoh that caused Alexander to believe that he might actually be a son of a god. So he journeyed to the temple of Siwa to ask for divine guidance on this point. What happened there is described in detail by all his early biographers and four declare that the chief priest of the oracle of Ammon (the one who held the position of prophet) announced that Alexander was the son of Ammon and further that Philip was not his actual father.

This well attested incident in the life of Alexander the Great is of immense significance. A human being is declared to be a son of a god, partly by accident of birth but largely as the result of a meritorious career. It is clear from the construction of the history of Alexander that he saw in this event that a god looked with such favor on him that he declared him to be his son. For the rest of his life, Alexander believed himself to be, and was believed by others to be, son of Ammon-Zeus. The precedent was set. *A historical human being could become a Son of God.*

Not just that, but Alexander learned that he was a son of a god as the result of a spiritual experience. A contrast between Alexander's apotheosis as a son of a god and his becoming a god is instructive. In the latter case, Alexander followed examples set by Lysander and Philip and in 324 demanded that the Greeks recognize him as an "invincible god."[25] This demand was received with a measure of sarcasm by the Greeks, though it was subsequently accepted by various political assemblies. At Siwa the prophet of a much-lauded oracle pronounced Alexander to be a son of Ammon. *Such an event was without parallel in the history of the western world until Jesus stood on the banks of the Jordan 350 years later.*

ALEXANDER AT SIWA

I submit that the way that the gospel narratives describe the declaration of Jesus as Son of God was modeled on Alexander's visit to Siwa three and a half centuries earlier. For Alexander is described as going into the desert to consider his origin and his mission; he going to a place on the edge of the desert where there is water (the oasis of Siwa) and where he is greeted by a prophet who hails him (on behalf of the god) as son of Ammon. Jesus goes to the edge of the desert to where there is water (the Jordan), where he is greeted by a prophet, John the Baptist, and where he is (apparently) hailed by a voice from heaven as "Son of God" (Chapter 4).

This asks two questions; was John really known as a prophet and was there really a voice from heaven? Firstly, though mainly known as the man who baptized Jesus[26] and who was beheaded for objecting to Herod the Tetrarch's marital arrangements[27], John is indeed referred to as a prophet.[28] Secondly, in the Pilate Cycle from the New Testament Apocrypha and Pseudepigrapha, John the Baptist describes himself as personally hearing the voice of God the Father speaking thus, "This is my beloved Son, in whom I am well pleased."[29] Though the Pilate Cycle comes from the fifth century CE, it incorporates early tradition and indicates that it was John, rather than a voice from heaven, who actually declared Jesus to be Son of God. So the story of Alexander at Siwa does indeed provide a complete paradigm for the story of Jesus on the banks of the Jordan.

It may be remarked that the words "this is my beloved son" do not only appear in the story of the baptism of Jesus; they appear in almost identical form in the story of the Transfiguration.[30] In this story, Peter, James and John go with Jesus up a mountain, they are covered by a cloud, the voice

---

25. Mosse, *Alexander*, 83.

26. Matt 3:3–17; Mark 1:2–11; Luke 3:2–22; John 1:19–34.

27. Matt 14:1–12; Mark 6:17–29; *Ant.* 18.5.2.116–9.

28. Mark 11:32 and parallels

29. *Des. Inf.* 2 [18] 2; Elliott, *The Apocryphal Jesus*, 165.

30 Matt 17:1–8; Mark 9:2–8; Luke 9:28–36.

from heaven declares Jesus to be the beloved Son (of God) and Jesus is seen talking with Moses and Elijah, his face shining with a holy light.

A paradigm for this account is found in the Book of Exodus. Moses goes up the Mountain of God; he is covered by a cloud; God speaks to him and his face shines with a holy light. It may be further noted that Elijah also goes up the same mountain and he also speaks with God who gives him a solemn commission.[31] *But to neither Moses nor Elijah does God infer that they are to be a son of God.* Though the mountain provides an excellent setting for a divine pronouncement, there is no epiphany for Moses or Elijah. It is only the story of Alexander at Siwa that offers the perfect paradigm for the epiphany of Jesus of Nazareth at the river Jordan.

A Paradigm for One of the Temptations

Diodorus recounts that when Alexander visited the shrine of Ammon at Siwa, the one who held the position of prophet, an elderly man, came to him and said, "Rejoice, son, take this form of address as from the god also." He (Alexander) replied, "I accept, father, for the future I shall be called thy son. But tell me if thou givest (Greek root—*didomi*) me the rule of the whole earth."[32]

Curtius tells the same story though with a different perspective: "Alexander was addressed as 'son' by the oldest of the priests, who claimed that this title was bestowed on him by his father Jupiter. Forgetting his mortal state, Alexander said he accepted and acknowledged the title, and he proceeded to ask whether he was fated to rule over the entire world. The priest, who was as ready as anyone else to flatter him, answered that he was going to rule over the whole earth."[33]

Reference is not made to world dominion by Trogus or Plutarch but Arrian does say that Alexander put his question to the oracle and received the answer that his heart desired.[34] All biographers agree that after his encounter with the prophet-priest, Alexander went out into the desert.[35]

According to Mark, after Jesus was acclaimed as God's beloved son, the Spirit drove him out into the wilderness [desert], and there he remained for forty days tempted by Satan.[36] It is left to Matthew and Luke to describe the

31. Exod 19:3, 9; 33:7–11; 1 Kgs 19:11–18.
32. Diod. 50.51.
33. Curtius, 4.7.25–26.
34. Arrian, 3.4
35. He had, in reality, nowhere else to go!
36. Mark 1:12–13.

temptations and they demonstrate that one of the temptations is significantly different from the other two. The first temptation in both gospels refers to turning stones into bread: "If you are the Son of God, tell these stones to become bread," suggests the tempter.[37] The second temptation in Matthew and the third in Luke concerns the suggestion that Jesus demonstrates his dependence on the power of God by hurling himself from the pinnacle of the temple: "If you are the Son of God," says the tempter, "throw yourself down (for) He will put his angels in charge of you, and they will support you in their arms, for fear you should strike your foot against a stone."[38] Both temptations begin with the words "If you are the Son of God. . ." and, as I have shown in Chapter 4; it is probable that each refers to a historical figure. Moses (in the desert) did feed the Israelites,[39] Elijah did fly through the air[40] and both performed great miracles. The two temptations seem to be that, if Jesus is the Son of God he can be Moses or he can be Elijah. Jesus is shown as rejecting both for a higher calling.

But the third temptation in Matthew (and the second in Luke) is different from the other two in that *there is no repetition of the words "if you are the Son of God."* The devil shows Jesus all the kingdoms of the world and says: "All these will I give you if you fall down and do me homage."[41] Now Diodorus shows Alexander being given (Gk. *didomi*) rule over all the kingdoms of the earth; Matthew shows Jesus declining the gift of the kingdoms because he will not worship Satan who is able to give (Gk. *didomi*) them to him. It is surely the case that Jesus is represented as treading in the footsteps of Alexander, though making a different and a better choice. Diodorus and Curtius describe Alexander's immediate response to receiving the title of son of Ammon—Zeus by asking if he was to achieve dominion of the kingdoms of the world. Matthew and Luke show Jesus being offered the same dominion but refusing and choosing a wiser path by serving God alone. Surely this shows that events at Siwa significantly influenced the portrayal of the life of Jesus as told by Matthew and Luke.

37. Matt 4:3; Luke 4:3.
38. Matt 4:6; Luke 4:9.
39. Exod 16.
40. I Kgs 18:12.
41. Matt 4:8–9, see also Luke 4:6–7.

Birth Stories: the Influence of Stories of Alexander's Birth

In their *Documents for the Study of the Gospels*,[42] Cartlidge and Dungan list Plato, Alexander, Augustus, Pythagoras and Heracles, along with Jesus of Nazareth, as having births involving some form of divine intervention. Setting aside Heracles who is a mythical character, Pythagoras (d. 497 BCE) is described as being sent down among men from the realm of Apollo; Plato (429—347 BCE) is described as being born without sex and Augustus is said to have been born after his mother had contact with a snake.[43] Though all these characters were born before Jesus of Nazareth, the stories of their births were written after the Gospels. The description of the birth of Pythagoras belongs to the writings of Iamblichus in fourth century CE, that of Plato to the writings of Diogenes Laertius in the third century CE and that of Augustus to the writings of Suetonius in the second century CE. However, Alexander's birth is described by Trogus, who tells of Olympias who bore in her womb [what] was certainly more than mortal[44] and by various passages in the *Romance* that almost certainly come from the first century BCE or before. Stories of his divine birth were clearly circulating in Alexander's former empire by the beginning of the first century CE.

It has been remarked that the story of the birth of Augustus was partially modeled on those told of Alexander and it would seem obvious that if Jesus was being described as Son of God, similar stories would be told of him. Alexander's birth stories gave as much encouragement to the writers of Matthew and Luke to generate extravagant stories of the birth of Jesus as they did to those who wrote about the births of Pythagoras, Plato and Augustus. To take one example; Alexander's birth is preceded by a thunderbolt (Appendix 1), Octavius dreams that the sun rose from the womb of the mother of Augustus[45] and Matthew tells of Jesus birth being foretold by a star.[46] From the time of Alexander, the births of the very great were attended by heavenly portents and Jesus was but one of these.

42. Cartlidge and Dungan, *Documents*, 129–36.

43. *Div. Aug.* 97.4.

44. *Trogus* 12.16.2.

45. *Div. Aug.* 19.4.

46. Matt 2:1–11.

DIRECT INFLUENCE OF AUGUSTUS ON THE LEGEND OF JESUS OF NAZARETH

Birth Stories: the Influence of Stories of Augustus Birth

Chapter 6 showed that Augustus, too, may have seriously influenced the use of the title Son of God for he became a son of the deified (*filius divi*), not because of a mystical experience (as had Alexander), nor because the ruler of Rome was divine or semi divine (as were the Pharaohs), but for the prosaic reason that his adopted father (Julius Caesar) had been deified. But so excellent were his life and career (or so well were these promoted!) that the title son of the deified ceased to be a factual description and became a title of honor and one to be received with adulation. So stories of a miraculous birth began to circulate, as described earlier in this chapter. Almost certainly such stories mirrored those told of Alexander, but equally certainly they were circulating in Palestine as the gospels were written. This must have had an effect on the birth stories of Jesus.

The Anarthrous uios theou

Appendix 3 fully rehearses the argument by Kim in his "The Anarthrous *uios theou* in Mark 15.39 and the Roman Imperial Cult" and only a brief summary is necessary here. Kim argues that *uios theou* without the definite articles is used only twice in Mark (1.1 and 15.39) and that all other references to Jesus as Son of God are rendered *ho uios tou theou* while Augustus was known from the beginning of his political career as *divi filius*, "son of god," which in Greek is written as *uios theou* or *theou uios* without the definite article. This, it seems, was a favorite title of Augustus. In brief, Kim and Bligh argue that Mark was deliberately using an imperial title as an appellation of Jesus in his opening and in the climactic utterance of the Centurion at the Cross.[47]

I find this part of their argument compelling (though not the rest of their thesis). To omit the definite article from *uios theou* at these two most important moments of his story must suggest that Mark was not just being careless. If he deliberately chose the anarthrous *uios theou* it must have been because he wished to dignify Jesus with imperial associations.

47. Bligh, *Note*, 53.

The Priene Calendar Inscription

It is C. A. Evans thesis[48] that the opening of Mark's Gospel bears comparison with the Priene Calendar Inscription. This was written in 9 BCE and in it Augustus is referred to as both savior and god, the description of his arrival on the Roman scene is referred to as his appearance and his birthday announce as revelation. Such language is redolent of the way the evangelists spoke about Jesus. Savior is specifically used of Jesus in Acts 5.31 and Jesus is referred to as "god" twice in the gospels.[49] It seems clear that the Priene inscription must have had some affect on the way the gospels provided titles for Jesus.

My Lord and My God

There can be little doubt that the recognition of the risen Jesus by Thomas, My Lord and my God, is a deliberate ascription to Jesus of Domitian's self designation, *Dominus et deus noster.*[50] This is a clear indication, if one is needed, that titles, given to Jesus by his gospellers, were taken from the imperial vocabulary. As already pointed out, Domitian seems to have believed he was the son of a divinity, not because his natural father was deified but because he held that his real parent was the goddess, Minerva.

INDIRECT INFLUENCES OF ALEXANDER THE GREAT ON THE LEGEND OF JESUS OF NAZARETH

In addition to the influences described above, there are other less definable affects that the story of Alexander had on the legend of Jesus. Alexander set the precedent for a historically attested human being who is accepted as a Son of God becoming a God; he believed in, and proved that he believed in, the brotherhood of man and so opened the way for Christian universalism and it may well be that his death at the age of 32 was responsible for the belief that Jesus died at that age. Each must be examined in turn.

48. Evans, *Jesus.*

49. John 1:1; 20:28.

50. Dio 67.7.7.

Sons of God can become Gods

It has been pointed out in Chapter 2 that in 324 Alexander was officially deified, following Heracles by advancing in rank from son of a god to being an actual god; the first historically attested human being to do this. As Bosworth puts it, the precedent for the worship of a living man was firmly established.[51] Augustus was to walk the same path (Chapter 6), though his official deification was to wait until his death. It was in the last decade of the first century, years after Augustus deification, that Jesus was to be described as God and it is difficult to believe that the path towards this event had not been indicated, if not actually created, by Alexander.

All Men are Brothers

After Alexander had left Siwa, he is said by Plutarch to have encountered the Egyptian philosopher Psammon. Following the encounter, the King of Macedon apparently said: "God was the common father of all of us, but more particularly to the best of us."[52] Plutarch further quotes remarks of Eratosthenes that Alexander believed "that he came as a heaven-sent governor for all, and as a mediator for the whole world. . . and he brought together in one body all men everywhere, uniting and mixing in one great loving-cup."[53] These comments prompt Tarn to say: "on the face of it, (this) is a plain statement that all men are brothers, and, if true, is the earliest known (such statement), at least in the western world."[54]

Chapter 2 established that to make so great a claim on behalf of Alexander on the basis of a single source would be regarded as questionable, were it not for Alexander's subsequent actions. He appointed Persians as governors;[55] dressed in a way which was a compromise between the simple dress of a Macedonian field officer and the court robes of the Great King of Persia; he attempted (but failed) to introduce prostration as a compromise between Macedonian and Persian greeting of the king[56] and he recruited local troops to replace his worn out Macedonian veterans to form a Macedonian-Persian army.[57] He was someone who clearly did believe that

51. Bosworth, *Alexander*, 290.
52. Plutarch, 27.6.
53. *Moralia*, 329.6.
54. Tarn, *Alexander* 2, 435.
55. Arrian 3.16.9.
56. Arrian 22.12, 13.
57. Arrian 7.9–12; Diod 17.108.

all men are brothers and he set a standard with which all great men who followed him must compete. It is difficult to see how any social thinker in antiquity could have avoided the vision provided by Alexander.

Certainly it seems to have affected Paul. His visit to the Greek peninsular began in about 50 CE and it has been established that it was in Macedonia that his mission direct to the Gentiles began, surely a significant non-coincidence. His altercation with Cephas (Peter) described in the letter to the Galatians, which was written about 55 CE, makes Paul's position and his authority clear. He declares: "I had been sent to preach to those who are uncircumcised as Peter to those who are circumcised."[58] And when Peter would not eat with the uncircumcised, Paul admonished him in front of the whole congregation with the words: "If you, a Jew born and bred, live like a Gentile, and not like a Jew, how can you insist that Gentiles must live like Jews?" Surely this makes it plain that, by the middle of the sixth decade of the first century CE, a full scale mission to the Gentiles was in progress. Luke underlines this by the story in Chapters 10 and 11 of the Acts of the Apostles about Cornelius, which ends with the Church in Jerusalem giving praise to God and saying, "this means that God has granted life-giving repentance to the Gentiles also."[59] And although it is doubtful that the letter to the Colossians was written by Paul himself, the members of the Pauline school that wrote it insist on the universalist message of the gospel: "You have discarded the old human nature and the conduct that goes with it, and have put on the new nature which is constantly being renewed in the image of its Creator and brought to know God. There is no question here of Greek and Jew, circumcised or uncircumcised, barbarian, Scythian, slave and freedman; but Christ is all, and is in all."[60] For Paul, the mission of Christianity was to all and the brotherhood of man promoted by Alexander certainly found resonance with him.

Though the writers of the Gospels do not show Jesus as promoting such a mission, a great deal of Jesus reported teaching had universal application. This is particularly true of the so-called Sermon on the Mount (Mt. 5–7). For though there are certain specific references in this speech that are rendered more comprehensible by knowledge of Judaism, the application of the Sermon is for all people throughout time. Similarly, to understand the Parable of the Sower requires no knowledge of Judaism, anymore than does the parable on forgiveness. My submission is that though the Jesus of Nazareth may have confined himself to healing and teaching to the Jews,

58. Gal 2:7.
59. Acts 11:18.
60. Col 3:9–11.

Paul's ideas (derived from Alexander's philosophy) caused the evangelists to attribute Universalist teachings to Jesus.

The Age of Jesus at his Death: a Suggestion

There is only one definite statement in the Gospels as to Jesus' age. Luke declares: "When Jesus began his work, he was about thirty years old." This was "In the fifteenth year of the emperor Tiberius [i.e. 28 CE]."[61] A date of birth for Jesus of 2 BCE seems indicated. But Matthew tells his readers that Jesus was born in the days of Herod the Great (37—4 BCE)[62] which suggests a date of birth prior to 4 BCE. Elsewhere Luke says that Jesus was born during the census, "when Quirinius was governor of Syria."[63] Quirinius was in fact governor from 6 CE,[64] which suggests that Jesus date of birth was after 6 CE. So Jesus is variously said to have been born between 6 BCE and 6 CE.

Josephus says that the marriage of Herod Antipas and Herodias took place in 33/34 CE and therefore the death of John the Baptist must have happened after that date, while Josephus tells of Pontius Pilate being Prefect in Judea from 26—36.[65] Since Herod believed that Jesus was in fact John the Baptist raised from the dead[66] and since all witnesses agree that Jesus died in the time of Pontius Pilate, the date of the crucifixion of Jesus must have been in 34/35 CE. This would set the age of Jesus when he died somewhere between thirty and forty years of age. But John tells of an altercation between the Jews at Jerusalem and Jesus in which the former say "You are not yet fifty years old,"[67] suggesting that Jesus may well have lived well into his forties.

On the above evidence, Jesus might have been born somewhere between 4 BCE and 8 CE, and died in 35 CE, making him somewhere between 27 and 39 years old at the time of his death. Lane Fox speculates that Jesus died when he was around fifty years old. It is not unreasonable to ask why Luke made his clear statement about Jesus age at the start of his ministry and though this question cannot be answered, I can offer a suggestion. If Jesus began his ministry when he was thirty years of age and it lasted about two years, this would mean he died aged thirty-two. *This was the age at which Alexander died.* To suggest that Luke deliberately chose the age at

61. Luke 3.
62. Matt 2:1.
63. Luke 2:2.
64. *War* 2.7.1.
65. *Ant.* 18.5, 1–2; Lane Fox, *Unauthorised Version*, 33–34.
66. Mark 6:16.
67. John 8:57.

which he ascribed Jesus death as that of Alexander's may sound fanciful. But it must be noted that neither Matthew nor Mark give any idea of Jesus age at the time of his death and that it is extremely unlikely that Luke engaged in any research on the issue. And if Jesus' age had to be guessed at or estimated, I would argue that the age at which Alexander the Great died is as good a model as any.

SUMMARY

This book has proposed that the Jesus portrayed in the gospels is an artificial character constructed from tales from the actual life of Jesus of Nazareth, interspersed with stories from the lives other people. It has sought to prove that when Jesus is spoken of as Son of God these latter stories owe an enormous amount to histories of Alexander the Great and the early Roman Emperors. It insists that the development of the appellation Son of God as a major Christian title depends upon three people.

Alexander, Augustus and Jesus

Born in the middle of the fourth century BCE, Alexander transformed the world in which he lived by virtue of his powers of conquest. In 336 BCE, when Darius III ascended the throne of Persia, probably only a handful of Persians had ever heard of Macedon. Five years later, Alexander was himself Great King of Persia and was able to introduce his ideas of the brotherhood of man and a single world society on a grand scale. He had also been acclaimed son of Ammon at Siwa and became a god before he died.

Born in the first century BCE, Augustus managed to hold plenipotentiary power in the Roman empire for many years by his skills as a diplomat. His ordering of Rome during the long period of rule was so excellent that he was able to transform the empire into a place of comparative peace, order and stability after a long period of civil war and civil strife. Adopted son of the deified Julius Caesar, he transformed "Son of the Deified" into a title to be held by a very great human being.

Born at the turn of the first millennium, Jesus of Nazareth (of whom little is known) was almost certainly a wandering Jewish exorcist who died by crucifixion in the fourth decade of the first century CE. He left behind a world that hardly noticed his passing and a small circle of friends who believed in his supreme significance to their world. But the movement he had begun among the Jews prospered when he was declared to be the Messiah and it was transformed by Paul into a movement for Gentiles as well as for Jews and prospered still more when Jesus was declared to be the Son of God. Stories remembered, borrowed or created of the life of Jesus were transcribed by Matthew, Mark, Luke and John as word portraits of him. The title Son of God played a part in the way these stories were put together and led (as Chapter 5 demonstrated) to it becoming Jesus' most important appellation.

The theme behind this thesis is that the use of the title "Son of God," as the major appellation of Jesus of Nazareth, was chosen by Paul as a title to proclaim the significance of Jesus to the Greeks and Macedonians that he encountered in their home land. Son of God was a title drawn from the mythological past but it had also been applied to Alexander, so it was inevitable that his shadow would be felt upon any human being to whom it was ascribed, with results that are shown throughout this book. Further, as the character of Jesus took shape within the writings that became the Gospels, the fact that the emperor of Rome was also a son of God influenced that character. There is more of Alexander and Augustus in the Gospels than has hitherto been realized. It is clear that Jesus was by no means the first historical person to be acclaimed Son of God and that the title had been prepared for him by others.

FULL CIRCLE; FANTASY OR FACT

Diodorus Siculus begins his work on Alexander: "Alexander accomplished great things in a short space of time, and by his acumen and courage surpassed in the magnitude of his achievements all kings whose memory is recorded from the beginning of time."[68] He ends: "He accomplished greater deeds than any, not only of kings who had lived before him but also those who were to come later, down to our time."[69] He begins and concludes with his hero's *achievements*. Mark begins his Gospel: "The beginning of the good news of Jesus Christ, the Son of God" and (virtually) ends it with the words of a centurion "Truly this man was God's Son!" By contrast with Diodorus, he begins and ends with his hero's *status*.

But there is a human side. Much has been made in this book of the remark in Mark 15.39 of the Roman centurion. Throughout this book, this utterance has been accepted as a literary device; I am sure that there never was a centurion at the scene of the death of Jesus who made such a comment. But, although it was never recorded and had no influence on the story of Jesus, I like to think that the remark was a historic one and had been

68. Diod. 17.1.3.
69. Diod. 17, 117.5.

made 350 years before. As Alexander lay dying, his troops gave one last spontaneous example of their love for him. They broke down the doors that guarded his quarters and insisted on being allowed to see him for one last moment. They filed past Alexander as he lay on a bed, too ill to move, and Arrian tells of how, though unable to speak, "in his eyes was a look of recognition for each individual that passed."[70] What these sorrowing troops said is not recorded but it cannot be doubted that there were some who looked back at the dying king who had achieved so much and said "Truly this man was a son of a god."

70. Arrian 7.26.

Endpiece
Limitations

Three figures of enormous significance to the world have been discussed in
this book and have this in common, that they were described by many people who either knew them or knew of them as sons of god. But Alexander,
Augustus and Jesus were three very different people and led very different
lives. The former two commanded huge armies, conquered many nations,
made laws, punished, tortured and killed many people. They may have been
loved by many and, indeed, by most of their subjects; the world may have
been the better for their reigns; art, culture and ideas may have flourished
under them but they were, and their existence depended upon it, fearsome
dictators. Jesus of Nazareth was a wandering exorcist and healer, probably
a teacher, possibly a rebel. He inspired the start of a religious movement in
which words and actions ascribed to him are seen by a billion people to be
the actions of the one, true, eternal God. There is very little he has in common with Alexander and Augustus and no suggestion is made in this book
that he had. The primary proposal of this thesis is that the appellation Son of
God, which had been made of Alexander and Augustus was a magnificent
and honorable title, to be later bestowed on Jesus of Nazareth. The second
proposition is that aspects of the life and thinking of Alexander and some
of the names used of Augustus and his successors provided concepts on
which some of the legend of Jesus was constructed, not least the fact that
Alexander and Augustus were eventually declared gods, just before or just
after they died.

Another limitation is that whereas much has been written about Augustus and Alexander by historians, nothing similar has been written about
Jesus. Though the Gospel narratives have the appearance of being histories,
they have been shown to be nothing of the kind but are rather theological
constructs, into which are interwoven some actual reminiscences of the life
of Jesus. The Jesus of the Gospels cannot be a rounded character, for nothing

is known of the negative side of his character. This may be encouraging to people of faith, who hold that his divine sonship produces a sinless and perfect being but poses a problem for the student who seeks what is to be thought of as the man behind the myth. To a keen Christian, such a search may be seen as heretical and have the taint of blasphemy. I would reply that though it is probably heretical, it is in no way blasphemous. The elusive Galilean I have sought through study throughout my life and who is the source of inspiration for any small bit of good I may have done is indeed a son of God. Blasphemy exists in misusing the name of God, not in trying to understand him.

Appendix 1

The Birth Stories of Alexander

THE ROMANCE OF ALEXANDER

The *Romance* is not a history but a human response to the person and character of Alexander and can therefore be compared with the gospel narratives, which are viewed by many in this way. Many of the stories told in the *Romance* have parallels in the five surviving biographies of Alexander from antiquity and it is not always easy to say what is history and what is legend. The body of literature which makes up the *Romance* is vast, and is to be found in Armenian, Syriac, Persian, Arabic, Hebrew and Latin as well as most western languages.[1] But the best known version in the English language is the 1991 edition of the *Greek Alexander Romance* published by Penguin Books and quotations in this appendix (except when otherwise stated) are taken from it.

The *Romance* describes many events in the life of its hero. Alexander is discovered flying up into the heavens on the back of an enormous bird and descending into the deep in a bathyscope; he is shown seeking the cave of the gods, mating with the Amazon women, slaughtering great beasts and demons, and consulting with holy men. The later Romance describes him as a Christian saint, a Muslim holy man, tells of his knocking on the gates of Paradise and visiting legendary cities (all described by Stoneman in *Alexander: A Life in Legend*). This dissertation is primarily concerned with Alexander's relationship with the god Ammon or Ammon–Ra, whom the Greeks call Zeus. Twice in the *Romance* Alexander calls Ammon his father. He begins a letter: "Alexander, the son of Ammon and Philip the king. . ." and his Will starts with the words "King Alexander, the son of Ammon and

1. Stoneman, *A Life in Legend,* 230–45.

149

Olympias . . ."[2] The *Romance* contains a brief reference to Alexander's visit to Siwa but only in connection with the foundation of Alexandria and not with Alexander's appellation as son of Ammon.

THE BIRTH STORIES

It is the birth stories of Alexander that encourage particular attention in this dissertation. Only two of the five surviving biographies from antiquity tell stories of his birth and both have all the appearance of legend. Trogus tells of Olympias, on the night of Alexander's conception, dreaming of being entwined with a huge snake and the dream did not mislead her, for what she bore in her womb was certainly more than mortal He tells also of two eagles perching on the palace, foretelling a double empire of Europe and Asia. Plutarch tells of Olympias dreaming of a thunderbolt from heaven falling upon her on the night before her wedding, while Philip was told to seal up his wife's body with the image of a lion's head.[3] Further he peeped through a door at the sleeping Olympias and saw a large serpent in her bed. When he asked the oracle at Delphi what this meant, he was told it was a god in the form of a snake. And Olympias was said by some to have told her son that he was of divine birth, though the ever just Plutarch says that others deny that she said any such thing.[4]

If such mythical events appear in the biographies, the reader must be prepared for even greater flights of fancy in the *Romance* and these are provided by the appearance of Nectabeno, the last native king of Egypt. He is a historical character who was dispossessed by Artaxerxes II of Persia in 343 BCE after which he fled to Nubia and vanished from history. In the *Romance* he appears as a magician at the Macedonian palace where he tells Olympias, "you must have intercourse with an incarnate god, become pregnant by him and bring him up." He then responds to her dream in which she tells him that she saw "the god Ammon whom you spoke of. I beg you, prophet, make him make love to me again. . ." Necabeno disguises himself as the god and has satisfactory sex with Olympias, which prompts her to ask "but will the god not come to me again? For it was very sweet with him." One of the authors of the *Romance* goes on to suggest that she may have seen through the deception. Apparently Ammon–Ra frequently appeared as a ram, though also as a snake or even a dragon and the reader is told that "Nectabeno turned himself into a serpent . . . and crept into the dining room

2. Stoneman, *Romance,* 1.35; 3.32.

3. *Trogus* 12.16.2–5.

4. Plutarch 2.1–6.

. . . Olympias, who recognised her special lover extended her right hand to him."[5]

This story does four things. First it declares Alexander as the rightful son of Nectabeno and hence legitimizes his claim to be Pharaoh and ruler of Egypt. Secondly, it makes him the son of Ammon and gives him every reason to wish to visit Siwa. Thirdly, since Ammon was identified by many Greeks as Zeus, it confirms Alexander as being indeed a son of Zeus. Fourthly, and perhaps most important of all, it establishes the principle that a historical figure can have an extraordinary birth worthy of legend and so opens the way for the birth story of Jesus of Nazareth.

5. Stoneman, *Romance*, 1.6–10.

Appendix 2

The Messiah (Anointed One) as Son of God

"Samuel took a vial of oil and poured it on his (i.e., Saul's) head, and kissed him; he said The Lord has anointed you ruler over his people Israel. You will reign over the people of the Lord and you will save them from their enemies all around."[1]

"Then Samuel took the horn of oil and anointed him (i.e., David) in the presence of his brothers; and the spirit of the Lord came mightily upon David from that day forward."[2]

"There the priest Zadok took the horn of oil from the tent and anointed Solomon."[3]

The above classic passages demonstrate that the first kings of Israel began their reign by being anointed with oil by a prophet. This custom seems to have ceased after the division of the kingdoms of Israel and Judah; neither Rehoboam nor Jeroboam are said to have been anointed, nor were their successors. It seems highly probable that early Messianism emerged as the hope of the restoration of an idealized monarch during the exile in Babylon[4]. Probably this is the cause of the statement of Deutero—Isaiah, "Thus says the Lord to his anointed, to Cyrus, whose right hand I have grasped . . ."[5] But after the failure of the hopes for Zerubbabel[6] Judah became a priestly state and Messianism only seems to have come into its own in the aftermath of the Maccabees. A better understanding of its significance has emerged with the discovery of the Dead Sea Scrolls.

1. 1 Sam 10:1.
2. 1 Sam 16:13.
3. 1 Kgs 1:39.
4. Collins and Collins, *King and Messiah*, 43.
5. Isa 45:1.
6. Hag 2:20–23.

DEAD SEA SCROLLS

Although the term Messiah seems originally to have been used of a king, Collins, in his book *The Scepter and the Star: The Messiahs of the Dead Sea Scrolls and Other Ancient Literature* produces evidence of *four* messiahs in the DSS. He refers to them as messianic paradigms and labels them as king, priest, prophet and heavenly messiah.[7] As an example of the messiah as king, Collins cites the *pesher* 4QPLSA, in which the messiah is given the title Branch of David.[8] The Messiah as priest is to be found in The Community Rule 1QS 9:11 where the Messiah of Aaron is clearly a priestly figure.[9] In the Damascus Document CD 7.18 and in 4Q174 the prophet (or teacher) Messiah is referred to as "The Teacher of Righteousness" or "Interpreter of the Law." The Heavenly Messiah, encountered in 4Q246, is introduced with the words "they will name him Son of the Most High," a passage that has been discussed in Chapter 3. There is considerable doubt as to whether this is a Son of God passage; Wolters and Collins argue that it refers rather to a future Messiah than to the Son of God.

PSEUDEPIGRAPHA

In a recent article, Stuckenbruck[10] points out that among the Pseudepigrapha that emerge from the Hebrew Scriptures is literature which deals with Messianism in the time of early Judaism. Though Judaism and Christianity may be described as overlapping in the latter part of the first century CE, it is reasonable to see in their literature evidence of a Judaism as yet not fully influenced by Christianity. Stuckenbruck focuses on four works: The Psalms of Solomon, Similitudes of 1 Enoch, 4 Ezra and 2 Baruch.

THE PSALMS OF SOLOMON

These were written some thirty years before the turn of the millennium and were hostile to Hasmonaean rule. "Two main features," writes Stuckenbruck, "mark the rule and character of this Messiah: (cultic) purity and justice, on the one hand, power and might on the other. This Messiah is to restore Jerusalem to an idealized purity under an equally idealized Davidic

---

7. Collins, *The Scepter and the Star*, 12; Wolters, *The Messiah*, 76.

8. Collins, *The Scepter and the Star*, 57–58; Wolters, *The Messiah*, 77.

9. Collins *The Scepter and the Star*, 77–83; Stuckenbruck, "Messianic Ideas,"78.

10. Ibid. 90–116.

rule and he is to exercise power over all the nations of the earth. However, he is not divine and has neither heavenly status nor pre-existence."[11]

SIMILITUDES

Though the Similitudes contain two brief references to Messiah, the texts say nothing directly about what sort of figure God's Anointed One is to be; and does not say whether he is human, angelic, or divine.

4 EZRA

The first clear and explicit allusion to "my son the Messiah" in Jewish literature occurs in 4 Ezra, which was written at the same time as the Fourth Gospel[12]. This pseudepigraphon was written some thirty year after the destruction of the Jerusalem temple and is believed to be heavily influenced by Christianity. Thus, though it refers to "my son the Messiah,"[13] it is impossible to say whether the ideas of Divine sonship have entered Judaism independently or because of the Christian developments already examined in Chapter 3.

2 BARUCH

This was written after 4 Ezra[14] and offers a confusing vision of many messianic possibilities. However, there is no suggestion of divinity; Baruch's Messiah is a warrior king. Collins gives examples of people who, following Baruch's suggestions, fulfill messianic expectations in the first two centuries and points out that all of them were marginalized by the power of Rome (including Bar Kokhba).[15]

Many scholars hold to the view that there are few grounds for seeing the Messiah as the Son of God. For example, Conzelmann holds that the title Son of God does not belong to contemporary Jewish designations of the Messiah.[16] Throughout his article "Messianic Ideas in the Apocalyptic and Related Literature of Early Judaism," Stuckenbruck sees that there is

11. Ibid. 93–95.

12. Dodd, *Interpretation*, 253.

13. Charlesworth, *Pseudepigrapha*, 7.29.

14. Stuckenbruck, "Messianic Ideas," 108

15. Collins, *The Scepter and the Star*, 196–204.

16. Conzelman, *Jesus*, 46–47.

no suggestion that the Messiah was necessarily divine. In his book *The The-ology of the Gospel of Mark,* Telford challenges the view that that Son of God was a *title* for the Messiah in first century Judaism, or that the terms were interchangeable.

Collins and Collins in their latest book *King and Messiah as Son of God* further address the issue. The first 63 pages of their book deal with refer-ences to the Messiah as potentially a son of God in the Hebrew Scriptures and cover the same ground as was dealt with in Chapter 3. They find that when the Son of God is referred to, he is the Messiah, but this does not make the Messiah a son of God. Many references to the Messiah do not involve suggestion divinity.

When Jesus was called Messiah or Christ, this certainly implied that he was the fulfillment of a widespread belief of an impending deliverer from the contemporary sufferings of the Jews. Some of the Messianic prophecies clearly could be interpreted as suggestive that the Messiah was divine (e.g. 2 Sam 7). But it is a long way from this to saying that when people referred to Jesus as the Christ or to Jesus Christ there was a suggestion that this meant Jesus, Son of God.

Appendix 3

Augustus and Jesus of Nazareth

In his "The Anarthrous Uios Theou in Mark 15.39 and the Roman Imperial Cult," Kim points out that *uios theou* is used only twice in Mark (1.1 and 15.39) and that all other references to Jesus as Son of God are rendered *ho uios tou theou*. However, he goes on to say that Augustus was known from the beginning of his political career as *divi filius,* "son of god," which in Greek is written as *uios theou* or *theou uios* without the definite article . He argues that it therefore seems plausible that the *anarthrous uios theou* in Mark 15.39 echoes the divine title of Augustus (*divi filius*) because of the absence of the definite article and the fact that it is ascribed to a Roman centurion. The absence of the definite article is deliberate, according to Kim, a conviction which prompts him to quote Bligh's argument that what the centurion actually meant was *"This* man (Jesus), not Caesar, is the Son of God!"[1]. Kim advances his argument further by giving a body of evidence that suggests that only Augustus used the title *filius divi* of himself and so (since Tiberius was on the throne) the centurion was saying that it was Jesus who was the true Son of God.

Kim's and Bligh's argument is hard to sustain. Firstly, as the Introduction to this book points out, the centurion in Mark 15 must have been a literary device of the author. Secondly, Mark was writing in the time of Vespasian, who was on the whole a popular emperor (not least because he stabilized the empire after the activities of Nero). Thirdly, though Augustus used the title *filius divi* more than other emperors, Chapter 6 gives clear proof that the appellation was used of other emperors, not least of Vespasian himself. But the suggestion that by ascribing the use of the anarthrous uios theou to the centurion, Mark was using an imperial title of Jesus is to be taken seriously, as is Kim's suggestion that *filius divi* was a favorite title of the

1. Bligh, "Note," 53.

great Augustus. The statement ascribed to the centurion, surely a climactic remark, grants Jesus a title dignified and deepened by its association with Augustus.

Bibliography

Aageson, J. W. *Paul, the Pastoral Epistles, and the Early Church.* Peabody, Ma.: Hendrickson, 2008.

Allen, J. E. "Why Pilate?" In *The Trial of Jesus*, edited by E. Bammel, 78–83. London: SCM, 1968.

Anderson, A. R. "Heracles and His Successors: A Study of a Heroic Ideal and the Recurrence of the Heroic Type." *HSCP* 39 (1928) 7–58.

Ando, C., ed. *Roman Religion.* Edinburgh: Edinburgh University Press, 2003.

Austin, M. M. *The Hellenistic World from Alexander to the Roman Conquest.* Cambridge: Cambridge University Press, 1981.

Badian, E. "Alexander Great—Green, P." *American Historical Review* 76:5 (1971)15–25.

————. "Alexander the Great—Fox, R. L." *JHS* 96 (1976) 229–30.

————. "Alexander the Great and the Unity of Mankind." *Journal of Ancient History* 7:4 (1958).

————. "The Deification of Alexander the Great." In *Colloquy 21: Center for Hermeneutical Studies in Hellenistic and Modern Culture.* Berkeley, 1976.

Balsdon, J. P. V. D. "The Divinity of Alexander the Great." *Historia* 1 (1950) 363–88.

Bamm, P. *Alexander the Great, Power as Destiny.* London: Thames and Hudson, 1996.

Barnard, L. W. *Justin Martyr: His Life and Thought.* Cambridge: Cambridge University Press, 1967.

Barr, J. "Daniel." In *Peake's Commentary on the Bible*, edited by M. Black and H. H. Rowley. London: Thomas Nelson and Sons, 1963.

Barrett, A. *Caligula: The Corruption of Power.* London: Batsford, 1989.

Barrett, C. K. *Acts: A Shorter Commentary.* London: T. & T. Clark, 2002.

————. *A Commentary on the Epistle to the Romans.* London: Adam and Charles Black, 1957.

————. *The Gospel According to St. John.* London: S. P. C. K., 1955.

————. *Paul: An Introduction to His Thought.* London: Geoffrey Chapman, 1998

Beale, G. K. *The Book of Revelation.* Cambridge: Eerdmans, 1999.

Beard, M. "Priesthood in the Roman Republic." In *Pagan Priests*, edited by M. Beard and J. North, 17–48. Ithaca, NY: Cornell University Press, 1990.

Beard, M., and M. Crawford. *Rome in the Late Republic, Problems and Interpretations.* Ithaca, NY: Cornell University Press, 1985.

Beard, M., J. North, and S. Price. *Religions of Rome.* 2 vols. Vol. 1 Cambridge: Cambridge University Press, 1998.

Beare, F. W. *The Earliest Records of Jesus.* Oxford: Basil Blackwell, 1964.

Bethune-Baker, J. F. *An Introduction to the Early History of Christian Doctrine.* London: Methuen, 1903.

Birley, A. *Marcus Aurelius.* London: Eyre & Spottiswoode, 1966.

Bligh, P. H. "A Note on Huios Theou in Mark 15.39." *ExpTim* 80 (1968) 53.

Blinzler, J. *The Trial of Jesus.* Westminster, Maryland: Newman, 1959.

Bobrinskoy, B. *The Mystery of the Trinity: Trinitarian Experience and Vision in Biblical and Patristic Tradition.* Translated by A. Gythiel. Crestwood, NY: SVSP, 1999.

Bockmuehl, M. *This Jesus: Martyr, Lord, Messiah.* Edinburgh: T. & T. Clark, 1994.

Bornkamm, G. "The Stilling of the Storm in Matthew." In *Traditions and Interpretations in Matthew*, edited by G. Bornkamm, G. Barth and H. J. Held. London: SCM, 1963.

Borza, E. N. "Alexander and the Return from Siwah." *Historia*, no. 16 (1967) 369.

Bosworth, A. B. "Alexander and Ammon." In *Greece and the Eastern Mediterranean in Ancient History and Prehistory: Studies Presented to Fritz Schachermeyr on the Occasion of His Eightieth Birthday*, edited by K. H. Kinzl, 51–75. New York: Walter de Gruyter, 1977.

———. "Alexander the Great and the Decline of Macedon." *JHS* 106 (1986) 1–12.

———. "Alexander, Euripides and Dionysos: The Motivation for Apotheosis." In *Transitions to Empire. Essays in Greco-Roman History, 360–146 B. C., in Honor of E. Badian*, edited by R. W. Wallace and E. M. Harris, 140–66. Norman: Univeristy of Oklahoma Press, 1996.

———. *Conquest and Empire: The Reign of Alexander.* Cambridge: Cambridge University Press, 1988.

———. "A Missing Year in the History of Alexander the Great." *JHS* 101 (1981) 7–39.

Bradford, E. *Hannibal.* Wordsworth Military Library, Ware: Wordsworth, 2000.

Brandon, S. G. F. *The Fall of Jerusalem and the Christian Church.* London: SPCK, 1951.

———. *Jesus and the Zealots: A Study of the Political Factor in Primitive Christianity.* Manchester: Manchester University, 1967.

———. *The Trial of Jesus of Nazareth.* London: Batsford, 1968.

Braund, D. *Rome and the Friendly King: The Character of Client Kingship.* London: Croom Helm, 1984.

Brent, A. *Ignatius of Antioch.* London: Continuum, 2007.

———. *Ignatius of Antioch and the Second Sophistic: A Study of Early Christian Transformation of Pagan Culture.* Studien und Texte zu Antike und Christentum 36. Tubingen: Mohr Siebeck, 2006.

Briant, P. *From Cyrus to Alexander: A History of the Persian Empire.* Translated by P. T. Daniels. Winona Lake, IN: Eisenbraun, 2002.

Briggs, C. A., and E. G. Briggs. *The Book of Psalms.* 2 vols. Edinburgh: T. & T. Clark, 1907.

Bright, J. A. *History of Israel.* Revised Edition. London: SCM, 1972.

Broad, W. E. L. "The History and the Significance of the Temple on Mount Gerizim and the Part Played by Alexander the Great in Its Establishment." MA diss., Durham University, 2008.

Broadhead, E. K. *Naming Jesus. Titular Christianity in the Gospel of Mark.* Sheffield: Sheffield Academic, 1999.

Bromiley, G. W. *Historical Theology: An Introduction.* Edinburgh: T. & T. Clark, 1978.

Brown, R. E. *The Gospel According to John.* The Anchor Bible. New York: Doubleday, 1966.

Bruce, F. F. "The Church of Jerusalem." *Christian Brethren Research Fellowship Journal* 4 (April 1964) 5–14.

———. *The Epistle to the Hebrews.* New Edition. Grand Rapids: Eeerdmans, 1990.

———. *The Gospel of John.* Basingstoke: Pickering, 1983.

Brugsch, H. K. *A History of Egypt under the Pharaohs.* London: J. Murray, 1879.

Bruns, J. E. "Jesus—Stranger from Heaven and Son of God—Jesus-Christ and Christians in Johannine Perspective—Dejonge, M." In *CBQ* 40:3 (1978) 437–38.

Bryant, J. M. "From Myth to Theology: Intellectuals and the Rationalization of Religion in Ancient Greece." In *Time, Place and Circumstance*, 71–85. Westport, CT: Greenwood, 1990.

Buchanan Gray, G. *Studies in Hebrew Proper Names.* London: A. and C. Black, 1896.

Budge, E. A.W. *The Gods of the Egyptians.* London: Methuen, 1904.

Bultmann, R. *Jesus and the Word.* New York: Scribners, 1935.

Burkert, W. *Greek Religion.* Translated by J. Raffan. Oxford: Blackwell, 1987.

Burn, A. R. *Alexander the Great and the Hellenistic Empire.* London: Hodder and Stoughton, 1947.

———. *The Penguin History of Greece.* London: Penguin, 1990.

———. *Persia and the Greeks.* London: Edward Arnold, 1962.

Byrne, B. "Sons of God." In *The Anchor Bible Dictionary*, vol. 6, edited by D. N. Freedman, 128–37. London: Yale University Press, 2008.

Byrne, J. "American Jesus: How the Son of God Became a National Icon." *CH* 75:1 (2006) 234–36.

Cadbury, H. J. *The Perils of Modernizing Jesus.* New York: Macmillan, 1937.

Cadoux, C. J. *The Historic Mission of Jesus.* London: Lutterworth, 1941.

Calame, C. "Greek Myth and Greek Religion." In *Cambridge Companion to Greek Mythology*, edited by R. Woodward, 259–85. New York: Cambridge University Press, 2007.

Carlson, R. A., *David the Chosen King.* Translated by E. J. Sharpe. Uppsala: Almquist and Wiksells, 1964.

Carrington, P. *The Early Christian Church.* Cambridge: Cambridge University Press, 1957.

Cartledge, P. "Alexander the Great—in Search of the Elusive Personality of the World's Greatest Hero." *HT* 54:7 (2004) 10–16.

———. *Alexander the Great: The Hunt for a New Past.* London: Macmillan, 2004.

———. *The Greeks: A Portrait of Self and Others.* Oxford: Oxford University Press, 2002.

Cartlidge, D. R., and D. L. Dungan, eds. *Documents for Study of the Gospel.* London: Collins, 1980.

Cary, M. *A History of Rome Down to the Reign of Constantine.* London: Macmillan, 1967.

Catchpole, D. R. "The Problem of the Historicity of the Sanhedrin Trial." In *The Trial of Jesus*, edited by E. Bammel, 47–65. London: SCM, 1968.

———. *The Trial of Jesus.* Leiden: Brill, 1971.

Chadwick, H. *Early Christian Thought and the Classical Tradition: Studies in Justin, Clement, and Origen.* Oxford: Clarendon, 1966.

———. *The Early Church.* Harmondsworth: Penguin, 1967.

Champlin, E. *Nero.* London: Harvard University Press, 2003.

Charles, R. H., ed. *The Book of Jubilees.* London: Adam and Charles Black, 1902.

Charlesworth, J. H. "From Jewish Messianology to Christian Christology: Some Caveats and Perspectives." In *Judaisms and Their Messiahs*, edited by J. Neusner. Cambridge: Cambridge University Press, 1987.

———. , ed. *The Old Testament Preudepigrapha*. 2 vols. London: Darton, Longman and Todd, 1983–5.

Charlesworth, M. P. "The Refusal of Divine Honours, an Augustan Formula." *Papers of the British School at Rome*, no. 15 (1939) 1–10.

———. "Some Observarions on the Ruler Cult, Especially in Rome." *HTR* 28 (1935) 5–44.

Chisholm, K., and J. Ferguson, *Rome: The Augustan Age*. Oxford: Oxford University Press, 1981.

Choksy, J. K. "Reassessing the Material Contexts of Ritual Fires in Ancient Iran." *IrAnt* 42 (2007) 229–69.

Classen, D. J. "The Libyan God Ammon in Greece before 331 BC." *Historia* 8 (1959) 349–55.

Coleman-Norton, P. R. *Roman State and Christian Church*. Vol. 1. London: SPCK, 1966.

Collins, A. Y. "Mark and His Readers: The "Son of God" among Greeks and Romans (Interpreting the Primitive Christian Proclamation of a Divine Jesus among Hellenistic Contemporaries)." *HTR* 93:2 (2000) 85–100.

Collins, A. Y. "Mark and His Readers: The Son of God among the Jews." *HTR* 92 (1999) 393–408.

Collins, A. Y. "The Origin of the Designation of Jesus as Son of Man." *HTR* 80:4 (1987) 391–407.

Collins, A. Y., and J. J. Collins. *King and Messiah as Son of God*. Cambridge: Eerdmans, 2008.

Collins, J. J. *The Scepter and the Star: The Messiahs of the |Dead Sea Scrolls and Other Ancient Literature*. New York: Doubleday, 1995.

Conzelman, H. *Jesus*. Philadelphia: Fortress, 1973.

Cornfeld, G. *The Historical Jesus: A Scholarly View of the Man and His World*. London: Macmillan, 1982.

Costadoat, S. J. J. "The Faith of Jesus, Foundation for Faith in Christ." *Theologia Y Vida* 48:4 (2007) 371–97.

Cranfield, C. E. B. *The Gospel According to St. Mark*. Ed. by C. F.D. Moule, Cambridge: Cambridge University Press, 1959.

———. *Romans: A Shorter Commentary*. Edinburgh: T. & T. Clark, 1985.

Cross, F. L. *The Oxford Dictionary of the Christian Church*. Oxford: Oxford University Press, 1958.

Currow, T. *The Oracles of the Ancient World*. London: Duckworth, 2004.

David, R. *Religion and Magic in Ancient Egypt*. London: Penguin, 2002.

Davies, P. R. *Daniel*. Sheffield: JSOT, 1985.

Davies, W. D., and D. C. Allison. *The Gospel According to St. Matthew*. Vol. 1. The International Critical Commentary. Edinburgh: T. & T. Clark, 1988.

De Boer, P. A.H. "The Son of God in the Old Testament." In *Syntax and Meaning: Studies in Hebrew Syntax and Biblical Exegesis*, edited by C. J. Labuschagne, 188–207. Leiden: Brill, 1973.

Devine, A. M. "Alexander's Propaganda Machine: Callisthenes as the Ultimate Source of Arrian, *Anabasis 1–3*." In *Ventures into Greek History*, edited by I. Worthington, 89 –104. Oxford: Clarendon, 1994.

Dhorme, E., *A Commentary on the Book of Job.* Translated by H. Knight. London: Thomas Nelson, 1967.

Dibelius, M. *Jesus.* 2nd ed. Berlin: de Gruyter, 1949.

Dodd, C. H. *The Founder of Christianty.* London: Macmillan, 1970.

———. *The Interpretation of the Fourth Gospel.* Cambridge: Cambridge University Press, 1968.

Doherty, P. *Alexander the Great: Death of a God.* London: Robinson, 2004.

Driver, S. R. *Notes on the Hebrew Text and the Topography of the Books of Samuel.* Oxford: Clarendon, 1913.

Driver, S. R., and G. B. Gray. *The Book of Job.* ICC Commentaries, Edinburgh: T. & T. Clark, 1921.

Droylsen, J. G. *History of Hellenism I: History of Alexander the Great.* Basel: Gotha, 1877.

Duchesne, L. *Early History of the Christian Church.* London: John Murray, 1910.

Dulles, A. R. *Apologetics and the Biblical Christ.* Westminster: Newman, 1963.

Duncan, G. S. *Jesus, Son of Man.* London: Nisbet, 1947.

Dunn, J. D. G. *Christianity in the Making.* Vol. 1 Cambridge: Eerdmans, 2003.

———. *The Evidence for Jesus.* London: SCM, 1985.

———. ed. *St. Paul.* Cambridge: Cambridge University Press, 2003.

Eder, W. "Augustus and the Power of Tradition." in *The Age of Augustus,* edited by K. Galinsky. Cambridge: Cambridge University Press, 2005, 13–32.

Edwards, M. J. "The Mysteries of the Life of Christ in Justin Martyr." *Journal of Theological Studies* 59 (2008) 340–42.

Ehrenberg, V. *Documents Illustrating the Reigns of Augustus and Tiberius.* London: Clarendon, 1955.

Ehrman, B. D., ed. *The Apostolic Fathers.* 2 vols. The LCL. London: Harvard University Press, 2003.

Ellingworth, P. *The Epistle to the Hebrews.* Grand Rapids: Eerdmans, 1993.

Elliott, J. K., ed. *The Apocryphal Jesus.* Oxford: Oxford University Press, 2008.

Ellis, E. E. *The Gospel of Luke.* London: Thomas Nelson, 1966.

Erman, A. *A Handbook of Egyptian Religion.* Translated by A. S. Griffiths. London: Archibald Constable, 1907.

Evans, C. A. *Jesus and His Contemporaries: Comparative Studies.* Leiden: Brill, 1995.

———. "Mark Incipit." In *Jesus and His Contemporaries: Comparative Studies,* 13. Leiden: Brill, 1995.

Evans, C. S. *The Historical Christ and the Jesus of Faith: The Incarnational Narrative as History.* Oxford: Clarendon, 1996.

Evans, G. R., ed. *The First Christian Theologians.* Oxford: Blackwell, 2004.

Eve, E. "Spit in Your Eye: The Blind Man of Bethsaida and the Blind Man of Alexandria." *NTS* 54:1 (2008) 1–17.

Fakhry, A. *Siwa Oasis.* Government, Bulaq, 1944.

Farmer, W. R. "Historical Essay on the Humanity of Jesus Christ." In *Christian History and Interpretation,* edited by W. R. Farmer et al., 101–126. Cambridge: Cambridge University Press, 1967.

Fears, J. R. "The Cult of Jupiter and Roman Imperial Ideology." *Aufstieg und Niedergang der Romischen Welt* 2, no. 17/1 (1981) 3–141.

Fee, G. D. *The Thessalonian Epistles.* Cambridge: Eerdmans, 2009.

Feldman, L. H. *Josephus, Judaism and Christianity.* Detroit: Wayne State University Press, 1987.

Fenton, J. C. *The Gospel of Matthew.* London: Penguin, 1963.

Ferguson, J. *The Religions of the Roman Empire.* Edited by H. H. Scullard. London: Camelot, 1970.

Fiorenza, E. S. "Eschatology of the New Testament." In *The Interpreters Dictionary of the Bible,* 271–77. Nashville: Abington, 1976.

Fishwick, D. "Prudentius and the Cult of Divus Augustus." *Historia* 39 (1990) 475–86.

Fisk, P. J. "Jonathan Edwards' Freedom of the Will and His Defence of the Impeccability of Jesus Christ." *Scottish Journal of Theology* 60 (2007) 309–25.

Fitzmyer, J. A. "4Q246: The Son of God Documents from Qumran." *Biblica* 74 (1993) 153–74.

Fossum, J. "Son of God." In *The Anchor Bible Dictionary,* edited by D. N. Freedman, 128–37. London: Doubleday, 1992.

Foster, P., ed. *The Writings of the Apostolic Fathers.* London: Continuum, 2007.

Fowler, W. W. *The Religious Experience of the Roman People, from the Earliest Times to the Age of Augustus: The Gifford Lectures for 1909-10, delivered in Edinburgh University.* London: MacMillan, 1911.

Frankfort, H. *Kingship and the Gods.* Chicago: University of Chicago Press, 1948.

Fredericksmeyer, E. A. "Alexander and the Kingship of Asia." In *Alexander the Great in Fact and Fiction,* edited by A. B. Bosworth and E. J. Baynham, 136–66. Oxford: Oxford University Press, 2000.

Fredriksen, P. *From Jesus to Christ: The Origins of the New Testament Images of Jesus.* London: Yale University Press, 1988.

Frend, W. H. C. *The Early Church.* London: Hodder and Stoughton, 1965.

Fried, L. S. "Cyrus the Messiah? The Historical Background to Isaiah 45.1." *HTR* 95:4 (2002) 373–93.

Fuller, J. F. C. *The Decisive Battles of the Western World.* 3 vols. London: Eyre and Spottiswoode, 1954.

———. *The Generalship of Alexander the Great.* Cambridge, MA: Perseus, 1960.

Fuller, R. H. *The Mission and Achievement of Jesus.* London: SCM, 1954.

Galinsky, K. *Augustan Culture.* Princeton NJ: Princeton University Press, 1996.

———, ed. *The Cambridge Companion to the Age of Augustus.* Cambridge: Cambridge University Press, 2005.

Gazik, P. "Early-Christian Transformation of the Greek Logos in the Philosophy of Justin Martyr." *Filozofia* 63:2 (2008) 169–73.

Globe, A. "The Caesarean Omission of the Phrase Son of God in Mark 1.1." *HTR* 2 (1982) 209–18.

Glover, T. R. *The Conflicts of Religions in the Eastern Roman Empire.* London: Methuen, 1909.

Goedicke, H. "Religion in Ancient-Egypt—Gods, Myths, and Personal Practice—Shafer, Be." *JNES* 54:1 (1995) 57–58.

Goodacre, M. *The Synoptic Problem: A Way through the Maze.* London: T. & T. Clark, 2001.

Goodenough, S. *Tactical Genius in Battle.* Oxford: Phaidon, 1979.

Goodman, M. *The Roman World. 44 BC—180 AD.* London: Routledge, 1977.

Gordis, R. *The Book of Job.* New York: The Jewish Theological Seminary of America, 1978.

Gordon, R. "From Republic to Principate: Priesthood, Religion and Ideology." In *Roman Religion*, edited by C. Ando, 62–83. Edinburgh: Edinburgh University Press, 2003.

———. "From Republic to Principate: Priesthood, Religion and Ideology." In *Pagan Priests: Religion and Power in the Ancient World*, edited by M. Beard and J. North, 177–98. Ithaca: Cornell University Press, 1990.

———. "Religion in the Roman Empire: The Civic Compromise and Its Limits." In *Pagan Priests: Religion and Power in the Ancient World*, edited by M. Beard and J. North, 233–56. London: Duckworth, 1990.

———. "The Veil of Power: Emperors, Sacrificers and Benefactors." In *Pagan Priests: Religion and Power in the Ancient World*, edited by M. Beard and J. North, 199–232. Ithaca: Cornell University Press, 1990.

Gradel, I. *Emperor Worship and Roman Religion.* Oxford: Clarendon, 2002.

Grant, M. *Jesus: An Historian's Review of the Gospel.* New York: Scribners, 1977.

———. *Jesus: An Historian's View of the Gospels.* New York: Macmillan, 1992.

———. *The Twelve Caesars.* London: Weidenfeld and Nicolson, 1975.

Grant, R. M. *The Early Christian Doctrine of God.* Charlottesville: University Press of Virginia, 1966.

Green, J. B., S. McKnight, and I. H. Marshall, eds. *Dictionary of Jesus and the Gospels.* Downers Grove: InterVarsity, 1992.

Green, P. *Alexander of Macedon.* Oxford: University of California Press, 1991.

Griffiths, G. T. *Alexander the Great: The Main Problems.* Cambridge: Cambridge University Press, 1966.

Grillmeier, A. *Christ in Christian Tradition.* 3 vols. London: Mowbray, 1975.

———. "Jesus-Christ, Kyriakos Anthropos." *TS* 38:2 (1977) 275–93.

Ha—Makdoni, A. *The Book of the Gests of Alexander of Macedon.* Translated by I. J. Kazis. Cambridge: The Medieval Academy of America, 1962.

Habel, N. C. *The Book of Job.* Cambridge: Cambridge University Press, 1975.

Hamilton, J. R. *Alexander the Great.* Pittsburg: University of Pittsburg Press, 1974.

Hammond, N. G. L. *Alexander the Great; King, Commander, Statesman.* London: Chatto and Windus, 1981.

———. *Sources of Alexander the Great.* Cambridge: Cambridge University Press, 1993.

———. *Three Historians of Alexander the Great: The So Called Vulgate Authors, Diodorus, Justin and Curtius.* Cambridge: Cambridge University Press, 1983.

Hanson, A. T. *Vindications: Essays on the Historical Basis of Christianity.* London: SCM, 1966.

Hartog, P. *Polycarp and the New Testament: The Occasion, Rhetoric, Theme, and Unity of the Epistle to the Philippians.* Tubingen: Mohr Siebeck, 2001.

Harvey, A. E., *Jesus and the Constraints of History.* London: Duckworth, 1982.

Heckel, W. *The Conquests of Alexander the Great.* Cambridge: Cambridge University Press, 2008.

Heckel, W., and J. C. Yardley, eds. *Alexander the Great: Historical Texts in Translation.* Oxford: Blackwell, 2003.

Hengel, M. *Acts and the History of Earliest Christianity.* London: SCM, 1979.

———. *The Son of God: The Origin of Christology and the History of Jewish-Hellenistic Religion.* Philadelphia: Fortress, 1976.

Herodotus. *Herodotus.* Translated by A. D. Godley. edited by G. P. Goold. 4 vols. The LCL. London: William Heinemann, 1920.

Hertzberg, H. W. *1 and 2 Samuel.* Old Testament Library. London: SCM, 1960.

Hesiod. "The Theogony of Hesiod." In *The Homeric Hymns and Homerica*, edited by G. P. Goold, 79–155. London: William Heinemann, 1982.

Hill, D. "Is the Search for the Historical Jesus Religiously Irrelevant?" *ExpTim* 88 (1976) 82–85.

———. "Jesus: A Prophet Mighty in Deed and Word." In *New Testament Prophecy*, edited by D. Hill, 48–69. Atlanta: John Knox, 1979.

Hoffman Lewis, M. W. "The Official Priests of Rome under the Julio-Claudians." *Papers and Monographs of the American Academy in Rome* 16 (1955) 1–179.

Homer. *The Iliad.* Translated by A. T. Murray. LCL 171–72. London: Heinemann, 1924–25.

———. *The Iliad.* Translated by E. V. Rieu. Edited by P. Jones. London: Penguin, 2003.

———. *The Odyssey.* Translated by A. T. Murray. LCL 104–5. Cambridge, MA: Harvard University Press, 1995.

———. *The Odyssey.* Translated by E. V. Rieu. Edited by P. Jones. London: Penguin, 2003.

Hooker, M. D. *The Gospel According to St. Mark.* London: Continuum, 2006.

———. *The Gospel According to St. Mark.* Black's New Testament Commentaries. London: Continuum, 1991.

Horbury, W. *Jewish Messianism and the Cult of Christ.* London: SCM, 1998.

Hornung, E. *Conceptions of God in Ancient Egypt: The One and the Many.* Translated by J. Baines. Ithaca: Cornell University Press, 1982.

Houlden, J. L. *A Commentary on the Johannine Epistles.* Edited by H. Chadwick. London: Charles and Adam Black, 1973.

Hunter, A. M. *Introducing the New Testament.* London: SCM, 1946.

Hurtado, L. W. *Mark.* Edited by W. Ward Gasque. Peabody, MA: Hendrickson, 1989.

Jeffery, A. "Abba." In *Dictionary of the Bible*, edited by F. C. Grant and H. H. Rowley, 2. Edinburgh: T. & T. Clark, 1963.

Johnson, E. S. "Mark—XV, 39 and the So-Called 'Confession of the Roman Centurion' (a Concise Discussion on the Grammatical, Literary and Historical Evidence of Declarations of Divinity Found in the Gospel of Mark)." *Biblica* 81:3 (2000) 406–13.

Johnson, L. T. *The Real Jesus: The Misguided Quest for the Historical Jesus and the Truth of the Traditional Gospels.* San Fransisco: Harper Collins, 1995.

Jones, B. W. *The Emperor Domitian.* London: Routledge, 1992.

Kakozy, L. "Zeus—Amon." In *Jubilee Volume of the Oriental Collection, 1951—1976*, 111–14. Budapest: Library of the Hungarian Academy of Sciences, 1978.

Kamesar, A., ed. *The Cambridge Companion to Philo.* Cambridge: Cambridge University Press, 2009.

Kammler, H. C. "The Son of God and the Cross—the Temptation Story in Matthew IV, 1–11 in the Context of the Gospel of Matthew." *ZTK* 100:2 (2003) 163–86.

Kazmierski, C. R. *Jesus, the Son of God: A Study of the Markan Tradition and Its Redaction by the Evangelist.* Wurzburg: Echter, 1982.

Kertlege, K. "The Epiphany of Jesus in the Gospel (Mark)." In *The Interpretation of Mark*, edited by W. R.Telford, 105–23. Edinburgh: T. & T. Clark, 1995.

Kilgallen, J. J. "Jesus First Trial: Messiah and Son of God in Luke-XXII, 66–71 (a Narratological Investigation of the So-Called 'Two-Source Hypothesis' Redaction of the Gospel of Luke)." *Biblica* 80, no. 3 (1999) 401–14.

Kim, S. *The Son of Man as the Son of God.* Tubingen: J. C.B. Mohr, 1983.

Kim, T. H. "The Anarthous *Uios Theou* in Mark 15.39 and the Roman Imperial Cult." *Biblica* 79 (1998) 221–41.

Kingsley, C. *The Heroes.* London: MacMillan, 1965.

Kloppenborg, J. S. *The Formation of Q.* Studies in Antiquity and Christianity. Philadelphia: Fortress, 1987.

Knibb, M. A. *The Ethiopic Book of Enoch.* Oxford: Oxford University Press, 1978.

Knight, J. *Revelation.* Sheffield: Sheffield Academic Press, 1999.

Kriwaczek, P. *In Search of Zarathustra.* London: Phoenix, 2003.

Kummel, W. G. *Promise and Fulfillment: The Eschatological Message of Jesus.* SBT 23. Naperville, IL: Trinity, 1957.

Kunz, Kriton. "Snake Symbolism in the Ancient Egyptian Book of the Dead." *Draco* 5:1 (2004) 54–63.

Ladd, G. E. "The Search for Perspective." *Int* 25 (1971) 41–62.

Lane Fox, R. *Alexander the Great.* London: Allan Lane, 1973.

———. *Pagans and Christians.* London: Viking, 1986.

———. *The Unauthorised Version: Truth and Fiction in the Bible.* New York: Vintage, 1993.

Larsen, A. O. "Alexander and the Oracle of Ammon." *CP* 27 (1932) 70–75.

Lawrence, S. E. "The God That Is Truly God and the Universe of Euripides Heracles." *Mnemosyne* 51:2 (1998) 129–46.

Lawson, J. *The Biblical Theology of Saint Irenaeus.* London: Epworth, 1948.

Leaney, A. R.C., *A Commentary of the Gospel According to St. Luke.* London: Charles and Adam Black, 1971.

———. *The Jewish and Christian World: 200 BC to AD 200.* Cambridge: Cambridge University Press, 1984.

Levick, B. *Claudius.* New Haven and London: Yale University Press, 1990.

———. *Tiberius the Politician.* London: Routledge, 1999.

———. *Vespasian.* London: Routledge, 1999.

Lieu, J. M. *I, II & III John.* London: Westminster John Knox, 2008.

Lincoln, A. T. *The Gospel According to St. John.* London: Continuum, 2005.

Logan, A. H. B. *Gnostic Truth and Christian Heresy.* Edinburgh: T. & T. Clark, 1996.

Macdonald, D. R. *The Homeric Epics and the Gospel of Mark.* New Haven: Yale University Press, 2000.

Mackie, S. D. "Confession of the Son of God in Hebrews." *NTS* 53:1 (2007) 114–29.

Mackinnon, J. *The Historic Jesus.* London: Longmans, 1931.

Macmullen, R. *Paganism in the Roman Empire.* London: Yale University Press, 1981.

Malitz, J. *Nero.* Translated by A. Brown. Oxford: Blackwell, 1999.

Manson, T. W. *The Sayings of Jesus.* London: Billing, 1949.

———. *The Servant Messiah: A Study of the Public Ministry of Jesus.* Cambridge: Cambridge University Press, 1953.

Manzi, F. "Human Faith and the Singular Realization of the Sonship of Jesus to God the Father in the Epistle to the Hebrews." *Biblica* 81:1 (2000) 32–62.

Marcus, J. *The Way of the Lord: Christological Exegesis of the Old Testament in the Gospel of Mark.* Edinburgh: T. & T. Clark, 1992.

Maritz, v. W., et al. "uios, uiothesia." In *Theological Dictionary of the New Testament,* vol. 8, edited and translated by G. W. Bromiley, 334–97. Grand Rapids: Eerdmans, 1972.

Marsh, J., *The Gospel of St. John.* Harmondsworth: Penguin, 1966.

Martial. *Epigrams.* Translated by W. C. A. Ker. London: Heinemann, 1920–25.

Matthews, E. "Names, Personal, Greek." In *OCD.* Oxford: Oxford University Press, 1996.

Mcconville, J. G. *Deuteronomy.* Leicester: Apollos, 2002.

Meecham, H. G. *The Epistle to Diognetus.* Manchester: Manchester University Press, 1949.

Mejer, J. *Diogenes Laertius and His Hellenistic Background.* Wiesebaden: Steiner, 1978.

Mellor, R. *The Worship of the Goddess Roma in the Greek World.* Göttingen: Vandenhoeck & Ruprecht, 1975.

Meyer, B. F. *The Aims of Jesus.* London: SCM, 1979.

Milik, J. T. "Les Modèles Araméens Du Livre DEsther dans la Grotte 4 De Qumrân." *RevQ* 15:1–2 (1991—1992) 321–406.

Millar, F. *The Emperor in the Roman World.* London: Duckworth, 1977.

———. *Study of Cassius Dio.* Oxford: Clarendon, 1964.

Millar, F., and E. Segal, eds. *Caesar Augustus: Seven Aspects.* Oxford: Clarendon, 1984.

Moffatt, J. *A Critical and Exegetical Commentary on the Epistle to the Hebrews.* Edited by A. Plummer. Edinburgh: T. & T. Clark, 1924.

Montefiore, H. W. *A Commentary on the Epistle to the Hebrews.* edited by H. Chadwick, Black's New Testament Commentaries: London: Adam and Charles Black, 1964.

Mosse, C. *Alexander: Destiny of a Myth.* Translated by J. Lloyd. Edinburgh: Edinburgh University Press, 2004.

Moule, C. F. D. *The Origin of Christology.* Cambridge: Cambridge University Press, 1977.

Muddiman, J. *The Epistle to the Ephesians.* London: Continuum, 2001.

Nickelsburg, G. W.E. *Jewish Literature between the Bible and the Mishnah.* Philadelphia: Fortress, 1981.

Nickelsburg, G. W. E., and J. C. Vanderkam, eds. *I Enoch: A New Translation.* Minneapolis: Fortress, 2004.

Nilsson, P. "The Problem of the History of Greek Religion in the Hellenistic and Roman Age." *HTR* 36:4 (1943) 225–75.

Nineham, D. E. "Et Hoc Genus Omne—an Examination of Dr. A. T.Hanson's Strictures on Some Recent Gospel Studies." In *Christian History and Interpretation*, edited by W. R. Farmer et al. London: SCM, 1967.

North, J. A. "Praeseus Divus." Review of Weinstock, S. (2004) Divus Julius. Oxford, Clarendon Press. *The Journal of Roman Studies* 65 (1975) 171 –77.

———. and M. Beard, eds. *Pagan Priests: Religion and Power in the Ancient World.* Ithaca: Cornell University Press, 1990.

Ogg, G. *The Chronology of the Public Ministry of Jesus.* Cambridge: Cambridge University Press, 1940.

Olmstead, A. T. *History of the Persian Empire.* Chicago: University of Chicago Press, 1948.

O'Neill, J. C. "The Charge of Blasphemy at Jesus Trial before the Sanhedrin." In *The Trial of Jesus*, edited by E. Bammell. London: SCM, 1968.

Osborn, E. "Justin Martyr." In *The First Christian Theologians: An Introduction to Theology in the Early Church*, edited by G. R. Evans, 115–20. Oxford: Blackwell, 2004.

Oxford English Dictionary. Oxford: Oxford University Press, 1968.

Parke, H. W. *Greek Oracles.* London: Hutchinson University Library, 1967.

———. *Oracles of Zeus*. Oxford: Blackwell, 1967.

Pearson, L. *The Lost Histories of Alexander the Great*. Oxford: Blackwell, 1960.

Perrin, N. "The Christology of Mark: A Study in Methodology." In *The Interpretation of Mark*, edited by W. R. Telford. Edinburgh: T. & T. Clark, 1995, 125–40.

Plummer, A. *A Critical and Exegetical Commentary on the Gospel According to St. Luke*. Edinburgh: T. & T. Clark, 1901.

———. *The Gospel According to St. Luke*. Edited by A Plummer, S. R. Driver, C. A. Briggs, Edinburgh: T. & T. Clark, 1901.

Plutarch. *Plutarch's Lives*. Edited by G. P. Goold. 11 vols. Vol. 1, The LCL. London: William Heinemann, 1914.

Polybius. *The Histories*. Translated by W. R. Paton. London: Harvard University Press, 2011.

Powell, A. "Order, Interaction, Authority: Ways of Looking at Greek Religion." In *Greek Religion. A Source Book*, edited by E. Kearns. New York: Routledge, 1995.

Preston, R. H., and A. T. Hanson. *The Revelation of St. John the Divine*. London: SCM, 1949.

Price, S. R.F. *Rituals and Power: The Roman Imperial Cult in Asia Minor*. Cambridge: Cambridge University Press, 1984.

Propp, W. H.C. *Exodus*. London: Doubleday, 1999.

Pseudo-Callisthenes, ed. *Historia Alexandri Magni. Vol. 1, Recensio Vetusta: (Pseudo-Callisthenes)*. edited by G. Kroll. Berolini: Weidmann, 1958.

Purcell, N. "Romans in the Roman World." In *The Cambridge Companion to the Age of Augustus*, edited by K. Galinsky. Cambridge: Cambridge University Press, 2005, 85–105.

Quek, T. M. "A Text-Critical Study of John 1.34." *New Testament Studies* 55, no. 1 (2009) 22–34.

Rahtz, P. A., and L. Watts. *Myth and Archaeology*. Stroud: Tempus, 2003.

Ramsay, B., *Beginning to Read the Fathers*. London: SCM 1993.

Rawlings, R. and H. Bowden, eds. *Herakles and Hercules*. Swansea: The Classic Press of Wales, 2005.

Rawlinson Jones, D. *Haggai, Zechariah and Malachi*. London: SCM, 1962.

Razmjou, S. "Religion and Burial Customs." In *Forgotten Empire: The World of Ancient Persia.*, edited by J. Curtis and N. Tallis. Berkeley, LA: University of California Press, 2005.

Renault, M. *The King Must Die*. London: Longmans, Green, 1958.

Richards, G. "Paul Tillich and the Historical Jesus." *Studies in Religion*, no. 4 (1974/5) 120–28.

Riches, J. K. "The Four Gospels and the One Gospel of Jesus Christ. An Investigation of the Collection and Origin of the Canonical Gospels." *Journal of Theological Studies* 53 (2002) 624–7.

Riley, G. J. "Mimesis of Classical Ideals in the Second Christian Century." In *Mimesis and Intertextuality in Antiquity and Christianity*, edited by D. R. MacDonald. Harrisburg, Pa: TPI, 2001, 91–103.

Robinson, J. A. T. *The Priority of John*. London: SCM Press, 1985.

Robinson, T. H. *The Epistle to the Hebrews*. edited by J. Moffatt, The Moffatt New Testament Commentaries, London: Hodder and Stoughton, 1933.

Rogers, R. W. *A History of Ancient Persia*. London: Charles Scribner, 1929.

Rose, H. J. *Ancient Greek Religion*. St. Albans: Gainsborough, 1946.

———. "The Evidence of Divine Kings in Greece." In *Myth and Ritual Theory*, edited by R. A. Segal, 381–87. Oxford: Blackwell, 1998.

Ross Taylor, L. "The Proskynesis and the Hellenistic Ruler-Cult." *JHS* 47 (1927) 53–62.

Rowe, R. D. *God's Kingdom and God's Son*. Leiden: Brill, 2002.

Rowley, H. H. *The Book of Job*. The New Century Bible Commentary. Grand Rapids: Eerdmans, 1976.

Rupke, J., ed. *A Companion to Roman Religion*. Oxford: Blackwell, 2007.

Porter, S. E., ed. *The Messiah in the Old and New Testaments* Grand Rapids, Mich.: William B. Eerdsmans, 2007.

Sanders, E. P. *Jesus and Judaism*. London: SCM, 1985.

Sanders, E. P., and M. Davies. *Studying the Synoptic Gospels*. London: SCM, 1989.

Sanders, J. N. "The Literature and Canon of the New Testament." In *Peake's Commentary on the Bible*, edited by M. Black, 676–82. London: Thomas Nelson, 1963.

Sanders, J. N., and B. A. Mastin. *A Commentary on the Gospel According to St. John*. Edited by H. Chadwick. London: Charles and Adam Black, 1968.

Schaberg, J. *The Illegitimacy of Jesus*. New York: Crossroad, 1990.

Schachermeyr, F. *Alexander Der Grosse, Ingenium Und Macht*. Vienna: Wissenschaften, 1949.

Schachter, A. "Heracles." In *OCD*. Oxford: Oxford University Press, 2003.

Schaff, P., ed. *The Apostolic Fathers with Justin Martyr and Irenaeus*. Grand Rapids,Mi: Eerdmans, 2001.

Scheid, J. "Augustus and Roman Religion: Continuity, Conservatism, and Innovation." In *The Cambridge Companion to the Age of Augustus*, edited by K. Galinsky, 175–193. Cambridge: Cambridge University Press, 2005.

———. *An Introduction to Roman Religion*. Edinburgh: Edinburgh University Press, 2003.

Schillebeeckx, E., et al., eds. *Jesus, Son of God?* Edinburgh: T. & T. Clark, 1982.

Schurer, E. *The Literature of the Jewish People in the Time of Jesus*. New York: Shocken, 1972.

Schweitzer, A. *The Quest of the Historical Jesus*. 3rd edition. London: A. and C. Black, 1963.

Schweizer, E. *The Good News According to Matthew*. London: S. P. C. K., 1976.

———. *Jesus*. Translated by D. E. Green London: SCM, 1968.

———. *Jesus, the Parable of God. What Do We Really Know About Jesus?* PTMS 37. Allison Park, PA: Pickwick 1994.

Scott, K. *The Imperial Cult under the Flavians*. Stuttgart: Kohlhammer, 1936.

Scullion, J. J. *Genesis*. Collegeville, MN: Liturgical, 1992.

Seager, R. *Tiberius*. Oxford: Blackwell, 1972.

Sealey, R. "The Olympic Festival in 324 B. C." *Classic Review* 10 (1960) 1985–86.

Shafer, B. E., ed. *Religion in Ancient Egypt: Gods, Myths, and Personal Practice*. Ithaca: Cornell University Press, 1991.

Shaltout, M., J. A. Belmonte, and M. Fekri. "On the Orientation of Ancient Egyptian Temples: Key Points at Lower Egypt and Siwa Oasis, Part II." *Journal for the History of Astronomy* 38 (2007) 413–42.

Shotter, D. *Augustus Caesar*. Lancaster Pamphlets. London: Routledge, 1991.

Siker, J. S. "Christianity in the Second and Third Centuries." In *The Early Christian World*, edited by P. F. Esler, 231–57. London: Routledge, 2000.

Silverman, D. P. "Divinities and Deities in Ancient Egypt." In *Religion in Ancient Egypt*, edited by B. E.Shafer, 7–87. London: Cornell University Press, 1991.

Simpson, C. A. "Joshua." In *Dictionary of the Bible*, edited by F. C. Grant and H. H. Rowley, 531–32. Edinburgh: T. & T. Clark, 1963.

Smalley, S. S. *1, 2, 3 John*. WBC 51. Waco, TX: Word, 1984.

Smith, H. P. *The Books of Samuel*. ICC. Edinburgh: T. & T. Clark, 1899.

Smith, M. *Jesus the Magician*. Berkeley, CA: Seastone, 1998.

Smith, R. H. "Pella." In *ABD*, edited by D. N. Freedman, 5:219–21. New York: Doubleday, 1992.

Southern, P. *Domitian: Tragic Tyrant*. London: Routledge, 1997.

Stanton, G. N. *The Gospels and Jesus*. Oxford: Oxford University Press, 1989.

———. *Jesus of Nazareth in New Testament Preaching*. SNTSMS 27. Cambridge: Cambridge University Press, 1974.

Stausberg, M. "On the State and Prospects of the Study of Zoroastrianism." *Numen* 55:5 (2008) 561–600.

Stevenson, J., ed. *A New Eusebius: Documents Illustrating the History of the Church to AD 337*. London: SPCK, 1987.

Stewart, S. "Zoroastrianism: An Introduction to an Ancient Faith." *ExpTim* 110:11 (1999) 378.

Stoneman, R. *Alexander the Great*. London: Routledge, 1997.

———. "Alexander the Great in Fact and Fiction." *Classical Review* 52:1 (2002) 103–5.

———. *Alexander the Great: A Life in Legend*. London: Yale University Press, 2008.

———. "Alexander. Destiny and Myth." *Classical Review* 55:1 (2005) 230–32.

———. "Darius in the Shadow of Alexander." *Classical Review* 56:2 (2006) 415–17.

———. "Naked Philosophers—the Brahmans in the Alexander Historians and the Alexander Romance." *JHS* 115 (1995) 99–114.

Streeter, B. H. *The Four Gospels: A Study of Origins*. London: Macmillan, 1924.

Stuckenbruck, L. T. "Messianic Ideas in the Apocalyptic and Related Literature of Early Judaism." in *The Messiah in the Old and New Testaments*, edited by S. E. Porter, pp. 90–113. Cambridge: Eerdmans, 2007.

———. "Qumran Cave—IV: Vol 7, Genesis to Numbers." *JSS* 43:1 (1998) 169–72.

Stuhlmacher, P. *Paul's Letter to the Romans*. Westminster: John Knox, 1994.

Sweet, L. M. *Roman Emperor Worship*. Boston: Gorham, 1916.

Syme, R. *The Roman Revolution*. Oxford: Oxford University Press, 2002.

Tarn, W. W. *Alexander the Great*. 2 vols. Vol. 1 Boston: Beacon, 1968.

———. *Alexander the Great*. 2 vols. Vol. 2 Cambridge: Cambridge University Press, 2002.

Taylor, L. R. *The Divinity of the Roman Emperor*. Middletown, CT: American Philology Association, 1931.

———. "The Worship of Augustus in Italy during His Lifetime." *Transactions of the American Philology Association* 51 (1920) 116–33.

Taylor, V. *The Person of Christ*. London: MacMillan, 1962.

Telford, W. R. "Mark." In *The Synoptic Gospels*, edited by J. K. Riches, W. R. Telford, and C. M. Tuckett, 128–249. Sheffield: Sheffield Academic, 2001.

———. *The Theology of the Gospel of Mark*. Edited by J. D.G. Dunn. Cambridge: Cambridge University Press, 1999.

Theissen, G. "From the Jesus of History to the Kerygma Son of God, Providing Sociological Analysis of the Comprehension Roles of Christology in the New Testament." *ETR* 83:4 (2008) 575.

Thomas, G. T. *Alexander the Great in His World.* Oxford: Blackwell, 2007.

Thompson, L. L. *The Book of Revelation.* Oxford: Oxford University Press, 1990.

Trakatellis, D. *The Pre-Existence of Christ in the Writings of Justin Martyr.* Missoula, MT: Scholars, 1976.

Trocme, E. "Is There a Marcan Christology?" In *Christ and Spirit in the New Testament. In Honour of Charles Francis Digby Moule,* edited by B. Lindars and S. S. Smalley, 3–13. Cambridge: Cambridge University Press, 1973.

Turcan, R. *The Cults of the Roman Empire.* Translated by A. Neville. Oxford: Blackwell, 1992.

Turner, H. E.W. *Historicity and the Gospels.* London: Mowbray, 1963.

Vanderkam, J., and P. Flint. *The Meaning of the Dead Sea Scrolls. Their Significance in Understanding the Bible, Judaism, Jesus and Christianity.* London: T. & T. Clark, 2002.

Vermes, G. *The Historical Figure of Jesus.* London: Allen Lane, 1993.

———. *Jesus the Jew: A Historians Reading of the Gospels.* London: Collins, 1973.

Von Rad, G. *Genesis: A Commentary.* Translated by J. H. Marks. London: SCM, 1956.

Wagner, W. H. *After the Apostles.* Minneapolis: Fortress, 1994.

Wallace-Hadrill, A. *Augustan Rome.* Classical World Series. Bristol: Bristol Classic, 2010.

Wardman, A. *Religion and Statecraft among the Romans.* London: Granada, 1982.

Warrior, V. M. *Roman Religion.* Cambridge: Cambridge University Press, 2006.

Waterhouse, J. W. *Zoroastrianism.* San Diego: The Book Tree, 1934.

Weinstock, S. *Divus Julius.* Oxford: Clarendon Press, 2004.

Weiser, A. *The Psalms.* Translated by H. Hartwell. London: SCM, 1962.

Wells, G. A. *The Historical Evidence for Jesus.* Buffalo, NY: Prometheus, 1982.

Werner, M. *The Formation of Christian Dogma.* 2nd Edition. London: A. & C. Black, 1957.

Westcott, B. F. *The Epistle to the Hebrews.* London: MacMillan, 1889.

Wieshofer, J. *Ancient Persia: From 550 B. C. To 650 A. D.* Translated by A. Azodi. London: J. B. Tauris, 1996.

Wilchen, U. *Alexander the Great.* Translated by G. C. Norton. New York: W. W. Norton, 1967.

Williamson, G. A. *The World of Josephus.* London: Secker and Warburg, 1964.

Wilson, A. N. *Jesus.* London: W. W. Norton, 1992.

Wilson, R. Mcl. *Hebrews.* Edited by R. E. Clements. Grand Rapids: Eerdmans, 1987.

Wolters, A. "The Messiah in the Qumran Documents." In *The Messiah in the Old and New Testaments,* edited by S. E. Porter, 75–89. Cambridge: Eerdmans, 2007.

Woolf, G. "Polis-Religion and Its Alternatives in the Roman Provinces." In *Roman Religion,* edited by C. Ando, 39–54. Edinburgh: Edinburgh University Press, 2003.

Worthington, I. *Alexander the Great: Man and God.* Harlow: Pearson Education, 2004.

Wright, N. T. "'Constraints' and the Jesus of History." *SJT* 39 (1986) 189–210.

———. *The Resurrection of the Son of God.* London: SPCK, 2003.

———. *Who Was Jesus.* London: SPCK, 1992.

Yavetz, Z. "The Res Gestae and Augustus Public Image." In *Caesar Augustus: Seven Aspects,* edited by F. Millar and E. Segal, 1–36. Oxford: Clarendon, 1984.

Young, F. *The Making of the Creeds.* London: SCM, 1991.

Zeitlin, I. M. *Jesus and the Judaism of His Time.* Oxford: Blackwell, 1988.

Index

Lightning Source UK Ltd.
Milton Keynes UK
UKOW06f0659100415

249390UK00002B/45/P